Gilbert Burnet

Dr. Burnet's Travels

Letters containing an account of what seemed most remarkable in Switzerland,

Italy, France and Germany

Gilbert Burnet

Dr. Burnet's Travels

Letters containing an account of what seemed most remarkable in Switzerland, Italy, France and Germany

ISBN/EAN: 9783337175740

Printed in Europe, USA, Canada, Australia, Japan

Cover: Foto ©Andreas Hilbeck / pixelio.de

More available books at **www.hansebooks.com**

Dr: BURNET'S TRAVELS,

OR LETTERS

CONTAINING
An ACCOUNT
Of what Seemed moſt Remarkable
IN
Switzerland, France, and
Italy, Germany, &c.

Written by
GILBERT BURNET, D.D.

TO THE
Honourable R. B. E'q; Fellow of the
Royal Society.

At, AMSTERDAM,
Printed, for *Peter Savouret* and *W. Fenner* in *Warmœs-ſtreet* near the *Dam*, 1687.

THE PRINTER TO THE READER.

THE Reverend Author's *Reflexions upon* Varilla's *his History of Heresie*, having met with the Reception owing to the merit of all his Productions, has made me sensible, that I can never mount to a higher strain of obliging the Publick, than in Continuing to entertain it with the Masterly pieces of the same hand; this Consideration induc'd me to go to Work upon these his incomparable Travelling Remarks, *and having in this, as well as I had in the* Reflexions, *the advantage of an* English *Gentleman to Correct and Over-see the Press, this*

Edition will be found to be altogether refined, from the gross and innumerable faults, with which the *Impression* of Rotterdam is not throughout only, blemisht, but almost render'd unintelligible. Thus, kind *Reader,* I may well expect from thee a due *Sense* of this my *Industrious Performance,* and that thou wilt have a suitable reguard for a *Present* of such inestimable value.

Vale.

P. Savouret.

LETTERS,

CONTAINING

An Account of what seemed most remarkable in *Switzerland*, in various Parts of *Germany* and *Italy*, &c.

LETTER I.

Zurich, the First of *September*, 1685.

SIR,

IT is so common to write Travels, that for one who has seen so little, and as it were in haste, it may look like a presumptuous Affectation to be reckoned among Voyagers, if he attempts to say any thing upon so short a Ramble, and concerning Places so much visited, and by consequence so well known:

known: Yet having had opportunities that do not offer themselves to all that travel, and having joyned to those a curiosity almost equal to the advantages I enjoyed, I fancy it will not be an ungrateful Entertainment, if I give you some account of those things that pleased me most in the Places through which I have passed: but I will avoid saying such things as occurr in ordinary Books, for which I refer you to the Prints; for as you know that I have no great inclination to copy what others have said; so a Traveller has not leisure nor humour enough for so dull an Employment.

As I came all the way from *Paris* to *Lyons*, I was amazed to see so much misery as appeared, not only in Villages, but even in big Towns, where all the marks of an extream Poverty, shewed themselves both in the Buildings, the Cloaths, and almost in the Looks of the Inhabitants. And a general dis-peopling in all the Towns, was a very visible effect of the hardships under which they lay.

I need tell you nothing of the irregular and yet magnificent Situation of *Lyons*, of the noble Rivers that meet there, of the Rock cut from so vast a height for a Prison, of the *Carthusians* Gardens, of the Town-House, of the Jesuits Colledge and Library, of the famous Nunnery of St. *Peter*, of the Churches, particularly St. *Irenees*, of the Remnants of the *Aqueducts*, of the Columns and the old Mosaick in the Abbey Dean: in short, Mr. *Spon* has given such an account of the Curiosities there, that it were a very presumptuous Attempt to offer to come after him.

The Speech of *Claudius* ingraven on a Plate of Brass, and set in the end of the low Walk in the Town-house, is one of the noblest Antiquities in the World; by which we see the way of Writing and Pointing in that Age very copiously. The Shield of Silver of twenty two pound weight, in which some Remains of gilding do yet appear, and that seems to represent that generous Action of *Scipio's*, of restoring a fair Captive to a

Celtiberian Prince, is certainly the noblest piece of Plate that is now extant: the embossing of it is so fine and so entire, that it is indeed unvaluable; and if there were an Inscription upon it to put us beyond conjecture, it were yet much more inestimable.

A great many Inscriptions are to be seen of the late and barbarous Ages, as *Bonum Memorium*, and *Epitaphium hunc*. There are twenty three Inscriptions in the Garden of the Fathers of *Mercy*, but so placed as it shews how little those who possess them do either understand or value them. I shall only give you one, because I made a little Reflection on it, tho' it is not perhaps too well grounded, because none of the Criticks have thought on it.

The Inscription is this, D. *M. Et Memoriae AEternae Sutiae Anthidis. Quae vixit Annis XXV. M. XI. DV. Quae dum Nimia pia fuit, facta est Impia: & Attio Probatiolo, Cecalius Calistio Conjux & Pater, & sibi vivo ponendum curavit & sub ascia dedicavit.* This must be towards the barbarous Age, as appears by the false Latin in *Nimia*: But the Inscription seems so extravagant, that a man dedicating a Burial-stone for his Wife and Son, and under which himself was to be laid, with Ceremonies of Religion, should tax his Wife of Impiety, and give so extraordinary an account of her becoming so through an excess of Piety, that it deserves some consideration.

It seems the Impiety was publick, otherwise a Husband would not have recorded it in such a manner; and it is plain that he thought it rose from an excess of Piety.

I need not examine the Conjectures of others; but will chuse rather to give you my own, and submit it to your censure.

It seems to me, that this *Sutia Anthis* was a Christian; for the Christians, because they would not worship the Gods of the Heathens, nor participate with them in their sacred Rites, were accused both of

B 2   Atheism

Atheism and Impiety. This is so often objected, and the Fathers in their Apologies have answered it so often, that it were lost labour to prove it: so this Wife of *Cerealius Califtia* having turned Christian, it seems he thought he was bound to take some notice of it in the Inscription. But by it he gives a honourable Character of the Christian Doctrine at the same time that he seems to accuse it; that through an excess of Piety his Wife was carried to it; since a mind seriously possessed with a true sense of Piety could not avoid the falling under a distaste of Paganism, and the becoming Christian.

At *Grenoble* there is not much to be seen. The learned Mr. *Chorier* has some Manuscripts of considerable Antiquity. In one of *Vegetius de re Militari*, there is a clear correction of a Passage that in all the printed Editions is not sense. In the Chapter of the size of the Souldiers, he begins; *Scio semper mensuram à Mario Consule exactam*: *à* is in no MS. and *Mario Consule* is a mistake for *trium Cubitorum*, for III which are for *trium* have been read *M*. and *C*, which stands for *Cubitorum*, as appears by all that follows, was by a mistake read *Consule*; so the true reading of that Passage, is, *Scio mensuram trium Cubitorum fuisse semper exactam.* He shewed me another MS. of about five or six hundred years old, in which St. *John*'s Revelation is contained, all exemplified in Figures; and after that came *Æsop*'s Fables, likewise all designed in Figures: from which he inferred, that those who designed those two Books valued both equally, and so put them together.

I will not describe the Valley of *Dauphine*, all to *Chambery*, nor entertain you with a Landskip of the Country, which deserves a better Pencil than mine, and in which the heighth and rudeness of the Mountains that almost shut upon it, together with the beauty, the evenness, and fruitfulness of the Valley, that is all along well watered with the River of *Liserre*, make such an agreeable mixture, that this vast diversity of

Objects

Objects that do at once fill the Eye, gives it a very entertaining Prospect.

Chambery has nothing in it that deserves a long Description; and *Geneva* is too well known to be much insisted on. It is a little State, but it has so many good Constitutions in it, that the greatest may justly learn at it. The Chamber of the Corn has always two years Provision for the City in store, and forces none but the Bakers to buy of it at a taxed price; and so it is both necessary for any Extremities under which the State may fall, and is likewise of great advantage; for it gives a good yearly Income, that has helpt the State to pay near a Million of Debt contracted during the Wars; and the Citizens are not oppressed by it; for every Inhabitant may buy his own Corn as he pleases, only Publick Houses must buy from the Chamber. And if one will compare the faith of *Rome* and *Geneva* together by this particular, he will be enforced to prefer the latter; for if good Works are a strong presumption, if not a sure Indication of a good Faith, then Justice being a good Work of the first form, *Geneva* will certainly carry it.

At *Rome*, the Pope buys in all the Corn of the Patrimony; for none of the Landlords can sell it either to Merchants or Bakers. He buys it at five Crowns their Measure, and even that is slowly and ill paid; so that there was eight hundred thousand Crowns owing upon that score when I was at *Rome*. In selling this out, the Measure is lessened a fifth part, and the price of the whole is doubled; so that what was bought at five Crowns, is sold out at twelve: and if the Bakers, who are obliged to take a determined quantity of Corn from the Chamber, cannot retail out all that is imposed upon them, but are forced to return some part of it back, the Chamber discounts to them only the first price of five Crowns: whereas in *Geneva* the measure by which they buy and sell is the same; and the Gain is so inconsiderable, that it is very little beyond the common Market price: so that upon the whole matter, the Chamber of the Corn is but the Merchant to the State. But if the Publick makes a moderate Gain by the Corn, that and all the other Revenues of this small Commonwealth are so well employed, that there is no cause of complaint given in the Administration of the publick Purse; which with the advantages that arise out of the Chamber of the Corn, is about one hundred thousand Crowns Revenue. But there is much to go out of this: Three hundred Souldiers are payed; an Arsenal is maintained, that in proportion to the State is the greatest in the World; for it contains Arms for more men than are in the State: there is a great number of Ministers and Professors, in all twenty four, payed out of it, besides all the publick Charges and Offices of the Government. Every one of the lesser Council of twenty five, having a hundred Crowns, and every *Syndic* having two hundred Crowns Pension: and after all this come the accidental Charges of the Deputies, that they are obliged to send often to *Paris*, to *Savoy*, and to *Zwitzerland*; so that it is very apparent, no man can enrich himself at the Cost of the Publick. And the appointments of the little Council are a very small recompence for the great attendance that they are obliged to give the Publick; which is commonly four or five hours a day. The Salary for the Professors and Ministers is indeed small, not above two hundred Crowns; but to ballance this, which was a more competent Provision when it was first set off a hundred and fifty years ago, the price of all things, and the way of living, being now much heightned, those Employments are here held in their due Reputation, and the richest Citizens in the Town breed up their Children so as to qualifie them for those Places: And a Minister that is sutable to his Character, is thought so good a Match, that generally they have such Estates, either by Succession or Marriage, as support them sutably to the rank they hold. And in

Geneva.

Geneva there is so great a regulation upon Expences of all sorts, that a small Sum goes a great way. It is a surprising thing, to see so much Learning as one finds in *Geneva*, not only among those whose Profession obliges them to Study, but among the Magistrates and Citizens; and if there are not many men of the first form of Learning among them, yet every body almost here has a good tincture of a learned Education; insomuch that they are Masters of the Latin, they know the Controversies of Religion and History, and they are generally men of good sense.

There is an universal Civility, not only towards Strangers, but towards one another, that reigns all the Town over, and leans to an excess; so that in them one sees a mixture of a *French* Openness, and an *Italian* Exactness: there is indeed a little too much of the last.

The publick Justice of the City is quick and good, and more commended than the private Justice of those that deal in Trade: a want of Sincerity is much lamented by those that know the Town well. There is no publick Lewdness tolerated, and the disorders of that sort are managed with great address. And notwithstanding their Neighbourhood to the *Switzers*, drinking is very little known among them. One of the best parts of their Law is the way of selling Estates; which is likewise practised in *Switzerland*, and is called *Subhastation*, from the *Roman* Custom of selling *Sub hasta*. A man that is to buy an Estate agrees with the Owner, and then intimates it to the Government; who order three several Proclamations to be made six Weeks one after another, of the intended Sale, that is to be on such a day: when the day comes, the Creditors of the Seller, if they apprehend that the Estate is sold at an under-value, may out-bid the Buyer; but if they do not interpose, the Buyer delivers the money to the State, which upon that gives him his Title to the Estate, which can never be so much as brought

under

under a Debate in Law; and the price is paid into the State, and is by them given either to the Debtors of the Seller, if he owes money, or to the Seller himself.

This Custom prevails likewise in *Swisse,* where also twelve Years Possession gives a Prescription; so that in no place of the World are the Titles to Estates so secure as here. The Constitution of the Government is the same both in *Geneva,* and in most of the *Cantons*. The Sovereignty lies in the Council of Two hundred, and this Council chuses out of its number Twenty five, who are the lesser Council; and the censure of the Twenty five belongs to the great Council: they are chosen by a sort of Ballet; so that it is not known for whom they give their Votes: which is an effectual method to suppress Factions and Resentments; since in a competition no man can know who voted for him or against him: yet the Election is not so carried, but that the whole Town is in an Intrigue concerning it: for since the being of the little Council leads one to the *Sindicat,* which is the chief Honour of the State; this Dignity is courted here with as active and sollicitous an Ambition, as appears elsewhere for greater matters. The Two hundred are chosen and censured by the Twenty five; so that these two Councils, which are both for Life, are checks one upon another. The Magistracy is in the one, and the Sovereignty in the other. The Number of Twenty five is never exceeded in the lesser Council; but for the greater, tho' it passes by the Name of the Council of Two hundred, yet there are commonly eight or ten more: so that notwithstanding the absence or sickness of some of the Number, they may still be able to call together near the full Number. There is another Council besides these two, composed of Sixty, consisting of those of the Two hundred that have borne Offices, such as Auditors, Attorney-Generals, or those that have been in other Employments, which are given for a determinate number of Years: This Court has

no

no Authority, but is called together by the Twenty five, when any extraordinary occasion makes it advisable for them to call for a more general Concurrence in the Resolutions that they are about to form. And this Council is of the nature of a Council of State that only gives Advice, but has no power in it self to enforce its Advices. The whole Body of the Burgesses chuses the Sindicks the first Sunday in the Year, and there are some other Elections that do likewise belong to them. The difference between the Burgesses and Citizens is, that the former degree may be bought or given to Strangers, and they are capable to be of the Two hundred: but none is a Citizen but he that is the Son of a Burgess, and that is born within the Town.

I need say no more of the Constitution of this little Republick: Its chief support is in the firm Alliance that has stood now so long between it and the *Cantons* of *Bern* and *Zurich*; and it is so visibly the Interest of all *Switzerland* to preserve it as the Key, by which it may be all laid open: that if the *Cantons* had not forgotten their Interest so palpably in suffering the *French* to become Masters of the *Franche Comté*, one would think that they would not be capable of suffering *Geneva* to be touch'd: for all that can be done in fortifying the Town, can signifie no more, but to put it in case to resist a Surprise or Scalade; since if a Royal Army comes against it to besiege it in form, it is certain, that unless the *Switzers* come down with a Force able to raise the Siege, those within will be able to make a very short resistance.

From *Geneva* I went through the Country of *Vaud* or the *Valley*, and *Lausanne*, its chief Town, in my way to *Bern*. The Town of *Lausanne* is situated on three Hills, so that the whole Town is ascent and descent, and that very steep, chiefly on the side on which the Church stands, which is a very noble Fabrick. The South-wall of the Cross was so split by an Earthquake about thirty years ago, that there was a rent made from
top

top to bottom above a foot wide; which was so closed up ten years after by another Earthquake, that now one only sees where the breach was. This extravagant situation of the Town was occasioned by a Legend of some Miracles wrought near the Church: which prevailed so much on the Credulity of that Age, that by it the Church, and so in consequence the Buildings near it, were added to the old Town, which stood on the other Hill, where there was a Town made on the High-way from the Lake into *Switzerland*, to which the chief Priviledges of the Town, particularly the judicature of Life and Death, do still belong. Between *Geneva* and this, lies the Lake which at the one end is called the Lake of *Geneva*, and at the other the Lake of *Lausanne*. I need not mention the Dimensions of it which are so well known, only in some Places the depth has never been found, for it is more than five hundred Fathom: The banks of the Lake are the beautifullest Plots of Ground that can be imagined, for they look as if they had been laid by art: the sloping is so easie and so equal, and the Grounds are so well cultivated and peopled, that a more delighting Prospect cannot be seen any where: The Lake is well stock'd with excellent Fish; but their Numbers do sensibly decrease, and one sort is quite lost: it is not only to be ascribed to the ravenousness of the Pikes that abound in it, but to another sort of Fish that they call *Moutails*, which were never taken in the Lake untill within six years last past: they are in the Lake of *Neuf-chastel*, and some of the other Lakes of *Switzerland*, and it is likely that by some conveyance under ground they may have come into Channels that fall into the Lake: the Water of the Lake is all clear and fresh. It is not only a great Pond made by the *Rhosne* that runs into it, but does not pass through it unmix'd, as some Travellers have fondly imagined, because sometimes a soft Gale makes a curling of the Waters in some places, which runs smooth in the places over which that soft breath

of

f Wind does not pa's, the Gale varying its place often. But it is believed that there are also many great Fountains all over the Lake: these Springs do very probably flow from some vast Cavities that are in the neighbouring Mountains, which are as great Cisterns that discharge themselves in the Valleys which are covered ove with Lakes. And on the two sides of the *Alps*, both North and South, there is so great a number of those little Seas, that it may be easily ghessed they must have vast Sources that feed so constantly those huge Ponds. And when one considers the height of those Hills, the chain of so many of them together, and their extent both in length and breadth; if at first he thinks of the old Fables of laying one Hill upon the top of another, he will be afterwards apt to imagine, according to the ingenious Conjecture of one that travelled over them oftner than once, that these cannot be the primary Productions of the Author of Nature, but are the vast ruines of the first World, which at the Deluge broke here into so many Inequalities.

One Hill not far from *Geneva*, called *Maudit*, or Cursed, of which one Third is always covered with Snow, is two miles of perpendicular height, according to the Observation of that incomparable Mathematician and Philosopher, *Nicolas Fatio Duilier*, who at Twenty two Years of Age is already one of the greatest men of his Age, and seems to be born to carry Learning some sizes beyond what it has yet attain'd.

But now I will entertain you a little with the State of *Bern*, for that Canton alone is above a third part of all *Switzerland*. I will say nothing of its Beginnings or History: nor will I enlarge upon the Constitutions which are all well known. It has a Counsel of Two hundred, that goes by that Name, tho' it consists almost of Three hundred; and another of Twenty five, as *Geneva*. The chief Magistrates are two *Advoyers*, who are not annual, as the Sindicks of *Geneva*, but are for life, and have an Authority not unlike that of the

Ro-

Roman Confuls; each being his Year by turns the *Advoyer* in Office. After them there are the four *Bannerets*, who anſwer to the Tribunes of the People in *Rome*: then come the two *Burſars* or Treaſurers, one for the ancient *German* Territory, the other for the *French* Territory or the Country of *Vaud*, and the two laſt, choſen of the Twenty five, are called the Secrets; for to them all Secrets relating to the State are diſcovered: and they have an Authority of ca'ling the Two hundred together when they think fit, and of accuſing thoſe of the Magiſtracy, the *Advoyers* themſelves not excepted, as they ſee cauſe; tho' this falls out ſeldom.

There are ſeventy two Bailiages, into which the whole Canton of *Bern* is divided, and in every one of thoſe there is a Bailiff named by the Council of Two hundred, who muſt be a Citizen of *Bern*, and one of the Two hundred, to which Council no man can be choſen till he is married. Theſe Bailiages are Imployments both of Honour and Profit; for the Bailiff is the Governour and Judge in that Juriſdiction: ſince tho' he has ſome Aſſeſſors who are choſen out of the Bailiage, yet he may by his Authority carry matters which way he will, againſt all their Opinions: and the Bailiffs have all the Confiſcations and Fines; ſo that Drinking being ſo common in the Country, and that producing many Quarrels, the Bailiff makes his advantage of all thoſe diſorders: and in the ſix years of his Government according to the quality of his Bailiage, he not only lives by it, but will carry perhaps twenty thouſand Crowns with him back to *Bern*; on which he lives till he can carry another Bailiage; for one is capable of being twice Bailiff: but tho' ſome have been thrice Bailiffs, this is very extraordinary. The Exactions of the Bailiff are the only Impoſitions or Charges to which the Inhabitants are ſubjected; and theſe falling only on the Irregularities and Diſorders of the more debauched, makes that this Grievance, tho' in ſome particular Caſes it preſſes hard, yet is not ſo univerſally

(13)

verfally felt: for a fober and regular man is in no danger. Many in this Canton are as in *England*, Lords of Caftles and Mannors, and have a Jurifdiction annexed to their Eftates, and name their Magiftrate, who is called the *Caftellan*. In matters of fmall confequence there lies no Appeal from him to the Bailiff; but beyond the value of two Piftols an Appeal lies; and no Sentence of Death is executed till it is confirmed at *Bern*. There lies alfo an Appeal from the Bailiff to the Council at *Bern*. There are many Complaints of the injuftice of the Bailiffs; but their Law is fhort and clear, fo that a Sute is foon ended: two or three Hearings is the moft that even an intricate Sute amounts to, either in the firft Inftance before the Bailiff, or in the fecond Judgment at *Bern*. The Citizens of *Bern* confider thefe Bailiages as their Inheritance, and they are courted in this State, perhaps, with as much Intrigue as was ever ufed among the *Romans* in the diftribution of their Provinces: and fo little fignifie the beft Regulations when there are intrinfick Difeafes in a State, that though there is all poffible Precaution ufed in the Nomination of thefe Bailiffs, yet that has not preferved this State from falling under fo great a mifchief by thofe little Provinces; that as it has already in a great meafure corrupted their Morals, fo it may, likely, turn in Conclufion to the Ruine of this Republick. All the Electors give their Voices by Ballot: fo that they are free from all after-Game in the Nomination of the Perfon; All the Kindred of the Pretenders, even to the remoteft degrees, are excluded from Voting, as are alfo all their Creditors; fo that none can vote, but thofe who feem to have no intereft in the Iffue of the Competition: and yet there is fo much Intrigue, and fo great Corruption in the diftribution of thefe Imployments, That the whole Bufinefs, in which all *Bern* is ever in motion, is the catching of the beft Bailiages, on which a Family will have its Eye for many Years before they fall. For

C the

the Counsellors of *Bern* give a very small share of their Estates to their Children when they marry them: all that they purpose is, to make a Bailiage sure to them: for this they feast and drink, and spare nothing by which they may make sure a sufficient number of Votes: but it is the Chamber of the *Bannerets* that admits the Pretenders to the Competition. When the Bailiff is chosen, he takes all possible methods to make the best of it he can, and lets few Crimes pass that carry either Confiscations or Fines after them: his Justice also is generally suspected. It is true, those of the Bailiage may complain to the Council at *Bern*, as the oppressed Provinces did anciently to the Senate of *Rome*: and there have been severe Judgments against some more exorbitant Bailiffs; yet as Complaints are not made, except upon great Occasions, which are not often given by the Bailiffs, so it being the general Interest of the Citizens of *Bern* to make all possible Advantages of those Imployments, the Censure will be but gentle, except the Complaint is crying.

In *Bern* there is very little Trade, only what is necessary for the support of the Towns They maintain Professors in the Universities of *Bern* and *Lausanne*, the one for the *German* Territory, which is the ancient Canton, and the other for the new Conquest, which is the *French*. In the former there are about three hundred Parishes, in the other there are but about a hundred and fifty: but in the Benefices of the *German* side, the ancient Rights of the Incumbents are generally preserved, so that some Benefices are worth a thousand Crowns; whereas in the *Païs des Vaud* the Provisions are generally from a hundred to two hundred Crowns. It is visible that those of *Bern* trust more to the Affections and Fidelity of their Subjects, than to the strength of their Walls: for as they have never finished them, so what is built cannot be brought to a regular Fortification; and it is not

pre-

preserved with any care, nor furnished with Canon; but if they have none on their Ramparts, they have good store in their Arsenal, in which they say there are Arms for forty thousand men.

The Peasants are generally rich, chiefly in the *German* side, and are all well armed: they pay no Duties to the Publick; and the Soil is capable of great Cultivation, in which some succeed so well, that I was shewed some that were by accident at *Bern*, who, as I was told, had of Estate to the value of a hundred thousand Crowns, but that is not ordinary; yet ten thousand Crowns for a Peasant is no extraordinary matter. They live much on their Milk and Corn, which in some Places, as about *Payern*, yields an increase of fifteen measures after one: they breed many Horses, which bring them in a great deal of money. The worst thing in the Country is the moisture of the Air, which is not only occasioned by the many Lakes that are in it, and the Neighbouring Mountains that are covered with Snow, some all the Summer long, and the rest till Mid-summer; but by the vast quantity of Woods of Fir-trees, which seem to fill very near the half of their Soil; and if these were for the most part rooted out, as they would have much more Soil, so their Air would be much purer; yet till they find either Coal or Turf for their Fewel this cannot be done. I was told that they had found Coal in some Places. If the Coal is conveniently situated, so that by their Lakes and Rivers it can be easily carried over the Country, it may save them a great extent of ground, that as it is covered with Wood, so the Air becomes thereby the more unwholsome.

They have some Fountains of Salt-water; but the making Salt consumes so much Wood, that hitherto it has not turn'd to any Account.

The Men are generally sincere, but heavy: they think it necessary to correct the moisture of the Air with liberal Entertainments, and they are well furnished with all necessary Ingredients: for as their Soil produces good Cattel, so their Lakes abound in Fish, and their Woods in Fowl, the Wine is also light and good. The Women are generally employed in their domestick Affairs, and the Wives even of the chief Magistrates of *Bern* look into all the Concerns of the House and Kitchin as much as the Wives of the meanest Peasants. Men and Women do not converse promiscuously together; and the Women are so much amused with the Management at home, and enter so little into Intrigues, that among them, as an eminent Physician there told me, they know not what Vapours are, which he imputed to the Idleness and Intrigues that abound elsewhere, whereas he said, among them the Blood was cleansed by their Labour, and as that made them sleep well, so they did not amuse themselves with much thinking, nor did they know what Amours were. The third Adultery is punished with Death, which is also the punishment of the fifth Act of Fornication; of which I saw an instance while I was at *Bern*: for, a Woman who confessed her self guilty of many Whoredoms, and designed to be revenged on some Men that did not furnish her liberally with Money, was upon that condemned and executed: the manner was solemn; for the *Advoyer* comes into an open Bench in the middle of the Street, and for the Satisfaction of the People, the whole Process was read, and Sentence was pronounced in the hearing of all; the Counsellors both of the great and lesser Council standing about the *Advoyer*, who after Sentence took the Criminal very gently by the hand, and pray'd for her Soul: and after Execution, there was a Sermon for the Instruction of the People.

The whole State is disposed for War, for every man that can bear Arms is listed, and knows his Post and Arms; and there are Beacons so laid over the Country, that the Signal can run over the whole Canton.

ton in a night: and their Military Lists are so laid, that every man knows whither he is to come out upon first or second, or not till the general Summons. They assured me at *Bern*, That upon a general Summons they could bring above eighty thousand Men together. The Men are robust and strong, and capable of great Hardship, and of good Discipline, and have generally an extream sense of Liberty, and a great Love to their Country; but they labour under a want of Officers. And tho' the Subjects of the State are rich, yet the Publick is poor: they can well resist a sudden Invasion of their Country; but they would soon grow weary of a long War: and the Soil requires so much Cultivation, that they could not spare from their Labour the Men that would be necessary to preserve their Country. They were indeed as happy as a People could be, when the Emperour had *Alsace* on the one hand, and the *Spaniards* had the *Franche Comté* on the other; they had no reason to fear their Neighbours: but now that both those Provinces are in the hands of the *French*, the case is quite altered; for as *Basil* is every moment in danger from the Garrison of *Hunningen*, that is but a Canon-shot distant from it; so all the *Pais de Vaud* lies open to the *Franche Comté*, and has neither fortified Places, nor good Passes to secure it; so that their Error in suffering this to fall into the hands of the *French* was so gross, that I took some pains to be informed concerning it, and will here give you this Account that I had from one who was then in a very eminent Post; so that as he certainly knew the Secret, he seemed to speak sincerely to me. He told me that the Duke of *Lorrain* had often moved in the Councils of War, That the Invasion of *France* ought to be made on that side in which *France* lay open, and was very ill fortified: This he repeated often, and it was known in *France*: so that the King resolved to possess himself of the *Comté*, but used that Precaution, that fearing to provoke the *Switsers*, he offred a Neutrality on that side;

side: but the *Spaniards* who judged right; that it was as much the interest of the Cantons, as it was theirs, to preserve the *Comté* in their hands, refused to consent to it; but they took no care to defend it, and seemed to leave that to the *Switsers*.

In the mean while the *French* Money went about very liberally at *Bern*, and after those that were most likely to make opposition were gained, the *French* Minister proposed to them the necesity in which his Master found himself engaged to secure himself on that side; but that still he would grant a *Neutrallity* on their account; if the *Spaniards* would agree to it; and with this, all the assurances that could be given in words were offered to them, that they should never find the least prejudice from the Neighbourhood of the *French*, but on the contrary all possible Protection. There was just cause given by the *Spaniards* to consider them very little in their Deliberation: for they would neither accept of the *Neutrality*, nor send a considerable force Force to preserve the *Comte*, so that it seem'd almost inevitable to give way to the *French* proposition; but one proposed that, which an anbyassed Assembly would certainly have accepted, that they should go themselves and take the *Comte*, and by so doing they would secure the *Neutrality*, which was all that the *French* pretended to desire, and they might easily satisfie the *Spaniards* and reimburse themselves of the Expence of the *Invasion*, by restoring the *Comté* to them when a General Peace should be made. He laid out the misery to which their Country must be reduced by so powerful a Neighbour, but all was lost labour, so he went out in a rage and published through the Town, that the State was Sold and all was lost. They now see their Error too late, and would repair it, if it were possible, but the truth is, many of the particular Members of this State, do so prey upon the publick, that unless they do with one consent reform those abuses, they will never be in condition to do
much:

much: for in many of their Bailiages, of which some are Abbeys, the Bailifs not only feed on the Subjects, but likewise on the State, and pretend they are so far super-expended, that they discount a great deal of the publick revenue, of which they are the receivers, for their reimbursement: which made Mr. *d'Erlach* once say, when one of those accounts was presented, that it was very strange if the Abbey could not feed the Monks. It is true, the power of their *Bannerets* is so great, that one would think they might redress many Abuses. The City of *Bern* is divided into four Bodies not unlike our Companies of *London*, which are the Bakers, the Butchers, the Tanners, and the Blacksmiths, and every Citizen of *Bern* does incorporate himself into one of these Societies, which they call *Abbeys*. For it is likely they were antiently a sort of a *Religious Fraternity*: every one of these chuses two *Bannerets*, who bear Office by turns, from *Four Years* to *Four Years*, and every one of them has a *Bailiaga* annexed to his Office, which he holds for Life. They carry their Names from the *Banners* of the several *Abbeys* as the *Gonfaloniers* of *Italy*: and the *Advoyers* carry still their Name from the ancient Titles *Ecdicus* or *Advocate*, that was the Title of the chief Magistrates of the Towns in the Times of the *Roman* Emperours. The Chamber of the four *Bannerets* that bear Office, has a vast power, they examine and pass all Accounts, and they admit all the competitors to any Offices, so that no man can be proposed to the Council of *Two Hundred* without their Approbation, and this being now the chief Intrigue of their State, they have so absolute an Authority in shutting men out from Employments, that their office, which is for life, is no less considerable than that of the *Advoyer*, tho' they are inferiour to him in Rank. They manage matters with great address, of which this instance was given me in a competition for the *Advoyership* not long ago: There was one whose temper was violent, that had

made

made it so sure among those who were qualified to vote in it, as being neither of his Kindred nor Alliance, that they believed he would carry it from the other Competitor, whom they favoured; so they set up a third Competitor, whose Kindred were the Persons that were made sure to him, whose Advancement they opposed; and by this means they were all shut out from voting: so that the Election went according to the Design of the *Bannerets*. The chief Man now in *Bern*, who was the reigning *Advoyer* when I was there, is Mr. *d' Erlack*, Nephew to that Mr. *d' Erlack* who was Governour of *Brisack*, and had a *Brevet* to be a Marshal of *France*. This is one of the noblest Families in *Bern*, that acted a great part in shaking of the *Austrian* Tyranny; and they have been ever since very much distinguished there from all the rest of their Nobility. The present Head of it is a very extraordinary Man; he has a great Authority in his *Canton*, not only as he is *Advoyer*, but by the particular esteem which is payed him; for he is thought the wisest and worthiest Man of the State, tho' it is somewhat strange how he should bear such a sway in such a Government, for he neither feasts nor drinks with the rest. He is a Man of great Sobriety and Gravity, very reserved, and behaves himself liker a Minister of State in a Monarchy, than a Magistrate in a Popular Government: for one sees in him none of those Arts that seem necessary in such a Government. He has a great Estate, and no Children, so he has no Projects for his Family, and does what he can to correct the Abuses of the State, tho' the disease is inveterate, and seems past Cure.

He had a Misfortune in a War that was thirty years ago, in the Year 1656, between the *Popish* and the *Protestant* Cantons, the Occasion of which will engage me in a short Digression. The Peace of *Switzerland* is chiefly preserved by a Law agreed on among all the Cantons, that every Canton may make what Regulations

tions concerning Religion they think fit, without prejudice to the general League. Now the *Popish* Cantons have made Laws, That it shall be capital to any to change their Religion; and on a set day every year they go all to Mass, and the Masters of Families swear to continue true to the State, and firm in their Religion to their lives end, and so they pretend they punish their falling into Heresie with Death and Confiscation of Goods, because it is a violation of the Faith which is so solemnly sworn. But on the other hand, in the *Protestant* Cantons such as turn are only obliged to go and live out of the Canton; but for their Estates they still preserve them, and are permitted to sell them. One cannot but observe more of the merciful Spirit of the Gospel in the one than in the other. In two Cantons, *Appenzel* and *Glaris*, both Religions are tollerated, and are capable of equal Priviledges; and in some Bailiages that were conquered in common by the Cantons of *Bern* and *Friburg*, in the Wars with *Savoy*, the two Cantons name the Bailiffs by turns, and both Religions are so equally tollerated, that in the same Church they have both Mass and Sermon, so equally, that on one Sunday the Mass begins and the Sermon follows, the next Sunday the Sermon begins and the Mass comes next, without the least disorder or murmuring.

But in the year 1656, some of the Canton of *Schwitz* changing their Religion, and retiring to *Zurich*, their Estates were confiscated; and some others that had also changed, but had not left the Canton, were taken and beheaded. *Zurich* demanded the Estates of the Refugies, but instead of granting this, the Canton of *Schwitz* demanded back their Subjects, that they might proceed against them as Delinquents; and they founded this on a Law, by which the Cantons are obliged to deliver up the Criminals of another Canton when they come among them, if they are demanded by the Canton to which they belong: but those of

Zurich and *Bern* thought this was both inhumane and unchristian, tho' the Deputy of *Basil* was of another mind, and thought that they ought to be delivered up, which extreamly disgusted those of *Zurich*. Those of *Schwitz* committed some Insolencies upon the Subjects of *Zurich*, and refused to give Satisfaction. Upon all which a War followed between the *Protestant* and *Popish* Cantons. The Cantons of *Bern* and *Zurich* raised an Army of Twenty five thousand Men, which was commanded by Mr. *d' Erlack*, but was dispersed in several Bodies: And the Papists had not above Six thousand, yet they surprised Mr. *d' Erlack* with a Body not much superiour to theirs: both sides, after a short Engagement, run: The Canon of the Canton of *Bern* was left in the Field a whole day; at last those of *Lucern* seeing that none stayed to defend the Canon, carried them off: This loss raised such a Tumult in *Bern*, that they seemed resolved to sacrifice Mr. *d' Erlack*; but he came with such a Presence of Mind, and gave so satisfying an Account of the Misfortune, that the Tumult ceased, and soon after the War ended. Upon this many thought, that tho' the *Papists* acted cruelly, yet it was according to their Laws, and that no other Canton could pretend to interpose or quarrel with those of *Schwitz*, for what they did upon that occasion. Within these few Years there were some Quarrels like to arise in the Canton of *Glaris*, where it was said the equal Priviledges agreed on to both Religions, were not preserved, but on this occasion the Pope's *Nuntio* acted a very different Part from that which might have been expected from him: for whereas the Ministers of that Court have been commonly the Incendiaries in all the Disputes that concern Religion, he acted rather the part of a Mediator; and whereas it was visible that the Injustice lay on the side of the Papists, he interposed so effectually with those of *Lucern*, which is the chief of the *Popish* Cantons, that the difference was composed. But

But to return to *Bern*. The Buildings have neither great Magnificence nor many Apartments, but they are convenient, and suited to the way of living in the Country. The Streets not only of *Bern* and the bigger Towns, but even of the smallest Villages, are furnished with Fountains that run continually; which as they are of great use, so they want not their Beauty. The great Church of *Bern* is a very noble Fabrick: but being built on the top of the Hill on which the Town stands, it seems the ground began to fail; so to support it they have raised a vast Fabrick, which has cost more than the Church it self: for there is a Platform made, which is a Square to which the Church is one side, and the farther side is a vast Wall, fortified with Buttresses about a hundred and fifty foot high. They told me, That all the Ground, down to the bottom of the Hill, was dug into Vaults: This Platform is the chief Walk of the Town, chiefly about Sun-set: and the River underneath presents a very beautiful Prospect; for there is a Cut taken off from it for the Mills, but all along as this Cut goes the Water of *Aar* runs, over a sloping bank of Stone, which they say was made at a vast Charge, and makes a noble and large Cascade.

The second Church is the *Dominicans* Chappel, where I saw the famous Hole that went to an Image in the Church, from one of the Cells of the *Dominicans*; which leads me to set down that Story at some length; for it was one of the most signal Cheats that the World has known: so it falling out about 20 years before the Reformation was received in *Bern*, it is very probable that it contributed not a little to the preparing of the Spirits of the People to that change. I am the more able to give a particular account of it, because I read the Original Process in the *Latin* Record signed by the Notaries of the Court of the Delegates that the Pope sent to try the matter. The Record is a hundred and thirty Sheets writ close and of all sides,

it

It being indeed a large Volume: and I found the Printed Accounts so defective, that I was at the pains of reading the whole Process; of which I will give here a true Abstract.

The two famous Orders that had possessed themselves of the esteem of those dark Ages were engaged in a mighty Rivalry. The *Dominicans* were the more learned, They were the eminentest Preachers of those Times, and had the Conduct of the Courts of Inquisition, and the other chief Offices in the Church in their hands. But on the other hand, the *Franciscans* had an outward Appearance of more Severity, a ruder Habit, stricter Rules, and greater Poverty: all which gave them such advantages in the eyes of the simple multitude, as were able to ballance the other Honours of the *Dominican* Order. In short, The two Orders were engaged in a high Rivalry; but the Devotion towards the Virgin being the prevailing Passion of those Times, the *Franciscans* upon this had great Advantages. The *Dominicans*, that are all engaged in the Defence of *Thomas Aquinas*'s Opinions, were thereby obliged to assert that she was born in Original Sin: this was proposed to the People by the *Franciscans* as no less than Blasphemy; and by this the *Dominicans* began to lose ground extreamly in the minds of the People, who were strongly prepossessed in favours of the immaculate Conception.

About the beginning of the fifteenth Century, a *Franciscan* happened to preach in *Francfort*, and one *Wigand* a *Dominican* coming into the Church, the *Cordelier* seeing him, brake out into Exclamations, praising God that he was not of an Order that profaned the Virgin, or that poisoned Princes in the Sacrament, (for a *Dominican* had poisoned the Emperour *Henry* the Seventh with the Sacrament.) *Wigand* being extreamly provoked with this bloody Reproach, gave him the Lye: upon which a Dispute arose, which ended in a Tumult, that had almost cost the *Dominican* his Life: yet

yet he got away. The whole Order resolved to take their Revenge, and in a Chapter held at *Vimpfen* in the Year 1504. They contrived a method for supporting the Credit of their Order, which was much sunk in the Opinion of the People, and for bearing down the Reputation of the *Franciscans* Four of the *Juncto* undertook to manage the Design; for they said since the People were so much disposed to believe Dreams and Fables, they must dream on their side, and endeavour to Cheat the People as well as the others had done. They resolved to make *Bern* the Scene in which the Project should be put in Execution; for they found the People of *Bern* at that time apt to swallow any thing, and not disposed to make severe enquiries into extraordinary matters. When they had formed their Design, a fit tool presented it self, for one *Jetzer* came to take their habit as a Lay-brother, who had all the dispositions that was necessary for the execution of their Project: For he was extream simple, and was much inclined to Austerities, so having observed his temper well, they began to execute their Project, the very Night after he took the habit, which was on Lady Day 1507. One of the Friers conveyed himself secretly into his Cell, and appeared to him as if he had been in Purgatory, in a strange figure, and he had a Box near his mouth upon which as he blew, fire seemed to come out of his mouth. He had also some Dogs about him that appeared as his tormentors, in this posture he came near the Frier while he was a Bed, and took up a celebrated Story that they used to tell all their Friers, to beget in them a great dread at the laying aside their habit, which was, that one of the Order, who was Superiour of their House at *Soloturn* had gone to *Paris*, but laying aside his Habit was killed in his Lay-habit. The Frier in the Vizar said he was that person, and was condemned to Purgatory for that Crime; but he added That he might be rescued out of it by his means, and he seconded this with

D

most

most horrible Cries, expressing the miseries which he suffer'd. The poor Frier (*Jetzer*) was excessively frighted, but the other advanced and required a promise of him to do that which he should desire of him, in order to the delivering him out of his torment. The frighted Frier promised all that he asked of him, then the other said he knew he was a great Saint, and that his Prayers and Mortifications would prevail, but they must be very great and extraordinary. The whole Monastery must for a week together discipline themselves with a Whip, and he must lie prostrate in the form of one on a Cross in one of their Chappels, while Mass was said in the sight of all that should come together to it; and he added, That if he did this, he should find the effects of the Love that the B. Virgin did bear him, together with many other extraordinary things: and said he would appear again accompani- with two other Spirits, and assured him that all that he did suffer for his deliverance should be most gloriously rewarded. Morning was no sooner come than the Frier gave an account of this Apparition to the rest of the Convent, who seemed extreamly surprised at it, they all pressed him to undergo the discipline that was enjoyned him, and every one undertook to bear his share, so the poor deluded Frier performed it all exactly in one of the Chappels of their Church: This drew a vast number of Spectators together, who all considered the poor Frier as a Saint, and in the mean while the four Friers that managed the imposture magnified the Miracle of the Apparition to the Skies in their Sermons. The Friers Confessor was upon the Secret, and by this means they knew all the little passages of the poor Frier's Life, even to his thoughts, which helped them not a little in the Conduct of the matter. The Confessor gave him an Hostie, with a piece of Wood, that was, as he pretended, a true piece of the Cross, and by these he was to fortifie himself, if any other Apparitions should come to him,

si ce

since evil Spirits would be certainly chained up by them. The night after that the former Apparition was renewed, and the masqued Frier brought two others with him in such Vizards, that the Frier thought they were Devils indeed. The Frier presented the Hosty to them, which gave them such a check, that he was fully satisfied of the vertue of this Preservative.

The Friar, that pretended he was suffering in *Purgatory*, said so many things to him relating to the secrets of his Life and Thoughts, which he had from the Confessor, that the poor Friar was fully possessed with the Opinion of the reality of the Apparition. In two of these Apparitions, that were both managed in the same manner, the Friar in the Mask talked much of the *Dominican* Order, which he said was excessively dear to the B. Virgin, who knew her self to be conceived in original sin, and that the Doctors who taught the contrary were in *Purgatory*; that the Story of St. *Bernard*'s appearing with a spot on him, for having opposed himself to the Feast of the Conception, was a Forgery; but that it was true that some hideous Flies had appeared on St *Bonaventure*'s Tomb who taught the contrary: that the B. Virgin abhorred the *Cordeliers* for making her equal to her Son, that *Scotus* was damned, whose Canonization the *Cordeliers* were then soliciting hard at *Rome*: and that the Town of *Bern* would be destroyed for harbouring such Plagues within their Walls. When the injoyned Discipline was fully performed, the Spirit appeared again, and said, He was now delivered out of *Purgatory*; but before he could be admitted to Heaven he must receive the Sacrament, having died without it, and after that he would say Mass for those who had by their great Charities rescued him out of his pains. The Friar fancied the Voice resembled the Priors a little: but he was then so far from suspecting any thing, that he gave no great heed to this suspicion. Some days after this, the same Friar appeared as a Nun all in glory, and told the poor Friar that she was St. *Barbara*, for whom he had a particular Devotion, and added, that the B. Virgin was so much pleased with his Charity, that she intended to come and visit him. He immediately called the Convent together, and gave the rest of the Friars an account of this Apparition, which was entertained by them all with great joy; and the Friar languished in desires for the accomplishment of the Promise that St. *Barbara* had made him. After some days the longed for delusion appeared to him, cloathed as the Virgin used to be on the great Feasts, and indeed in the same Habit: there were about her some Angels, which he afterwards found were the little statues of Angels which they set on the Altars on the great Holidays. There was also a pulley fastned in the Room over his head, and a Cord tied to the Angels, that made them rise up in the Air, and flie about the Virgin, which increased the Delusion. The Virgin, after some endearments to himself, extolling the merit of his Charity and Discipline, told him, That she was conceived in original sin, and that Pope *Julius* the Second, that then reigned, was to put an end to the Dispute, and was to abolish the Feast of her Conception, which *Sixtus* the Fourth had instituted, and that the Friar was to be the Instrument of perswading the Pope of the truth in that matter. She gave him three drops of her Sons Blood, which were three tears of Blood that he had shed over *Jerusalem*; and this signified that she was three hours in original Sin, after which she was, by his mercy, delivered out of that State: for it seems the *Dominicans* were resolved so to compound the matter, that they should gain the main Point of her Conception in Sin, yet they would comply so far with the Reverence for the Virgin, with which the World was possessed, that she should be believed to have remained a very short while in that State. She gave him also five drops of Blood in the

for m

form of a Cross, which were Tears of Blood that she had shed while her Son was on the Cross. And, to convince him more fully, she presented an Hosty to him, that appeared as an ordinary Hosty, and of a sudden it appeared to be of a deep red colour. The Cheat of those supposed Visits was often repeated to the abused Friar; at last the Virgin told him that she was to give him such marks of her Son's Love to him, that the matter should be past all doubt. She said, That the five Wounds of St. *Lucia* and St. *Catharine* were real Wounds, and that she would also imprint them on him, so she bid him reach his hand: he had no great mind to receive a Favour in which he was to suffer so much: but she forced his hand and struck a Nail through it; the Hole was as big as a Grain of Pease, and he saw the Candle clearly through it: this threw him out of a supposed Transport into a real Agony: but she seemed to touch his Hand, and he thought he smelt an Oyntment with which she anointed it, tho' his Confessor perswaded him that that was only an Imagination: so the supposed Virgin left him for that time.

The next Night the Apparition returned, and brought some linnen Cloaths, which had some real or imaginary vertue to allay his torment: and the pretended Virgin said, they were some of the linings in which *Christ* was wrapped, and with that she gave him a soporiferous draught, and while he was fast asleep, the other four Wounds were imprinted on his body in such a manner that he felt no pain.

But in order to the doing of this, the Friars betook themselves to Charms, and the Subprior shewed the rest a Book full of them: but he said that before they could be effectual they must renounce God: and he not only did this himself, but by a formal Act put in Writing, signed with his Blood, he dedicated himself to the Devil: it is true he did not oblige the rest to this, but only to renounce God. The Composition of the Draught was a mixture of some Fountain-water and Chrisme, the Hairs of the Eye-brows of a Child, some Quick-silver, some Grains of Incense, somewhat of an Easter Wax-candle, some consecrated Salt, and the Blood of an unbaptized Child. This Composition was a Secret which the Subprior did not communicate to the other Friars. By this the poor Friar *Jetzer* was made almost quite insensible. When he was awake and came out of this deep sleep, he felt this wonderful Impression on his Body, and now he was raished out of measure, and came to fancy himself to be acting all the parts of our Saviour's Passion. He was exposed to the people on the great Altar, to the amazement of the whole Town, and to the no small Mortification of the *Franciscans*. The *Dominicans* gave him some other Draughts, that threw him into Convulsions: and when he came out of those, a Voice was heard, which came through that Hole which yet remains and runs from one of the Cells along a great part of the Wall of the Church: for a Friar spoke thro' a Pipe, and at the end of the Hole there was an Image of the Virgins with a little *Jesus* in her Arms, between whom and his Mother the Voice seemed to come; the Image also seemed to shed Tears: and a Painter had drawn those on her Face so lively, that the People were deceived by it. The little *Jesus* ask'd why she wept; and she said it was because his Honour was given to her, since it was said, That she was born without sin. In conclusion, the Friars did so over-act this Matter, that at last ev'n the poor deluded Frier himself came to discover it, and resolved to quit the Order.

It was in vain to delude him with more Apparitions, for he well nigh kill'd a Frier that came to him, personating the Virgin in another shape, with a Crown on her Head. He also o'er-heard the Friers once talking amongst themselves of the Contrivance and Success of the Imposture, so plainly, that he discovered the whole matter, and upon that, as may be easily imagined

ned, he was filled with all the horror with which such a Discovery could inspire him.

The Friers fearing that an Imposture, which was carried on hitherto with so much success, should be quite spoiled, and be turned against them, thought the surest way was to own the whole matter to him, and to engage him to carry on the Cheat. They told him in what esteem he would be, if he continued to support the Reputation that he had acquired, that he would become the chief person of the Order, and in the end they persuaded him to go on with the Imposture. But at last they, fearing lest he should discover all, resolved to poyson him: of which he was so apprehensive, that once a Loaf being brought him that was prepared with some Spices, he kept it for some time, and it growing green, he threw it to some young Wolves Whelps that were in the Monastery, who died immediately. His Constitution was also so vigorous, that tho' they gave him Poyson five several times, he was not destroyed by it. They also prest him earnestly to renounce God, which they judg'd necessary, that so their Charms might have their effect on him; but he would never consent to that: at last they forced him to take a poisoned Hosty, which yet he vomited up soon after he had swallowed it down: that failing, they used him so cruelly, whipping him with an iron Chain, and girding him about so strait with it, that to avoid farther torment, he swore to them, in a most imprecating stile, That he would never discover the Secret, but would still carry it on: and so he deluded them, till he found an opportunity of getting out of the Convent, and of throwing himself into the Hands of the Magistrates, to whom he discovered all.

The four Friers were seised on, and put in Prison, and an account of the whole Matter was sent, first to the Bishop of *Lausanne* and then to *Rome*; and it may be easily imagined, that the *Franciscans* took all possible

like care to have it well examined; and the Bishops of *Lausanne* and of *Zyon*, with the Provincial of the *Dominicans*, were appointed to form the Process. The four Friers first excepted to *Jetzers* Credit, but that was rejected; then being threatned with the Question they put in a long Plea against that: but tho' the Provincial would not consent to that, yet they were put to the Question: some endured it long, but at last they all confessed the whole progress of the Imposture. The Provincial appeared concerned: for tho' *Jetzer* had opened the whole matter to him, yet he would give no credit to him; on the contrary, he charged him to be obedient to them; and one of the Friers said plainly, that he was on the whole Secret, and so he withdrew, but he died some days after at *Constance*, having poison'd himself, as was believed. The matter lay asleep some time: but a year after that, a *Spanish* Bishop came, authorised with full Powers from *Rome*, and the whole Cheat being fully proved, the four Friers were solemnly degraded from their Priesthood, and eight days after, it being the last of *May* 1509, they were burnt in a Meadow on the other side of the River over against the great Church. The place of their Execution was shewed me, as well as the Hole in the Wall thro' which the Voice was conveyed to the Image. It was certainly one of the blackest, and yet the best carried on Cheat, that has been ever known; and no doubt had the poor Frier died before the Discovery, it had passed down to Posterity as one of the greatest Miracles that ever was; and it gives a shrewd Suspicion, that many of the other Miracles of that Church were of the same nature, but more successfully finished.

I shall not entertain you any farther with the State of *Bern*, but shall only add one general Remark, which was too visible not to be observed every where; and of too great Importance not to deserve a particular Reflection: it belongs in general to all the Cantons, but

I give

cause I had more occasion to make it
seen it more, and stayed longer in it
r Canton.
es between *France* and *Italy*, that are
untries incomparably more rich, and
with all the Pleasures and Conveni-
in it is; and yet *Italy* is almost quite
the People in it are reduced to a mi-
arce be imagined by those who have
France is in a great measure dispeo-
Inhabitants are reduced to a poverty
all the Marks in which it can shew it
eir Houses, Furniture, Cloaths, and

ary, *Switzerland* is extream full of peo-
y place, in the Villages as well as in
e sees all the Marks he can look for of
lth: Their Houses and Windows are
e High-ways are well maintained, all
cloathed, and every one lives at his
ervation surprised me yet more in the
Grisons, who have almost no Soil at all,
Va'eys that are almost washed away
nts that fall down from the Hills, and
ks sometimes so vio'ently and so sud-
many places the whole Soil is wash-
et those Valleys are well peopled, and
happy and at ease, under a gentle
hilst other rich and plentiful Countries
uch misery, that as many of the Inha-
d to change their Seats, so those who
scarce live and pay those grievous Im-
e laid upon them. The rude People
n very simply when they enter into
Government; but they feel true, tho'
so an easie Government, tho' joyn-
l, and accompanied with great Incon-
s, or at least keeps people in it, whereas

as a severe Government, tho' in general Idea's it may appear reasonable, drives its Subjects even out of the best and most desirable Seats.

In my way from *Bern* to this place I passed by *Soloturn*, as I came through *Fribourg* in my way from *Lausanne* to *Bern*, these are two of the Chief of the *Popish* Cantons, after *Lucerne*, and one sees in them a heat and a bigottry beyond what appears either in *France* or *Italy:* long before they come within the Church-doors they kneel down in the Streets when Mass is a saying in it. The Images are extream gross. In the chief Church of *Soloturn* there is an Image of God the Father, as an Old man with a great black beard, having our Saviour on his knees, and a Pigeon over his head. Here also begins a devotion at the *Ave-Mary-Bell*, which is scarce known in *France*, but it is practised all *Italy* over: At Noon and at Sun-set the Bell rings, and all say the *Ave-Mary*, and a short Prayer to the Virgin; but whereas in *Italy* they content themselves with putting off their Hats; in *Switzerland* they do for the most part kneel down in the Streets, which I saw no where practised in *Italy* except at *Venice*, and there it is not commonly done. But notwithstanding this extream bigotry, all the *Switzers* see their common Interest so well, that they live in very good understanding one with another. This is indeed chiefly owing to the Canton of *Lucern*, where there is a Spirit in the Government very different from what is in most of the other *Popish* Cantons: the residence of the *Spanish* Ambassadour and of the *Nuntio* in that Town, contributes also much to the preserving it in so good a temper, it being their interest to unite *Switzerland*, and by this means the heat and indiscretion of the rest is often moderated. The *Jesuits* begin to grow as powerful in *Switzerland* as they are elsewhere: they have a noble Colledge and Chappel situated in the best place of *Friburg*. It is not long since they were received at *Soloturn*, where there was a Revenue of

One

One Thousand Livres a Year, set off for the maintenance of ten of them, with this provision, That they should never exceed that number; but where they are once setled they find means to break through all limitations, and they are now become so rich there, that they are raising a Church and Colledge, which will cost before it is finished above Four hundred thousand Livres, to which the *French* King gives ten thousand Livres for the frontis-piece: For this being the Canton in which his Ambassadour resides, he thought it suteable to his glory to have a monument of his bounty raised by an Order that will never be wanting to flatter their benefactors, as long as they find their account in it.

In the same Canton there is an Abbey that has One hundred thousand Livres of Revenue, there is also a very rich House of Nuns that wear the *Cupuchins* Habit, that as I was told had Sixty thousand Livres of Revenue, and but Sixty Nuns in it, who having thus One thousand Livres a piece, may live in all possible plenty in a Country where a very little money goes a great way. But that which surprises one most at *Solothurn*, is the great Fortification that they are building of a Wall about the Town, the noblest and solidest that is any where to be seen: The Stone with which it is faced is a sort of course Marble, but of that bigness, that many Stones are ten foot long, and two foot of breadth and thickness: but tho' this will be a Work of vast expence and great Beauty, yet it would signifie little against a great Army that would attack it vigorously. The Wall is finished on the side of the River, on which the Town stands: the Ditch is very broad, and the Counterscarp and Glasier are also finished, and they are working at a Fort on the other side of the River, which they intend to fortifie in the same manner. This has cost them near two Millions of Livres; and this vast Expence has made them often repent the Undertaking: and it is certain,

that

that a Fortification that is able to refist the Rage of their Peaſants in the caſe of a Rebellion, is all that is needful. This Canton has two *Advoyers*, as *Bern*: the little Council conſiſts of Thirty ſix; they have twelve Bailiages belonging to them, which are very profitable to thoſe that can carry them; they have one *Burſar* and but one *Banneret*. All the Cantons have their Bailiages; but if there are Diſorders at *Bern* in the Choice of their Bailiffs, there are far greater among the *Popiſh* Cantons, where all things are ſold, as a Foreign Miniſter that reſides there told me, who tho' he knew what my Religion was, did not ſtick to own frankly to me, That the *Catholick* Cantons were not near ſo well governed as the *Proteſtant* Cantons. Juſtice is generally ſold among them; and in their Treaties with Foreign Princes, they have ſometimes taken money both from the *French* and *Spaniſh* Ambaſſadors, and have ſigned contradictory Articles at the ſame time.

Baden has nothing in it that is remarkable, except its convenient Situation, which makes it the Seat of the general Diet of the Canton, tho' it is not one of them, but is a Bailiage that belongs in common to eight of the ancient Cantons. At laſt I came to this Place, which as it is the firſt and moſt honourable of all the Cantons, ſo with relation to us it has a precedence of a higher Nature, it being the firſt that received the Reformation.

This Canton is much leſs than *Bern*, yet the Publick is much richer: They reckon that they can bring fifty thouſand Men together upon twenty four hours warning: their Subjects live happy; for the Bailiffs here have regulated Appointments, and have only the hundredth Penny of the Fines; ſo that they are not tempted as thoſe of *Bern* are, to whom the Fine belongs entirely, to ſtrain matters againſt their Subjects; and whereas at *Bern* the conſtant Intrigue of the whole Town is concerning their Bailiages, here, on
the

the contrary it is a Service to which the Citizens are bound to submit according to their Constitution, but to which they do not aspire. The Government is almost the same as at *Bern*, and the Magistrate that is called the *Advoyer* at *Bern*, is here called the *Bourgemaster*. The Revenue of the State is here justly accounted for, so that the publick purse is much richer than at *Bern*; the Arsenal is much better furnished, and the Fortifications are more regular. There is a great Trade stirring here, and as their Lake that is Twenty four miles long and about two or three broad, supplies them well with provisions, so their River carries their Manufacture to the *Rhine*, from whence it is conveyed as they please. One of their chief Manufacturies is Crape, which is in all respects the best I ever saw. I will not describe the Situation of the Town, but shall content my self to tell you that it is extream pleasant the Country about it is Mountanous, and the Winters are hard; for the Lake freezes quite over, only in some places the Ice never lies, which is believed a mark that some Springs rise there, which cause that heat; so also in the Lake of *Geneva*, tho' it is never quite frozen, yet great boards of Ice lie in several parts, but these are never seen in some parts of the Lake, which is supposed to flow from the same Cause.

But to return to *Zurich*, one sees here the true ancient simplicity of the *Switzers*, not corrupted with Luxry or Vanity, their Women not only do not converse familiarly with Men, except those of their near Kindred, but even on the Streets do not make any returns to the Civility of Strangers; for it is only Strangers that put off their Hats to Women, but they make no courtesies: and here as in all *Switzerland*, Women are not saluted, but the Civility is expressed by taking them by the Hand. There is one thing singular in the Constitution of *Zurich*, that is their Little Council consists of Fifty Persons, but there sit in

E

it only Twenty five at a time, and so the two halves of this Council, as each of them has his proper Bourgomaster, have also the Government in their hands by turns, and they shift every six Months, at *Midsummer* and at *Christ Mass*. The whole Canton is divided into nine great Bailiages, and 21 *Cast llaneries*; in the former the Bailiff resides constantly, but the *Castellan* who is also one of the great Council, has so little to do that he lives at *Zurich*, and goes only at some set-times of the Year to do Justice.

The vertue of this Canton has appeared signally in their adhering firmly to the antient Capitulations with the *French*, and not slackening in any Article, which has been done by all the other Cantons, where Money has a Soveraign influence: but here it has never prevailed. They have converted the ancient Revenues of the Church, more generally to pious uses than has been done any where else, that I know of. They have many Hospitals well entertained, in one as I was told, there was Six hundred and fifty Poor kept: but as they support the real Charities, which belongs to such Endowments, so they despise that vain magnificence of buildings which is too generally affected elsewhere; for theirs are very plain, and one of the Government there said to me very sensibly, that they thought it enough to maintain their Poor as Poor, and did not judge it proper to lodge them as Princes.

The Dean and Chapter are likewise still continued as a Corporation, and enjoy the Revenues which they had before the Reformation, but if they subsist plentifully, they labour hard, for they have generally two or three Sermons a day, and at least one: the first begins at Five a Clock in the morning. For at *Geneva*, and all *Switzerland* over, there are daily Sermons, which were substituted upon the Reformation to the Mass. But the Sermons are generally too long, and the Preachers have departed from the first design of these Sermons, which were intended to be an explication of of a whole Chapter, and an exhortation upon it, and if this were fo contrived that it were in all not above a quarter of an hour long, as it would be heard by the people with lefs Wearinefs and more Profit, fo it would be a vaft advantage to the Preachers; For as it would oblige them to ftudy the Scriptures much, fo having once made themfelves Mafters of the practical parts of the Scripture, fuch fhort and fimple difcourfes would coft them lefs pains, than thofe more laboured Sermons do, which confume the greateft part of their time, and too often to very little purpofe.

Among the Archives of the Dean and Chapter, there is a vaft collection of Letters, written either to *Bullinger*, or by him; they are bound up, and make a great many Volumes in *Folio*, and out of thefe no doubt but one might difcover a great many particulars relating to the Hiftory of the Reformation: For as *Bullinger* lived long, fo he was much efteemed. He procured a very kind reception to be given to fome of our *Englifh* Exiles in Queen *Maries* Reign, in particular to *Sands* afterwards Arch-bifhop of *York*, to *Horn* afterwards Bifhop of *Winchefter*, and to *Jewel* Bifhop of *Salisbury*. He gave them Lodgings in the Clofe, and ufed them with all poffible kindnefs, and as they prefented fome Silver Cups to the College, with an Infcription acknowledging the kind reception they had found there, which I faw, fo they continued to keep a conftant Correfpondence with *Bullinger*, after the happy re-eftablifhment of the Reformation under Queen *Elizabeth*: Of which I read almoft a whole Volume while I was there: Moft of them contain only the general News, but fome were more important, and relate to the Difputes then on foot, concerning the Habits of the Clergy, which gave the firft beginnings to our unhappy divifions: and by the Letters, of which I read the Originals, it appears that the Bifhops preferved the ancient Habits rather in compliance with the Queens inclinations, then out of any

E 2 liking

liking they had to them; so far they were from liking them, that they plainly exprest their dislike of them. *Jewel*, in a Letter bearing date the Eighth of *February*, 1566. wishes that the Vestments together with all the other remnants of Popery might be thrown both out of their Churches, and out of the minds of the People, and laments the Queens fixedness to them, so that she would suffer no change to be made. And in *January* the same year, *Sands* writes to the same purpose, *Contenditur de vestibus Papisticis utendis vel non utendis, dabit Deus his quoque finem.* Disputes are now on foot concerning the *Popish* Vestments whether they should be used or not, but God will put an end to those things. *Horn*, Bishop of *Winchester*, went farther: for in a Letter, dated the Sixteenth of *July* 1565. he writes of the Act concerning the Habits with great regret, and expresses some hopes that it might be repealed, next Session of Parliament, if the *Popish* Party did not hinder it; and he seems to stand in doubt whether he should conform himself to it or not, upon which he desires *Bullinger's* Advice. And in many Letters writ on that Subject, it is asserted, That both *Cranmer* and *Ridley* intended to procure an Act for abolishing the Habits, and that they only defended their Lawfulness, but not their Fitness; and therefore they blamed private Persons that refused to obey the Laws. *Grindal*, in a Letter dated the Twenty seventh of *August*, 1566. writes, That all the Bishops, who had been beyond Sea, had at their Return dealt with the Queen to let the matter of the Habits fall; but she was so prepossessed, that tho' they had all endeavoured to divert her from prosecuting that matter, she continued still inflexible. This had made them resolve to submit to the Laws, and to wait for a fit opportunity to reverse them. He laments the ill effects of the opposition that some had made to them, which extreamly irritated the Queens Spirit, so that she was now much more heated in those matters than formerly:

He

Bullinger for the Letter that he had the lawful use of the Habits, which he great Service. *Cox*, Bishop of *Ely*, in ers, laments the Aversion that they rliament to all the Propositions that the reformation of Abuses. *Jewel*, in he Two and Twentieth of *May* 1559, e Queen refused to be called Head of d adds, That that Title could not be ny Mortal, it being due only to *Christ*, icles had been so much abused by *Anti-* ought not to be any longer continued. sages I will make no Reflections here: own only to shew what was the sense hurch-men at that time, concerning which have since engaged us into such y Disputes; and this may be no incon- ction to one that intends to write the time. The last particular with which d this Letter, might seem a little too ere writing to a less knowing Man than

some pains in my Travels to examine t Manuscripts of the New Testament, t doubted Passage of St. *John's* Epistle, *that bear Witness in Heaven, the Father, the Spirit, and these three are one.* Bul- much of it, because he found it not in n Manuscript at *Zurich*, which seems to hundred years old; for it is written in egan to be used in *Charles* the Great's d the Manuscript, and found the Passage : but this was certainly the error or Copier: for before the General Epistles. ript, the Preface of St. *Jerom's* is to be ch he says, that he was the more exact ion, that so he might discover the Fraud, who had struck out that Passage concerning the Trinity. This Preface is printed in *Lira's* Bible; but how it came to be left out by *Erasmus*, in his Edition of that Father's Works, is that of which I can give no Account: for as on the one hand *Erasmus*'s Sincerity ought not to be too rashly censured, so on the other hand, that Preface being in all the Manuscripts, ancient or modern, of those Bibles that have the other Prefaces in them that I ever yet saw, it is not easie to imagine what made *Erasmus* not to publish it: and it is in the Manuscript Bibles at *Basle*, where he printed his Edition of St. *Jerom*'s Works. In the old Manuscript Bible of *Geneva*, that seems to be above seven hundred Years old, both the Preface and the Passage are extant, but with this difference from the common Editions, that the common Editions set the Verse concerning *the Father, the Word, and the Spirit*, before that of *the Water, the Blood, and the Spirit*; which comes after it in this Copy. And that I may in this place end all the Readings I found of this Passage in my Travels, there is a Manuscript in St. *Mark*'s Library in *Venice* in three Languages, *Greek*, *Latin*, and *Arabick*, that seems not above four hundred Years old, in which this Passage is not in the *Greek*, but it is in the *Latin* set after the other three, with a *sicut* to joyn it to what goes before. And in a Manuscript *Latin* Bible in the Library of St. *Laurence* at *Florence*, both St. *Jerom*'s Preface and this Passage are extant: but this Passage comes after the other, and is pinned to it with a *sicut*, as is that of *Venice*; yet *sicut* is not in the *Geneva* Manuscript. There are two *Greek* Manuscripts of the Epistles at *Basle*, that seem to be about five hundred years old, in neither of which this Passage is to found: they have also an ancient *Latin* Bible, which is about eight hundred years old; in which tho' St. *Jerom*'s Prologue is inserted, yet this Passage is wanting. At *Strasburg* I saw four very ancient Manuscripts of the *New Testament* in *Latin*: three of these seemed to be about the time of *Charles* the Great; but the fourth seemed

seemed to be much ancienter, and may belong to the seventh Century: in it neither the Prologue nor the Place is extant; but it is added at the foot of the Page with another hand. In two of the other the Prologue is extant, but the Place is not; only in one of them it is added on the Margent. In the fourth, as the Prologue is extant, so is the Place likewise; but it comes after the Verse of the other three, and is joyned to it thus, *Sicut tres sunt in cœlo.*

It seem'd strange to me, and it is almost incredible, that in the *Vatican* Library there are no ancient *Latin* Bibles, where above all other places they ought to be lookt for; but I saw none above four hundred years old. There is indeed the famous *Greek* Manuscript of great value, which the Chanoine *Shelstrat*, that was Library-Keeper, asserted to be One thousand four hundred years old, and proved it by the great similitude of the Characters with those that are upon St. *Hippolite's* Statue, which is so evident, that if his Statue was made about his time, the Antiquity of this Manuscript is not to be disputed. If the Characters are not so fair, and have not all the marks of Antiquity that appears in the King's Manuscript at St. *James's*, yet this has been much better preserved, and is much more entire. The Passage that has led me into this Digression, is not to be found in the *Vatican* Manuscript, no more than it is in the King's Manuscript. And with this I will finish my Account of *Zurich*. The publick Library is very noble: the Hall in which it is placed is large and well contrived: there is a very handsome Cabinet of Medals; and so I will break off. But when I have gone so much farther that I have gathered materials for another Letter of this Volume, you may look for a second Entertainment, such as it is, from

Your &c.

POSTSCRIPT.

I told you, that in *Bern* the Bailiages are given by a fort of a Ballot, which is fo managed, that no mans Vote is known: but I muſt now add, that ſince I was firſt there, they have made a conſiderable Regulation in the way of voting, when Offices are to be given; which approaches much nearer the *Venetian* method, and which expoſes the Competitors more to chance, and by conſequence may put an end to the Intrigues; that are fo much in uſe for obtaining thoſe Imployments. There is a number of Balls put into a Box, equal to the number of thoſe that have right to Vote; and that are preſent; of theſe the third part is gilt, and two parts are only ſilvered; ſo every one takes out a Ball; but none can vote, except thoſe who have the gilt Balls: ſo that hereafter a man may have more than two thirds ſure, and yet be caſt in a Competition.

There is one thing for which the *Switzers*, in particular thoſe of *Bern*, cannot be enough commended: they have ever ſince the Perſecution began firſt in *France*, opened a Sanctuary to ſuch as have retired thither, in ſo generous and ſo *Chriſtian* a manner, that it deſerves all the honourable Remembrances that can be made of it: ſuch Miniſters and others, that were; at firſt, condemned in *France*, for the affair of the *Cevennes*, have not only found a kind Reception here, but all the Support that could be expected, and indeed much more than could have been in reaſon expected. For they have aſſigned the *French* Miniſters a Penſion of five Crowns a month, if they were unmarried, and have increaſed it to ſuch as had Wife and Children, ſo that ſome had above ten Crowns a month penſion. They diſperſed them over all the *Pais de Vaud*: but the greateſt number ſtaid at *Lauſanne* and *Vevay*. In order to the ſupporting of this Charge, the Charities of *Zurich* and the other neighbouring *Proteſtant* States, were

were brought hither. Not only the *Protestant Cantons*, but the *Grisons*, and some small States that are under the protection of the Cantons, such as *Neufchastel*, *S. Gall*, and some others that have sent in their Charities to *Bern*, who dispence them with great discretion, and bear what further charge this relief brings upon them, and in this last total and deplorable dispersion of those Churches, the whole Country has been animated with such a Spirit of Charity and Compassion, that every Mans house and purse has been opened to the Refugies that have passed thither in such numbers, that sometimes there have been above Two thousand in *Lausanne* alone, and of these there were at one time near Two hundred Ministers, and they all met with a kindness and free-heartedness, that lookt more like somewhat of the Primitive Age reviv'd, than the degeneracy of the Age in which we live.

I shall Conclude this Postscript, which is already swell'd to the bigness of a Letter, with a sad Instance of the Anger and Heat that rises among Divines concerning matters of very small consequence.

The middle way that *Amirald*, *Daillé*, and some others in *France* took in the matters that were disputed in *Holland*, concerning the Divine Decrees and the extent of the death of *Christ*, as it came to be generally followed in *France*, so it had some assertors both in *Geneva* and *Switzerland*, who denied the imputation of *Adam*'s Sin, and asserted the Universality of *Christ*'s death, together with a sufficient Grace given to all men, asserting with this a particular and free Decree of Election, with an efficacious Grace for those included in it: these came to be called *Universalists*, and began to grow very considerable in *Geneva*: two of the Professors of Divinity there being known to favour those Opinions. Upon this those who adhered strictly to the opposite Doctrine, were inflamed, and the Contention grew to that height, that almost the whole

whole Town came to be concerned, and all were divided into parties. If upon this the Magistrates had enjoyned silence to both parties, they had certainly acted wisely: for these are speculations so little certain, and so little essential to Religion, that a diversity of Opinions ought not to be made the occasion of heat or faction. But tho' the party of the *Universalists* were considerable in *Geneva*, it was very small in *Switzerland*, therefore some Divines there, that adhered to the Old received Doctrine, drew up some Articles in which all these Doctrines were not only condemned, together with some speculations that were asserted concerning *Adam*'s Immortality, and other qualities belonging to the state of Innocency; but because *Capel* and some other Criticks had not only asserted the novelty of the points, but had taken the liberty to correct the reading of the *Hebrew*; supposing that some Errors had been committed by the coppiers of the Bible, both in the vowels and consonants, in opposition to this, they condemned all corrections of the *Hebrew* Bible, and asserted the Antiquity of the points, or at least of the power and reading according to them, by which tho' they did not engage all to be of *Buxtorfs* Opinion, as to the Antiquity of the points, yet they shut the door against all Corrections of the present punctuation. If this consent of Doctrine, for so they termed it, had been made only the standard against which no man might have taught, without incurring Censures, the severity had been more tollerable: but they obliged all such as should be admitted either to the *Ministry*, or to a Professors Chair to sign *sic sentio*, so I think, and this being so setled at *Bern* and *Zurich*, it was also carried by their authority at *Geneva*: but for those in Office, the Moderator and Clerk signed it in all their Names: and thus they were not contented to make only a Regulation in those matters, but they would needs, according to a maxim that has been so often fatal to the Church,

Church, enter into peoples Confciences, and either fhut out young-men from Emp'oyments, or impote a Teft upon them, which perhaps fome ha e figned, not without ftruglings in their Confcience. Yet fome that fet on this Teft or Content, are men of fuch extraordinary wer h, that I am confident they have acted in this ma ter out of a fincere zeal for that wh ch they believe to be the truth, only I wifh they had larger and freer Souls.

The only confiderable Tax under which the *Switzers* lie, is, that when Eftates are fold, the fifth part of the Price belongs to the Pub ick. and all the Abatement that the bailiff can make is to bring it to a fixth part. This they call the *Lod*, which is derived from *Alodium*: only there a e fome Lands that are *Frankalod*, which lie not under this Tax : but this falling only on the fellers of Eftates. it was thought a juft Punifhment, and a wife reftraint on ill Husbands of their Eftates.

I was the more confirmed in the Account I have given you of the Derivation of *Advoyer*, when I found hat in fome fma'l Towns in the Canton of *Bern* the hief Magiftrate is ftil' fo called; as in *Payerne*: fo hat I make no doubt, but as the Ancient Magiftrates n the time of the *Romans*, that were to give an account of the Town, were called *Advocates*; and afterwards the Judge in Civil Matte s, that was named by the Bifhops, was cal'ed at firft *Advocate*, and afterwards *Vilam* or *Vicedominus*; fo this was the Title that was ftill continued in *Bern*, while they were under the *Auftrian* and *German* Yoke, and was preferved by them when they threw it off.

I have, perhaps, touch'd too flightly the laft diffeence that was in *Switzerland*, which related to the Can on of *Glaris* In the Canton of *Apenzell*, as the wo Religions are tolerated, fo they are feparated in different Quarters, thofe of one Religion have the one half of the Canton, and thofe of the other Religion have

have the other half, so they live apart; but in *Glaris* they are mixt: and now the number of the *Papists* is become very low: so e assured me there were not above two hundred Families of that Religion, and those are also so poor, that their Necessities dispose some of them every day to change their Religion. The other *Popish* Cantons seeing the danger of losing their Interest entirely in that Canton, and being set on by the Intrigues of a Court that has understood well the Policy of imbroiling all other States, made great use of some Complaints that were brought by the *Papists* of *Glaris*, as if the prevailing of the other Religion exposed them to much injustice and oppression; and upon that they proposed that the Canton should be equally divided into two halves, as *Appenzel* was: this was extreamly unjust, since the *Papists* were not the tenth or perhaps the twentieth part of the Canton. It is true it was so situated in the midst of the *Popish* Cantons, that the *Protestant* Cantons cou'd not easily come to their Assistance: but those of *Glaris* resolved to die rather than suffer this injustice; and the *Protestant* Cantons resolved to engage in a War with the *Popish* Cantons if they imposed this matter on their Brethren of *Glaris*. At last this Temper was found, that in all Sutes of Law between those of different Religions, two Thirds of the Judges should be always of the Religion of the Defendant. But while this Contest was on foot, those, who as is believed, fomented it, if they did not set it on, knew how to make their advantage of the Conjuncture; for then was the Fortification of *Huninghen* at the Ports of *Basle* much advanced, of the importance of which they are now very apprehensive when it is too late. There are six Noble Families in *Bern* that have still this Priviledg, That when any of them is chosen to be of the Council, they take place before all the Ancient Counsellors; whereas all the rest take place according to the Order in which they were chosen to be of the Council.

LETTER

LETTER II.

Millan, the First of *October*, 1685.

After a short stay at *Zurich* we went down the Lake, where we past under the Bridge at *Ripperswood*, which is a very noble Work for such a Countrey; the Lake is there, about half a mile broad, the Bridge is about twelve foot broad, but hath no Rails on either side, so that if the wind blows hard, which is no extraordinary thing there, a man is in great danger of being blown into the Lakes: and this same defect I found in almost all the Bridges of *Lombardy*, which seemed very strange; for since that defence is made upon so small an expence, it was amazing to see Bridges so naked: and that was more surprizing in some places where the Bridges are both high and long: yet I never heard of any Mischief that followed on this, but those are sober Countries where drinking is not much in use. After two days journey we came to *Coire* which is the chief Town of the *Grisons*, and where we found a general Diet of the three Leagues sitting, so that having staid ten days there, I came to be informed of a great many particulars concerning those Leagues, which are not commonly known: The Town is but little, and may contain between four and five thousand Souls; it lies in a bottom upon a small brook, that a little below the Town falls into the *Rhine*. It is enironed with Mountains on all hands, so that they have a very short Summer, for the Snow is not melted till *May* or *June*; and it began to Snow in *September* when I was there: On a rising ground at the *East*-End of the Town is the Cathedral, the Bishop's

Bishop's Pallace, and the Close, where the Dean and six Prebendaries live; all within the Close are *Papists*, but all the Town are *Protestants*, and they live pretty Neighbourly together. Above a quarter of a mile high in the Hill one goes up by a steep ascent to S. *Lucius* Chappel; my Curiosity carryed me thither, tho'. I gave no Faith to the Legend of King *Lucius*, and of his coming so far from home to be the Apostle of the *Grisons*. His Chappel is a little Vault about ten Foot square, where ther is an Altar, and where Mass is said upon some great Festivites; it is situated under a natural Arch that is in the Rock, which was thought proper to be given out to have been the Cell of a Hermit, from it some drops of a small Fountain fall down near the Chappel; the Bishop assured me it had a miraculous vertue for weak eyes, and that it was Oily: but neither Tast nor Feeling could discover to me any Oilyness: I believe it may be very good for the Eyes, as all Rock-water is; but when I offered to shew the good Old Bishop that the legend of *Lucius* was a Fable in all the parts of it; but most remarkably in that which related to the *Grisons*; and that we had no Kings in *Brittain* at that time, but were a Province to the *Romans*, that no ancient Authors speak of it, *Bede* being the first that mentions it; and that the pretended Letter to Pope *Eleutherius*, together with his Answer, has evident Characters of Forgery in it, all this signified nothing to the Bishop, who assured me that they had a Tradition of that in their Church, and it was inserted in their Breviary which he firmly believ'd. He also told me the other legend of King *Lucius*'s Sister S. *Emerita*, who was burnt there, and of whose Veil there was yet a considerable remnant reserved among their Relicks; I confess I never saw a Relick so ill disguised, for it is a piece of worn linnen Cloth lately washt, and the burning did not seem to be a month old; and yet when they took it out of the Case to shew it me, there were some there that with great Devotion rub'd ub'd their beads upon it. The Bishop had some Conꝶs with his Dean, and being a Prince of the Empire ie had proscribed him: the Dean had also behaved iimself so insolently, that by an order of the Diet, to vhich even the Bishop, as was believed, consented, ie was put in Prison as he came out of the Cathedral. 3y the common consent both of the *Popish* and *Pro-estant* Communities, a Law was long ago made against Ecclesiastical Immunities: this attempt on the Dean vas made four years ago; as soon as he was let out, ie went to *Rome*, and made great Complaints of the 3ishop, and it was thought the *Popish* Party intended o move in the Diet while we were there, for the Re->ealing of that Law, but they did it not. The foun-lation of the quarrel between the Bishop and Dean, vas the Exemptions to which the Dean and Chapter >retended, and upon which the Bishop made some nvasion. Upon which I took occasion to shew him he novelty of those Exemptions, and that in the Pri-nitive Church it was believed that the Bishop had the Authority over his Presbyters by a Divine Right; and f it was by a Divine Right, then the Pope cou'd not :xempt them from his Obedience: but the Bishop vould not carry the matter so high, and contented iimself with two maxims; the one was, *That the Bishop was* Christ's *Vicar in his Dioceß*: and the other vas, *That what the Pope was in the Catholick-Church, he Bishop was the same in his Dioceß.*

He was a good natured man, and did not make use of the great Authority that he has over the *Papists* :here, to set them on to live uneasily wth their Neigh->ours of another Religion. That Bishop was anti-:ntly a great Prince, and the greatest part of the League that carries still the Name of *The House of God*, belonged to him, tho' I was assured that *Pregallia*, one of these Communities was a Free-State above Six hundred years ago, and that they have Records yet extant that prove this: The other Communities to

F 2 this

this League bought their Liberties from several Bishops some considerable time before the Reformation, of which the Deeds are yet extant: So that it is an impudent thing to say, as some have done, That they shook off his Yoke at that time.

The Bishop hath yet reserved a Revenue of about One thousand pound sterling a year, and every one of the Prebendaries hath near Two hundred pound a year. It is not easie to imagine out of what the Riches of this Countrey is raised, for one sees nothing but a tract of vast Mountains that seem barren Rocks, and some little Vallies among them not a mile broad, and the best part of these is washed away by the *Rhine*, and some Brooks that fall into it; but their wealth consists chiefly in their Hills, which afford much Pasture, and in the hot Months, in which all the Pasture of *Italy* is generally parched, the Cattle are driven into these Hills, which brings them in a Revenue of above Two hundred thousand Crowns a year. The Publick is indeed very poor, but particular persons are so rich, that I knew a great many there, who were believed to have Estates to the value of One hundred thousand Crowns. Mr. *Schovestein* that is accounted the richest man in the Country, is believed to be worth a million, I mean of Livres. The Government here is purely a Common-wealth, for in the Choice of their Magistrates every man that is above sixteen years Old hath his voice, which is also the Constitution of some of the small Cantons. The three Leagues are, the League of the *Grisons*; that of the *House of God*, and that of *The Ten Jurisdictions*.

They believe that upon the incursions of the *Goths* and *Vandals*, as some fled to the *Venetian* Islands, out of which arose that famous Common-Wealth; so others came and sheltred themselves in those Valleys. They told me of an ancient Inscription lately found, of a Stone where on the one side is graven *Omitte*
R. betys

Rhetos Indomitos, and *ne plus Ultra* is on the other; which they pretend was made by *Julius Cæsar*; the Stone on which this Inscription is is upon one of their Mountains, but I did not pass that way, so I can make no judgment concerning it. After the first forming of this People, they were cast into little States, according to the different Valleys which they inhabited, and in which Justice was administred, and so they fell under the power of some little Princes that became severe Masters; but when they saw the Example that the *Switzers* had set them, in shaking off the *Austrian* Yoke above two hundred years ago, they likewise combined to shake off theirs; only some few of those small Princes used their Authority better, and concurred with the People in shaking off the yoke, and so they are still parts of the body; only *Haldenstein* is an absolute Soveranity, it is about two miles from *Coire* to the *West*, on the other side of the *Rhine*; the whole Territory is about half a mile long at the foot of the *Alps*, where there is scarce any breadth. The Authority of these Barons was formerly more absolute than it is now, for the Subjects were their Slaves: but to keep together the little Village, they have granted them a power of naming a list for their Magistrates, the person being to be named by the Baron; who hath also the Right of Pardoning, a Right of Coining, and every thing also that belongs to a Soveraign. I saw this little Prince in *Coire*, in an Equipage not suitable to his quality, for he was in all points like a very ordinary Gentleman. There are Three other Baronies that are members of the Diet, and subject to it; the chief belonged to the Arch-Dukes of *Inspruck*; the other two belong to *Mr. Schovenstein* and *Mr. de Mont*, they are the Heads of those Communities of which their Baronies are composed; they name the Magistrates out of the lists that are presented to them by their Subjects; and they have the Right of Pardoning and of Confiscations: That belonging

longing to the House of *Austria* is the biggest, it hath five voices in the Diet, and it can raise Twelve hundred Men. One *Travers* bought it of the Emperour in the year 1679. he entred upon the Rights of the ancient Barons, which are specified in an Agreement that past between him and his Peasants, and was confirmed by the Emperour. *Travers* made many incroachments upon the Priviledges of his Subjects, who upon that made their complaints to the league; but *Travers* would have the matter judged at *Infpruck*, and the Emperour supported him in this pretension, and sent an Agent to the Diet: I was present when he had his Audience, in whiah there was nothing but general Complements: But the Diet stood firm to their Constitution, and asserted that the Emperour had no Authority to judge in that matter which belonged only to them, so *Travers* was forced to let his Pretensions fall.

All the other parts of this State are purely Democratical, there are Three different Bodies or Leagues, and every one of these are an intire Government, and the Assembly or Diet of the Three Leagues, is only a Confederacy like the United Provinces or the Cantons: There are Sixty-seven Voices in the general Diet, which are thus divided: the league of the *Grisons* hath twenty-eight Voices, that of the *House of God* hath twenty four, and that of the *Jurisdictions* hath fifteen. The *Jurisdictions* belonged anciently to the House of *Austria*, but they having shaken off that Authority, were incorporated into the Diet, but in the last Wars of *Germany*, the *Austrians* thought to have brought them again under their yoke, yet they defended their Liberty with so much vigour, that the *Austrians* it seems thought the Conquest not worth the while, and that it would not quit the cost. They were affrighted by two extraordinary actions; in one Village which was quite abandoned by all the Men belonging to it, who left the Women in it, some hundreds, as I was

told,

told, were quartered, and were apprehensive of no danger from their Hostesses; but the Women intended to let their Husbands see that they were capable of contriving and executing a bold design; tho' it must be confest it was a little too rough and barbarous for the Sex: They entred into a Combination to cut the Throats of all the Souldiers at one time; the Woman that proposed this had four lodged with her, and she with her own hands dispatcht them all, and so did all the rest, not one Souldier escaping to carry away the News of so unheard of a Rage. In another place a Body of the *Austrians* came into a Valley that was quite abandoned, for the Men that had no Arms but their Clubs and Staves, got up to the Mountains; but they took their measures so well, and possessed themselves so of the Passes, that they came down upon the Souldiers with so much fury, that they defeated them quite, so that very few escaped, and it is certain that the subduing them would have proved a very hard work. It is true they are not in a condition to hold out long, the publick is so poor; so that tho' particular persons are extream rich, yet they have no publick Revenue, but every man is concerned to preserve his Liberty, which is more intire here than in *Switzerland*, but this often swells too much, and throws them into great convulsion. The league of the *Grisons* is the first and most ancient, and it is composed of eight and twenty Communities, of which there are eighteen *Papists*, and the rest are *Protestants*; the Communities of the two Religions live Neighbourly together, yet they do not suffer those of another Religion to live among them, so that every Community is intirely of the same Religion, and if any one changes he must go into another Community. Each Community is an intire State within it self, and all Persons must meet once a year to chuse the Judge and his Assistants, whom they change or continue from year to year as they see cause: There is no difference
made

made between Gentleman and Peasant, and the Tenant hath a Vote as well as his Landlord, nor dare his Landlord use him ill when he Votes contrary to his Intentions, for the Peasants would look upon that as a common Quarrel. An Appeal lies from the Judge of the Community to the Assembly of the League, where all matters end; for there lies no Appeal to the general Diet of the three Leagues, except in matters that concern the conquered Countries, which belong in common to all the three. There is one chosen by the Deputies for the Assembly of the League, who is called the head of the League, that can call them together as he sees cause, and can likewise bring a cause that hath been once judged, to a second hearing. *Ilants* is the chief Town of this League, where their Diet meets. The second League is that of the *House of God*, in which there are four and twenty Communities; the Burgomaster of *Coire* is always the head of this League: This League is almost wholly *Protestant*, and the two Valleys of the upper and lower *Engedin* are pointed out by the *Papists*, as little less than *Cannibals* towards such *Catholicks* as come among them; but Frier *Sfondrato*, Nephew to Pope *Gregory* the fourteenth, whose Mother the Marquess of *Borgomaniero*, that was in *England*, hath married, found the contrary of all this to be true, to his great regret. About eighteen years ago he was believed to have wrought Miracles, and he became so much in love with the Crown of Martyrdom, that he went through the *Engedin*, not doubting but he would find there that which he desired. His Brother had come sometime before into the Countrey to drink mineral Waters, and was well known to the Gentry, so some of these hearing of the Friers coming, went and waited on him; and he was entertained by them in their Houses and conveyed him through the Countrey; tho' he took all possible ways to provoke them, for he was often railing at their Religion, but to all that they

made

made no anfwer, only they continued their Civilities ftill, which did fo inrage the warm Frier, that he went to *Bormio*, and there (as was believ'd) he died of Grief. An accident fell out five year ago, that the People of the Country efteemed a fort of a Miracle. The *Papifts* in their Proceffions go fometimes out of one Community into another, and when they pafs through *Proteftant* Communities they lower the Crofs, and give over Singing till they are again upon *Popifh* ground; but then they went on bearing up the Crofs, and finging as they went, upon which the *Proteftants* ftopt them, and would not fuffer them to go on in that manner: they finding that they were not equal in number to the *Proteftants*, fent to a *Catholick* Community, and defired them to come to their Affiftance: Two thoufand came, and by all appearance the difpute would have had a bloody iffue: for the *Proteftants* were refolved to maintain the Rights of their Community, and the others were no lefs refolved to force their way : but an extraordinary thick mift arofe, and through it the *Papifts* fancied they faw a vaft body of men, which was no other then a Wood: but terrified with the appearance of fuch a Number they retired, and this faved a little Battel that probably would not only have ended in the fhedding much Blood, but might have very much diforder'd the whole Conftitution and union of their Leagues.

The *Papifts* of Quality endeavour much to keep their People in order, but they acknowledged to my felf, that the *Proteftants* were much peaceabler than the *Catholicks*. The Jurifdictions have fifteen Votes in the general Diet, yet they are generally called the ten Jurifdictions, and the greater part of them are likewife of the Religion; for upon the general computation of the three Leagues, the *Proteftants* are about two thirds. In their Diets there are three Tables, one in the middle and two on either fide, at every Table fits
the

the head of the League and Secretary near him, and from the Table there goes down Benches on both hands for the Deputies from the communities of that league: They ho'd their Diets by turns in the chief Towns of the several Leagues, and it hapened to be the turn of the House of God when I was there, so they met at Coire.

The three Leagues have a conquered Country in *Italy* divided into three Districts, the *Valteline*, *Chavennes*, and *Bormio*. When *John Galeasse* possessed himself of the Dutchy of *Milan*, and drove out *Barnabas*, *Mastinus* one of *Barnabas*'s Sons, to whom his Father had given those three Branches of the Dutchy of *Milan*, retired to *Coire*, and being hospitably received and entertained by the Bishop, when he died he gave his Right to those Territories to the Cathedral of *Coire*: but here was a Title without a force able to make it good. But when the Wars of *Italy* were on foot, the three Leagues being much courted by both the Crowns, since they were Masters of the Passes by which either the *Switzers* or *Germans* could come into *Italy*, they resolved to lay hold on that opportunity; yet they had not zeal enough for their Bishop to engage deep upon his account: so they agreed with him to pay him such a Revenue, and he transferred his Title to them; and they were so considerable to the *Spaniards*, that without much ado, they yielded those parcels of the Dutchy of *Milan* to them, and by this means they are possessed of them. Those Accessions to this State are much better than the principal; for as certainly the *Valteline*, which is above forty miles long and two broad, is one of the richest Valleys in the World, in which there are three Harvests some years, so the *Chavennes* and *Bormio* are much preferable to the best Valleys of the *Grisons*; yet the engagement that people have to their native homes appears signally here, since the *Grisons* have not forsaken their Country that they might situate themselves so advantageously

ously: but they love their rugged Valleys, and think the safety they enjoy in them beyond the Pleasures of their acquired Dominions, so they govern them by Bailiffs and *Pedestas*, and other Officers whom they send among them; and all the advantages that they draw from them, is, That the Magistrates whom they send to govern them, do inrich themselves, as the Bailiffs in *Switzerland* do. All those Offices go round the several Communities who have the right of Nomination in their turn: but if there is none of the Community proper for the Employment, any one of another Community may buy of them the Nomination for that turn, and the Community distribute among them the money that he gives them. The Publick draws nothing out of those Parts, except the Fines, which in some years amounts to no considerable Sum, and ten or twelve thousand Crowns is thought a great deal to be raised out of them in a Year, so that their Subjects live happy and free of all Taxes, which made their last Revolt appear the more extraordinary; and it was indeed the effect of a very surprising Bigotry, when a People under the gentlest Yoke in the World, who had no other Grievance, but that now and then their Magistrates were of another Religion, and that the *Protestant* Religion was tolerated amongst them, would therefore throw off their Masters, cut the Throats of their Neighbours, and cast themselves into the hands of the *Spaniards*, who are the terriblest Masters in the World.

But to give a more particular relation of that matter, and to tell the Circumstances which seem a little to lessen that Rebellion and Massacre, I must give an account of a part of this Constitution that is very terrible, and which makes the greatest men in it to tremble. The Peasants come sometimes in great Bodies and demand a Chamber of Justice from the general Diet; and they are bound to grant it always when it is thus demanded, which comes about generally once in twenty years:
commonly

commonly this Tumult of the Peasants is set on by some of the male-contented Gentry, and generally there are a great many Sacrifices made. This Court is composed of ten Judges out of every League, and twenty Advocates, who manage such Accusations as are presented to them: this Court is paramount to Law, and acts like a Court of Inquisition; they give the Question, and do every thing that they think necessary to discover the Truth of such Accusations as are presented to them: and the decisions of this Court can never be brought under a second review, tho' there is an Exception to this; for about a hundred Years ago, one Court of Justice reversed all that another had done: but that is a single Instance. The Peasants are in as great a Jealousie of the *Spaniards*, as the *Switzers* are of the *French*, and the good men among them are extream sensible of a great dissolution of Morals that the *Spanish* Service brings among them; for there is a *Grison* Regiment kept still in Pay by the *Spaniards* there are in it twelve Companies of Fifty a-piece, and the Captains have a thousand Crowns Pay, tho' they are not obliged to attend upon the Service. This is upon the matter a Pension paid under a more decent Name, to the most considerable Men of the Country and this is shared among them without any distinction of *Protestant* and *Papist*, and is believed to sway their Councils much. The Peasants are apt to take fire, and to believe they are betrayed by those Pensioners of *Spain*; and when Rumours are blown about among them, they come in great numbers to demand a Chamber of Justice. The common question that they give which is also used all *Switzerland* over, and in *Geneva* is, that they tye the Hands of the suspected person behind his Back, and pull them up to his Head, and so draw them about, by which the Arms, and chiefly the Shoulder-blades, are disjoynted. And when a Person put to the Question confesses his Crime, and is upon that condemned to die, he is obliged to renew

his

his confession upon oath at the place of execution, and if he goes off from it then, and faith that his confession was extorted by the violence of the torture, he is put again to the question: for this passes for a maxime that no man must die unless he confesseth himself guilty: Generally when the fury of demanding this Chamber is spread among the people, the Gentry run away and leave the whole matter in the power of the Peasants, for they know not where it will end, and so the Peasants being named to be Judges, the Justice go s quick till some sacrifices appease the rage. Two year ago upon the sale of a common to the Bishop of *Como*, to which he had an ancient pretension, the Peasants having no more the liberty of the common, were inraged at their Magistrates, and a report was spread abroad, of which the first Author could never be discovered, that the *Spaniards* had sent a hundred thousand Crowns among them to corrupt all their Magistrates, upon this they were so set on fire, that it was generally thought there would have been many sacrifices made to this fury: but the Gentry hapned to be then so much united, that there was none of them ingaged among the Peasants, or that managed their rage: a Chamber of Justice was granted, but the matter was so ordered that it did not appear that any one was guilty, yet some that had dealt in that transaction were fined, not so much for any fault of theirs, is to raise a fonds to pay the expences of the Chamber, and because they could not find colour enough to raise so much out of the fines, there was a fine of ive hundred Livers laid on every one of the *Spanish* Companies. I hope this digression will not appear edious to you, and the rather because you will oon see that it was a little necessary to open the natter of the Rebellion and Massacre in the Valteline.

G

In the year 1618. there was a report set about, that the *Spaniards* had a treaty on foot to tear away the *Valteline* from the leagues, this was supported by the Fort *Fuentes*, that the Governor of *Milan* was building upon the Lake of *Como*, near the *Valteline*. There was one *Ganatz* a Minister, but a bloody and perfidious Man, that set on and managed the rage of the Peasants, and there was great reason to suspect some underhand dealing, tho he threw it which way he pleased. A Chamber of Justice was appointed to sit at *Tossane*, which is a considerable Town twelve miles from *Coire*, on the way to *Italy*, near *Alta Rhetia*, which is a high and small Hill, to which there is no access but on one side, where there are yet the ruines of a Castle and a Church, and which they believe was the Pallace of *Rhetus* the first Prince of the Countrey: There was severe justice done in this Chamber, a Priest was put to the question, and so ill used that he died in it, which is a crying thing among them. The chief suspicion lay upon one *Pianta*, who being of one of the best Families of the *Grisons*, was then one of the Captains in the *Spanish* Regiment; he withdrew himself from the storm, but the Peasants led on by *Ganatz* pursued him so, that at last they found him and hewed him in pieces, *Ganatz* himself striking the first stroke with an Ax, which was taken up and preserved by his Friends, and four and twenty years after fifty or sixty of his Friends fell upon *Ganatz* in *Coire*, and killed him with the same Ax, which they brought along with them, that they might execute their design by the same tool with which their Friend was murthered. *Ganatz* had during the Wars abandoned both his Religion and Profession, being, indeed, a disgrace to both, and had served first in the *Venetian*, and then in the *Spanish* Troops. After the peace was made he became so considerable, being supported

ted by the *Spanish* Faction, that he was chosen Governor of *Chavennes*, and was come over to *Coire* to a Diet, he being then in so important a charge: but he was so much hated, that tho the murthering of a Magistrate in Office, and at a publick assembly in so terrible a manner ought to have been severely punished, yet no inquiry was made into the crime, nor was any man so much as questioned for it. In that Chamber, many that were put to the question confessed enough to hang them, some indured the question and escaped with the loss of the use of their Arm. Those of the *Valteline* have made use of this severity, as that which gave the rise to the Massacre, and it is very probable this might have drawn in some, that would have been otherwise more moderate, and that it did likewise precipitate that barbarous action: yet it was afterwards found out that the Plot had been formed long before, so that the industry and rage of the Priests managed by *Spanish* Emissaries, working upon the bigotry of the people was the real cause, and this was only made use of as a pretext to give some more plausible colours to the Massacre, which was executed some months after this Chamber was dissolved. It began while the *Protestants* were at Church, there were some hundreds destroyed, the rest got all up to the Mountains, and so escaped into the Countrey of the *Grisons*, and those of *Chavennes* got likewise up to the Hills, for they are scituated just at the bottom of them.

I shall not prosecute the rest of that War, the *French* saw of what advantage it was to them not to let this pass from *Italy* into *Germany* fall into the hands of the *Spaniards*; so *Bassompiere* was sent to *Madrid*, and obtained a promise, that all things should be put in the same state in which they were before the year 1618, but when that

G 2   order

order vvas fent to the Governour of *Milan*, it vvas plain he had fecret orders to the contrary, for he refufed to execute it: fo a War follovved, in vvhich the *Grifons* found it vvas not eafie for them to fupport the charge of it, vvithout imploying the affiftance of the *French*. But the *Spaniards* pretended to have no other intereft in the affairs of the *Valteline* then the prefervation of the Catholick Religion, and to fhevv their fincerity, they put the Countrey into the Pope's hands, knovving that he could not preferve it but by their affiftance, nor reftore it vvithout fecuring it from all change of Religion. The *French* vvillingly undertook the caufe of the *Grifons*, and becaufe the Duke of *Rohan* vvas like to be the moft favourable General, as being of the Religion, he vvas fent to command fome forces that marched thither: But he favv that if the *French* once made themfelves Mafters of the paffes of the Countrey, it vvould turn to their ruine, and finding the *Grifons* repoled an intire confidence in him, he thought it unbecoming him to be an inftrument in that vvhich he favv muft be fatal to them. The *Spaniards* feeing the *French* ingage in the quarrel, and fearing left they fhould poffefs themfelves of the paffes, offered to reftore all the Territory in *Italy*, for *Chavennes* and *Bormio* had likevvife revolted, only the *Preteftants* got avvay fo quick upon the diforders in the *Valteline*, that they prevented the rage of the Priefts. The *Spaniards* ask'd thefe conditions, that an Amnefty fhould be granted for vvhat vvas paft, that there fhould be no exercife of the *Proteftant* Religion tolerated in the Countrey, and that even the Bailiffs and other Magiftrates of the Religion, that came to be fent into the *Valteline*, fhould have no exercife of their Religion, and as for other perfons, that none of the Religion might ftay above fix vveeks at a time in the Countrey. The

Duke

Duke of *Rohan* seeing that conditions of so much advantage to the Leagues were offered to them, did underhand advise those of the Religion to accept of them, at the same time that he seemed openly to oppose the treaty set on foot on those terms, and that he might get out of this imployment with the less dishonour, he advised their clapping him up in prison till they had finished their treaty with the *Spaniards*. So that they very gratefully to this day own that they owe the preservation of their Countrey to the wise advices of that great Man. Many that were of the Religion returned to their Houses and Estates, but the greatest part fearing such another *Massacre*, have since changed their Religion, others have sold their Estates and left the Country, some stay still and go two or three hours journey to some of the *Protestant* communities, where they have the exercise of the Religion: And tho they may not stay in the *Valteline* above six weeks at a time, yet they avoid that by going for a day or two out of the Countrey once within that time, nor is that matter at present so severely examined, so that there is a calm among them as to those matters. But when it comes to the turn of the *Protestant* communities to send one of the Religion to those imployments, he is often much embarassed by the Bishop of *Como*, to whose Diocess those Territories belong, for if the Bishop fancies that they do any thing contrary to the Ecclesiastical immunities, he excommunicates them, and tho this may appear a ridiculous thing, since they are already in a worse state by being Hereticks, yet it produces a very sensible effect, for the people that are extreamly superstitious, will not after that come near such Magistrates, so that about three years ago a Bailiff found himself obliged to desire to be recalled, tho his time was not out, since being excommunicated he could no longer maintain the Government in his own person.

Among the *Grisons* the *Roman* Law prevails, modified a little by their Customs. One that was a little particular, was executed when I was there.

A Man that hath an Estate by his Wife, enjoys it after her Death as long as he continues a Widower, but when he marries again he is bound to divide it among the Children that he had by her. The Justice is short and simple; but it is oft thought that Bribes go here, tho' but meanly in proportion to their Poverty, as well as in other Places. The married Women here do scarce appear abroad except at Church, but the young Women have more Liberty before they are married. There is such a plenty of all things, by reason of the gentleness of the Government and the industry of the People, that in all the ten days in which I stayed at *Coire*, I was but once ask'd an Alms in the Streets. There are two Churches in *Coire*, in the one there is an Organ that joyns with their Voices in the singing of the Psalms; and there was for the honour of the Diet, while we were there, an Anthem sung by a set of Musicians very regularly. In all the Churches both of *Switzerland* and the *Grisons*, except in this only, the Minister preaches covered, but here he is bare-headed. And I observed a particular Devotion used here in saying of the Lord's Prayer, that the Ministers who wear Caps put them off when it was said. The Women here, as in *Bern*, turn all to the *East* in time of Prayer, and also in their private Devotions before and after the publick Prayers: many also bow at the Name of *Jesus*. They *Christen* discovering the whole Head, and pouring the Water on the hind-head, using a trine Aspersion, which is also the practice of the *Switzers*. It was matter of much Edification, to see the great Numbers both here and all *Switzerland* over, that come every day to Prayers morning and evening. They give here in the middle of the Prayer a good in-

ter-

terval of Silence for the private Devotions of the Assembly. The Schools here go not above *Latin*, *Greek*, and *Logick*: and for the rest they send their Children to *Zurich* or *Basil*. The Clergy here are very meanly provided: for most part they have nothing but the benevolence of their People: they complained much to me of a great coldness in their People in the matters of Religion, and of a great Corruption in their morals. The Commons are extream insolent, and many Crimes go unpunished if the Persons that commit them have either great credit or much money. The poor Ministers here are under a terrible slavery: for the *Grisons* pretend that in all times they had not only the Patronage of their Churches, but a power to dismiss their Church-men as they saw cause. How it is among the *Papists* I cannot tell, but the Dean of the Synod of the *House of God* told me they had an ill custom of ordaining their Ministers without a Title, upon an Examination of their Qualifications and Abilities, which took them up generally six or seven hours: and when this Tryal was thus dispatched, if the Person was found qualified, they ordained him; and it was too ordinary for those that were thus ordained, to endeavour to undermine the Ministers already in Employment, if their people grew disgusted at them, or as they became disabled by Age: and often the Interest and Kindred of the Intruder carried the matter against the Incumbent without any colour or pretence; and in that case the Synod was bound to receive the Intruder. In one half of the Country they preach in *High Dutch*, and in the other half in a corrupt *Italian*, which they call *Romanish*, that is a mixture of *French* and *Italian*. In every League they have a Synod, and as the People chuse their Ministers, so in imitation of the *Switzers* every Synod chuses their *Antistes* or Superintendant; he is called the Dean among the *Grisons*, and hath a
sort

fort of an Episcopal Power, but he is accountable to the Synod. The Office is for life, but the Synod, upon great cause given, may make a change. The people of this Country are much more lively than the *Switzers*, and they begin to have some tincture of the *Italian* Temper. They are extream civil to Strangers; but it seems in all Commonwealths Inn-keepers think they have a right to exact upon Strangers, which one finds here as well as in *Holland* or in *Switzerland*.

I shall conclude what I have to say concerning the *Grisons*, with a very extraordinary Story, which I had both from the Ministers of *Coire* and several other Gentlemen, that saw in *April* 1685. about five hundred persons of different Sexes and Ages that past through the Town, who gave this account of themselves. They were the Inhabitants of a Valley in *Tirol*, belonging for the greatest part to the Archbishoprick of *Saltsburg*, but some of them were in the Diocesses of *Trent* & *Bresse*; they seemed to be a Remnant of the old *Waldenses*, they worshipped neither Images nor Saints, and they believed the Sacrament was only a commemoration of the Death of Christ; and in many other Points they had their peculiar Opinions different from those of the Church of *Rome*: they knew nothing neither of *Lutherians* nor *Calvinists*, and the *Grisons* tho' their Neighbours, had never heard of this nearness of theirs to the *Protestant* Religion. They had Mass said among them, but some years since some of the Valley going over *Germany* to earn somewhat by their labour, hapned to go into the *Palatinate*, where they were better instructed in matters of Religion; and these brought back with them into the Valley the *Heidelberg* Catechism, together with some other *German* Books, which run over the Valley; and they being before that in a good disposition, those Books had such an

effect

effect upon them, that they gave over going to Mass any more, and began to worship God in a way more suitable to the Rules set down in Scripture: some of their Priests concurred with them in this happy Change, but others that adhered still to the Mass, went and gave the Archbishop of *Saltsburg* an account of it: upon which he sent some into the Country to examine the truth of the matter, to exhort them to return to Mass, and to threaten them with all severity if they continued obstinate: so they seeing a terrible Storm ready to break upon them, resolved to abandon their Houses and all they had, rather than sin against their Consciences. And the whole Inhabitants of the Valley, old and young, Men and Women, to the number of two thousand, divided themselves into several Bodies: some intended to go to *Brandenburgh*, others to the *Palatinate*, and about five hundred took the way of *Coire*, intending to disperse themselves in *Switzerland*. The Ministers told me they were much edified with their Simplicity and Modesty, for a Collection being made for them, they desired only a little Bread to carry them on their way. From *Coire* we went to *Toffane*, and from that through the way that is justly called *Via Mala*. It is through a bottom between two Rocks, through which the *Rhine* runs, but under ground for a great part of the way. The Way is cut out in the middle of the Rock in some places, and in several places the steepness of the Rock being such that a Way could not be cut out, there are beams driven into it, over which, Boards and Earth are laid: this way holds an hour. After that, there is for two hours good way, and we past through two considerable Villages: there is good Lodging in both. From thence there is, for two hours Journey, terrible Way, almost as bad as the *Via Mala*: then an hours Journey good way to *Splugen*, which is a large Village of above two hundred Houses, that

are

are well built, and the Inhabitants seem all to live at their ease, tho' they have no sort of Soil but a little Meadow ground about them. This is the last *Protestant* Church that was in our Way, it was well endowed, for the Provision of the Minister was near two hundred Crowns. Those of this Village are the Carriers between *Italy* and *Germany*, so they drive a great Trade, for there is here a perpetual Carriage going and coming, and we were told that there pass generally a hundred Horses through this Town one day with another: and there are above five hundred Carriage-Horse that belong to this Town. From this place we went mounting for three hours, till we got to the top of the Hills, where there is only one great Inn. After that the way was tollerably good for two hours, and for two hours there is a constant-descent, which for the most part is as steep as if we were all the while going down Stairs. At the foot of this is a little Village, called *Campdolcin*, and here we found we were in *Italy*, both by the vast difference of the Climate; for wherea we were freezing on the other side, the heat of the Sun was uneasie here, and also by the number of the Beggars, tho' it may seem the reverse of what one ought to expect, since the richest Country of *Europ* is full of Beggars; and the *Grisons*, that are one of th poorest States, have no Beggars at all. One thing i also strange, that among the *Grisons*, the rich Win of the *Valteline*, after it is carried three days Journey is sold cheaper than the Wine of other Countrie where it grows at the door: but there are no Taxe nor Impositions here. From *Campdolcin* there is thre hours Journey to *Chavennes*, all in a slow Descent, an in some places the way is extream rugged and stoney *Chavennes* is very pleasantly scituated at the very foo of the Mountains: there runs through the Town pleasant little River. It is nobly built, and hath great many rich Vineyards about it; and the reboun f the Sun-beams from the Mountains, oth so increase the heats here, that the il is as rich here as in any place of *Italy*. Here one begins to see a Noble rchitecture in a great many houses; short all the marks of a rich Soil nd a free Government appear here. he Town stood a little more to the North, about five hundred year ago, but Slice of the Alps came down upon it, nd buried it quite, and at the upper nd of the Town there are some Rocks hat look like Ruines; about which here hath been a very extraordinary xpence to divide them one from another, and to make them fit places or Forts, and Castles: the marks of he Tools appeared all over the Rock n one place. I measured the breadth f the one from the other, which is wenty foot, the length is four hundred and fifty foot, and as we could uess the Rock was two hundred foot igh, cut down on both sides in a line s even as a wall; towards the top of ne the name *Salvius* is cut in great Letters a little *Gothick*. On the tops of hose Rocks which are inaccessible, except on the one side, and to that the ascent s extream uneasie, they had Garrisons

during

during the Wars of the *Valteline*: there were 1500 in Garrison in that which is in the middle: There falls down frequently slice from the Hills that do extreamly fatten the ground which they cover, so that it becomes fruitful beyond expression, and I saw a Lime tree that was planted 38 year ago, in a piece of ground which had been so covered, that was two fathom, & a half of compass. On both sides of the River the Town and the Gardens belonging to it, cover the whole Bottom that lies between the Hills, and at the roots of the Mountains they dig great Cellars, and grottoes, and strike a hole about a foot square, ten or twelve foot into the Hill, which all the Summer long blows a fresh Air into the Cellar, so that the Wine of those Cellars drinks almost as cold as if it were in Ice; but this wind-pipe did not blow when I was there, which was towards the end of *September*: For the Sun opening the pores of the Earth, & rarifying the exterior Air, that which is compressed within the cavities that are in the Mountains, rushes out with a constant Wind; but when the operation of the Sun is weakned, this course of the Air is less sensible. Before or over those Vaults they build little pleasant Rooms like Summer-houses, and

in

to Collation generally at night in
er saw bigger Grapes then grow
ne sort bigger then the biggest Da-
iat we have in *England*.
t of Wine here and in the *Valteline*,
eard named any where else, that is
k Wine, and as the tast makes one
a compofition, for it tasts like a
wn off Spices, so its strength being
Brandy, difpofes one to believe
a natural Wine, and yet it is the
e Grape without any mixture. The
gular, I informed my felf particu-
ly of preparing is: the Grapes
drinks white; they let the Grapes
'ines till *November* that they are
hen they carry them to their Gar-
em all upright on their ends by one
o or three months, then they pick
nd throw away those in which there
arance of rottenness, so that they
ound Grapes: after they are prefsed
juor in an open Veffel, in which it
a, which they take off twice a day,
re fcum comes up, which according
of the feafon is fooner or later, for
um comes no more after eight days,
mes it continues a Fortnight, then
close Veffel; for the first year it is
nd luscious, but at the end of the
it a little higher then the middle of
oft two thirds from the bottom, and
it cometh fo low, and then every
up a new: once a year in the month
ments, and cannot be drunk till that
continues a month, but their other
not at that time. *Madam Salu* a

H   Lady

I*ly of that Country who entertained us three days with a magnificence equal to what can be done in *London* or *Paris*, had Wine of this composition that was forty years old, and was so very strong that one could hardly drink above a spoonful, and it tasted high of Spicery, tho she assured me there was not one grain of Spice in it, nor of any other mixture whatsoever. Thus the heat that is in this Wine, becomes a fire and distils it self, throwing up the more spirituous parts of it to the top of the Hogs-Head.

Both here and in the *Grisons* the meat is very juycy, the Fowl is Excellent, their Roots and Herbs very tastful, but the Fish of their Lakes is beyond any thing I ever saw. They live in a great simplicity as to their habit and furniture, but they have plenty of all things, and are extream Rich, the Family where we were so Nobly Entertained is believed to have about two hundred thousand Crowns: here the *Italian* custom of one only of a Family that Marries takes place generally. There is a sort of Pots of Stone that is used not only in all the Kitchins here, but almost all *Lombardy* over, called *Lavege*, the Stone feels oyly and scaly, so that a scale sticks to ones Finger that touches it, and is somewhat of the nature of a slate, there are but three Mines of it known in these parts, one near *Chavennes*, another in the *Valteline*, and the third in the *Grisons*, but the first is much the best, they generally cut it in the Min: round, of about a foot and a half Diameter, and about a foot and a quarter thick, and they work it in a Mill, where the Chizzels that cut the Stone are driven about by a Wheel that is set a going by Water, and which is so ordered that he who manages the Chizzel, very easily draws forward the Wheel out of the course of the Water; they turn off first the outward Coat of this Stone till it is

exactly

xactly smooth, and then they separate one Pot after another by those small and hooked Chizzels, by which they make a nest of Pots all one within another, the outward and biggest being as big as an ordinary Beef-pot, and the inward Pot being no bigger than a small Pipkin; these they arm with hooks and circles of Brass, and so they are served by them in their Kitchins. One of these Stone-pots takes heat and boils sooner than any Pot of Mettle; and whereas the bottoms of Mettle-pots transmit the heat so intirely to the Liquor within, that they are not insufferably hot, the bottom of this Stone pot, which is about twice so thick as a Pot of Mettle, burns extreamly; it never cracks, neither gives it any sort of taste to the Liquor that is boiled in it, but if it falls to the ground it is very brittle, yet this is repaired by patching it up, for they piece their broken Pots so close, tho without any cement, by sowing with Iron-wire the broken Parcels together, that in the holes which they pierce with the Wire, there is not the least breach made, except that which the Wire both makes and fills. The passage to this Mine is very inconvenient, for they must creep into it for near half a mile through a Rock that is so hard that the passage is not above three foot high, and so those that draw out the Stones creep all along upon their Belly, having a Candle fastned in their forehead, and the Stone laid on a sort of Cushion made for it upon their hips: The Stones are commonly two hundred weight.

But having mentioned some falls of Mountains in those parts, I cannot pass by the extraordinary fate of the Town of *Pleurs*, that was about a league from *Chavennes* to the North in the same bottom, but on a ground that is a little more raised: The Town was half the bigness of *Chavenness*, the number of the Inhabitants was about two and twenty hundred persons, but it was much more nobly Built; for besides the great Palace of the *Francken*; that cost some millions, there were many other Palaces that were built by several rich Factors both of *Milan* and the other parts of *Italy*, who liked the scituation and Air, as well as the freedom of the Government of this place, so they used to come hither, during the heats, and here they gave themselves all the Indulgences that a vast wealth could furnish. By one of the Palaces that was a little distant from the Town, which was not overwhelmed with it, one may judge of the rest: It was an out-house of the Family of the *Francken*, and yet it may compare with many Palaces in *Italy* and certainly House and Gardens could not cost so little as one hundred thousand Crowns. The voluptuousness of this place became very crying, and Madam *de Salis*, told me that she heard her Mother often relate some passages of a *Protestant* Ministers Sermons, that preached in a little Church, which those of the Religion had there, and warned them often of the terrible judgments of God, which were hanging over their heads, and that he believed would suddenly break out upon them. On the 25th of *August*, 1618: An Inhabitant came and told them to be gone, for he saw the Mountains cleaving, but he was laughed at for his pains: He had a Daughter whom he perswaded to leave all and go with him, but when she was gone out of Town with him, she called to mind that she had not locked the Door of a Room, in which she had some things of value, and so she went back to do that, and was buried with the rest; for at the hour of Supper the Hill fell down and buried the Town and all the Inhabitants, so that not one person escaped: The fall of the Mountains did so fill the Channel of the River, that the first news those of *Chavennes* had of it was by the failing of their River; for three or four hours there came not a drop of Water, but the River wrought for it self a new course

and

and returned to them. I could hear no particular character of the Man who escaped, so I must leave the secret reason of so singular a preservation to the great discovery at the last day of those steps of Divine Providence that are now so unaccountable. Some of the Family of the *Francken* got some Miners to work under ground, to find out the wealth that was buried in their Palace; for besides their Plate and Furniture there was a great cash and many Jewels in the House: the Miners pretended they could find nothing, but they went to their Countrey of *Tirol*, and built fine Houses and a great wealth appeared, of which no other visible account could be given but this, that they had found some of that treasure. The chief Factors of *Italy* have been *Grisons*, and they told me that as the Trade of Banking began in *Lombardy*, so that all *Europe* over a *Lombard* and a Bank signified the same thing, so the great Bankiers of *Lombardy* were *Grisons*, and to this day the *Grisons* drive a great Trade in money; for a Man there of a hundred thousand Crowns Estate, hath not perhaps a third part of this within the Countrey, but puts it out in the neighbouring States: And the liberty of the Countrey is such, that the Natives when they have made up Estates elsewhere, are glad to leave even *Italy* and the best parts of *Germany*, and to come and live among those Mountains; of which the very sight is enough to fill a Man with horror.

From *Chavennes* we went for two hours through a plain to the Lake of *Chavennes*, which is almost round, and is about two mile Diameter. This Lake falls into the Lake of *Como* over against the Fort *Fuentes*; when we passed there, the Water was so low that the Boat could not easily get over a Bank that lay between the two Lakes. The Lake of *Como* is about eight and forty miles long and four broad, it runs between two ranges of Hills: I did not stay

long

long enough in *Como* to give any defcription of it, for I thought to have returned that way from a little Tour that I made into the Baliages that the *Switzers* have in *Italy*, of *Lugane*, *Locarmo* and *Bellinzona*: But I took another courfe, fo I faw nothing in *Como*; the beft thing in it is a fine Chappel, which the prefent Pope, who is a native of *Como*, is building. From *Como*, we went eight miles to *Codelago*, which belongs to the *Switzers*, and from thence to *Lugane* we had eight miles of Lake: this Lake doth not run in an even current as the other Lakes that rife under the Alps; but the fcituation of the Hills about it throws it into feveral courfes.

The *Switzers* have here feveral little Provinces or Baliages, of which during the Wars of *Italy*, between the Dukes of *Milan* and the two Crowns in *Francis* the Firft, and *Charles* the Fifths time, they poffeffed themfelves as a pledge for payment of their Arrears, and they were then fuch confiderable Allies, that they made both the Competitors for the Dutchy of *Milan* Court them by turns, and became the peaceable Poffeffors of almoft all that Tract that lies between the Lake of *Como*, to the Countrey of the *Valeffii* or the Valleys. The Inhabitants here are fo well ufed, they live to free of all Impofitions, and the *Switzers* Government is fo gentle, that here I muft tell you another Paradox, this is the worft Countrey, the leaft Productive, the moft expofed to cold, and the leaft capable of Trade of all *Italy*, and yet is by far the beft peopled of any that I faw in all *Italy*: There belongs to the Baliage of *Lugane* alone ninety nine Villages, of which a great many are very large, and all are full of people. The twelve ancient Cantons have their turns of all the Baliages and other Officers here: but when it comes to the turn of thofe of the Religion, their Bayliff, muft be contented with private Devotions in their own Houfe, but can have no publick exercifes,

cifes, nor fo much as a Minifter in their Houfes. For here as in the *Valteline* when the *Spaniards* confirmed the right of the Cantons to thofe Territories, they made an exprefs provifion, that no Religion except the *Popifh* fhould be tolerated here; fo that the Bayliff who is the Prince often hath not the free Liberty of his Religion in thefe parts. The Bayliffs here make their advantages as well as in the other parts of *Switzerland*, but yet with more caution, for they take great care not to give the natives any diftaft, tho the miferies to which they fee all their Neighbours expofed, and the abundance and liberty in which they live fhould by all appearance deliver their Mafters from any great apprehenfions of a revolt: A great many Mechanicks of all forts live in thefe parts, who go all Summer long over *Italy*, and come back hither with what they have gained, and live free of all Taxes.

I was told that fome Nephews of *Popes*, in particular the *Barberines* had Treated with the *Switzers* to buy this Country from them, and fo to erect it into a principality, and that they had refolved to offer twelve thoufand Crowns to the twelve Cantons, but they found it would certainly be rejected, fo they made not the propofition to the Diet of the Cantons as they once intended, and it is certain whenfoever this Country is brought under a yoke like that which the reft of *Italy* bears it will be foon abandoned, for there is nothing that draws fo many people to live in fo ill a foil, when they are in fight of the beft foil of *Europe*, but the eafinefs of the Goverment. From *Lugane* I went to the *Lago Maggiore*, which is a great and Noble Lake, it is fix and fifty miles long, and in moft places fix miles broad; and a Hundred Fathom deep about the middle of it, it makes a great Bay to the VVeftward, and their lies here two Iflands called the *Borromean*
Iflands

Iflands, that are certainly the lovelieſt ſpots of ground in the VVorld, there is nothing in all *Italy* that can be compared to them, they have the full view of the Lake, and the ground riſes ſo ſweetly in them that nothing can be imagined like the Terraſſes here, they belong to two Counts of the *Borromean* Family. I was only in one of them which belongs to the head of the Family, who is Nephew to the Famous *Cardinal* known by the name of *S. Carlo* : on the VVeſt-end lies the Palace, which is one of the beſt of *Italy*, for the lodgings within, tho the Architecture is but ordinary, there is one Noble apartment above four and twenty foot high, and there is a vaſt addition making to it, and here is a great Collection of Noble Pictures beyond any thing I ſaw out of *Rome*: The whole Iſland is a Garden except a little corner to the *South* ſet off for a Village of about forty little Houſes, and becauſe the figure of the Iſland was not made regular by nature, they have built great Vaults and *Portaca's* along the Rock, which are all made Groteſque, and ſo they have brought it to a regular form by laying Earth over thoſe Vaults. There is firſt a Garden to the *Eaſt* that riſes up from the Lake by five rows of *Terraſſes*, on the three ſides of the Garden that are watered by the Lake, the Stairs are Noble, the VValls are all covered with Oranges and Citrons, and a more beautiful ſpot of a Garden cannot be ſeen: There are two buildings in the two corners of this Garden, the one is only a milne for fetching up the VVater, and the other is a noble Summer houſe all wainſcotted, if I may ſpeak ſo, with Alabaſter and Marble of a fine colour inclining to red, from this Garden one goes in a level to all the reſt of the Allies and parterres, Herb-Gardens and Flower-Gardens, in all which there are varieties of Fountains and Arbors, but the great parterre is a ſurprizing thing, for as it is well furniſhed

with

(45)

ith Statues and Fountains, and is of a vast extent, id justly scituated to the Palace, so at the further-id of it there is a great Mount, that face of it at looks to the Parterre is made like a Theater all ll of Fountains and Statues, the height rising up five several rows, it being about Fifty foot high, id about Fourscore foot in front, and round this ount answering to the Five rows into which the heater is divided, there goes as many terrasses of ble walks, the Walls are all as close covered with ranges and Citrons as any of our Walls in *England* are with Lawrel; the top of the Mount is venty foot long and Forty broad, and here is a ist Cistern into which the Mill plays up the Wa-r that must furnish all the Fountains: The Foun-ins were not quite finished when I was there, but hen all is finished this place will look like an Inchan-d Island. The freshness of the Air, it being both in a ike and near the Mountains, the fragrant smell, the autiful prospect, and the delighting variety that is re makes it such a habitation for Summer, that per-ips the whole World hath nothing like it. From this went to *Sestio*, a miserable Village at the end of the ike, and here I began to feel a mighty change being w in *Lombardy*, which is certainly the beautifullest ountry that can be imagined, the ground lies so even, it so well watered, so sweetly divided by rows of Trees iclosing every piece of ground of an Acre or two cres compass, that it cannot be denied that here is vast extent of soil above Two Hundred miles long, nd in many places a Hundred miles broad, where ie whole Country is equal to the loveliest spots in ll *England* or *France*, it hath all the sweetness that *Holland* or *Flanders* have, but with a warmer Sun nd a better Air, the Neighbour-hood of the Moun-ains causes a freshness of Air here, that makes the il the most desirable place to live in that can be en, if the Government were not so excessively se-

I   vere

vere, that there is nothing but poverty over all the rich Country. A Traveller in many places finds almost nothing, and is so ill furnished, that if he does not buy provisions in the great Towns, he will be obliged to a very severe Diet, in a Country that I should think flowed with Milk and Honey; but shall say more of this hereafter. The *Lago Maggiore* discharges it self in the River *Tesine*, which runs with such a force that we went Thirty miles in three hours, having but one Rower, and the Water was no way swelled. From this we went into the *Canale*, which *Francis* the first cut from this River to the Town of *Milan*, which is about Thirty foot broad, and on both its banks there are such provisions to discharge the Water when it rises, to such height, that it can never be fuller of Water then intended it should be; it lies also so even that sometimes for six miles together one sees the line so exact that there is not the least crook; it is Thirty miles long, and is the best advantage that the Town of *Milan* hath for Water carriage.

I will not entertain you with a long description of this great City, which is one of the noblest in the World, to be an Inland Town that hath no great Court, no commerce either by Sea or any Navigable River, and that is now the Metropolis of a very small State; for that which is not Mountainous in this state, is not above sixty miles square, and yet it produces a wealth that is surprizing: It paies for an establishment of Seven and Forty Thousand Men and yet there are not Sixteen Thousand Souldiers effectively in it, so many are eat up by those in whose hands the Government is lodged: But the vastness of the Town, the Nobleness of the Buildings, and above all the surprizing riches of the Churches and Convents are signs of great wealth: The Dome hath nothing to commend it of Architecture, it being built in the rude *Gothick* manner, but for the vastness

ess and riches of the Building, it is equal to any in Italy, S. *Peters* it self not excepted. It is all marble, both pavement, and Walls both outside and inside, and on the top it is all flagg'd with Marble; and there is the vastest number of niches for Statues of Marble, both within and without, that are any where to be seen. It is true the Statues in some of the niches are not proportioned to the niches themselves; the Frontispiece is not yet made, it is to be all over covered with Statues and *bas reliefs*; and the Pillars of which there are Four rows in the body of the Church, have each of them Eight niches at the top for so many Statues; and though one would think this Church so full of Statues, that almost every Saint hath his statue, yet I was assured they wanted Seven Thousand to finish the design, but these must chiefly belong to the Frontispiece: The Church as I could measure it by walking over it in a equal pace, is Five Hundred foot long, and Two Hundred wide; the Quire is wainschotted and carved in so extraordinary a manner, that I never saw a fashion so well expressed in Wood; it contains Sixty stalls, and they have almost all the Histories of the Gospel represented in them. Just under the Cupulo lies S. *Carlo*'s body, as I was told, in a great case of Cristal of vast value, but I could not come near it; for we were there on two Holy-days, and there was a perpetual crowd about it; and the superstition of the People for his body, is such, that on a Holy-day one runs a hazard that comes near it without doing some reverence. His Canonization cost the Town a Hundred Thousand Crowns, they pretend they have miracles too, for Cardinal *Frederigo Borromee*; but they will not set about his Canonization, the price is so high. The Plate and other presents made to S. *Carlo* are things of a prodigious value; some services for the Altar are all of Gold, some very massie and set with Jewels, others

I 2 so

so finely wrought that the fashion is thought equal to the value of the mettle; the Habits and all the other Ornaments for the Function of his Canonization are all of an incredible Wealth. He was indeed a Prelate of great merit, and according to the answer that a Frier made to *Philip de Comines*, when he asked him how they came to qualifie one of the worst of their Princes with the Title of Saint in an Inscription which he read, which was that they gave that Title to all their Benefactors; never Man deserved of a Town this Title so justly as Cardinal *Borromee* did, for he laid out a prodigious Wealth in *Milan*, leaving nothing to his Family, but the honour of having produced so great a Man, which is a real temporal Inheritance to it, for as there have been, since that time, two Cardinals of that Family, so it is esteemed a *Casa Santa*; and every time that it produces an Ecclesiastick of any considerable merit, he is sure, if he lives to it, to be raised to this Arch-bishoprick, for if there were one of the Family capable of it, and that did not carry it that alone might dispose the State to a Rebellion, and he were a bold Man that would adventure on a competition with one of this Family. He laid out a great deal on the Dome and consecrated it, though the work will not be quite finished yet for some Ages, that being one of the crafts of the *Italian* Priests never to finish a great design, that so by keeping it still in an unfinisht estate, they may be always drawing great donatives to it, from the superstition of the People. He built the Arch-Bishops Palace, which is very noble, and a seminary, a Colledge for the *Switzers*, several Parish Churches, and many Convents. In short the whole Town is full of the marks of his Wealth. The riches of the Churches of *Milan* strike one with amazement, the Building, the Painting, the Altars, and the Plate, and every thing in the Convents, except their Libraires, prairies, are all signs both of great Wealth and of a very powerful superstition, but their Libraires not only here, but all *Italy* over are scandalous things, the room is often fine and richly adorned, but the Books are few, ill bound, and worse chosen, and the ignorance of the Priests both Secular and Regular is such, that no Man that hath not had occasion to discover it, can easily believe it. The Convent of S. *Victor* that is without the Town, is by much the richest, it is composed of Canons Regular, called in *Italy* the Order of *Mount Olive*, or *Olivetan*, that of the *Bernabites* is extream rich, there is a Pulpit and a Confessional all inlaid with Agates of different colours, finely spotted Marbles, and of *Lapis Lazulis* that are thought almost inestimable. S. *Laurence* has a noble *Cupulo*, and a Pulpit of the same form with that of the *Bernabites*. The *Jesuits*, the *Theatines*, the *Dominicans*, and S. *Sebastians* are very rich. The Cittadel is too well known to need a description, it is very regularly built, and is a most effectual restraint to keep the Town in order, but it could not stand out against a good Army three days; for it is so little, and so full of buildings, that it could not resist a showr of Bombs. The Hospital is indeed a Royal Building, I was told it had Ninety Thousand Crowns Revenue: The old Court is large, and would look noble if it were not for the new Court that is near it, which is Two Hundred and Fifty foot square, and there are three rows of Corridors or Galleries all round the Court, one in every stage according to the *Italian* manner, which makes the Lodgings very convenient, and gives a Gallery before every door: It is true these take up a great deal of the Building, being ordinarily Eight or Ten foot broad; but then here is an open space that is extream cool on that side where the Sun doth not lie, for it is all open to the Air, the Wall being only supported by Pillars, at the distance of Fifteen or

Twenty

Twenty foot one from another. In this Hospital there are not only Galleries full of Beds on both sides, as is ordinary in all Hospitals; but there are also a great many Chambers in which Persons whose condition was formerly distinguished are treated with a particular care. There is an out-house which i called the *Lazarette*, that is without the Walls which belongs to this Hospital, it is an exact quarter of a mile square, and there are Three Hundred and Sixty Rooms in it, and a Gallery runs all along before the Chambers, so that as the service is convenient, the sick have a covered walk before their Doors. In the middle of this vast square there i an *Octangular* Chappel, so contrived that the sicl from all their Beds may see the elevation of the Hostie and adore it: This House is for the Plague or for infectious Feavers, and the Sick that want a freer Air, are also removed hither.

As for the devotions of this place, I saw here the *Ambrosian* Office, which is distinguished from the *Roman*, both in the Musick which is much simpler, and in some other rites: the Gospel is read in a high Pulpit at the lower end of the Quire, that so it may be heard by all the People, though this is needless since it is read in a Language that they do not understand; when they go to say high Mass, the Priest comes from the high Altar to the lower-end of the Quire, where the Offertory of the Bread and the Wine is made by some of the Laity, they were Nuns that made it when I was there, I heard a *Capucin* Preach here; it was the first Sermon I heard in *Italy*, and I was much surprized at many Comical expressions and gestures, but most of all with the conclusion; for there being in all the Pulpits of *Italy* a Crucifix on the side of the Pulpit towards the Altar; he, after a long address to it, at last in a forced transport, took it in his Arms and hugged it and kissed it: But I observed that before he kiss'd it; he seeing some dust on on it, blew it off very carefully, for I was juſt under the Pulpit: He entertained it with a long and tender careſs, and held it out to the People, and would have forced tears both from himſelf and them, yet I ſaw none ſhed. But if the Sermon in the Morning ſurprized me, I wondred no leſs at two diſcourſes that I heard in one Church, at the ſame time, in the afterhoon; for there were two bodies of Men ſet down in different places of the Church all covered, and two Lay-men in ordinary habits were entertaining them with diſcourſes of Religion in a Catechetical ſtile: Theſe were Confrairies, and thoſe were ſome of the more devout that inſtructed the reſt. This I never ſaw any where elſe, ſo I do not know whether it is peculiar to *Milan* or not. My Conductor could not ſpeak *Latin*, and the *Italian* there is ſo different from the true *Tuſcan*, which I only knew, that I could not underſtand him when he was engaged in a long diſcourſe, ſo I was not clearly informed of this matter; but I am apt to think it might have been ſome inſtitution of Cardinal *Borromees*. The *Ambroſian* Library founded by Cardinal *Frederick Borromee* is a very noble Room and well furniſhed, only it is too full of School-men and Canoniſts, which are the chief ſtudies of *Italy*, and it hath too few Books of a more ſolid and uſeful learning. One part of the diſpoſition of the Room was pleaſant, there is a great number of Chairs placed all round it at a competent diſtance from one another, and to every Chair there belongs a Desk with an Ecritoire that hath Pen, Ink, and Paper in it, ſo that every Man finds tools here for ſuch extracts as he would make. There is a little Room of Manuſcripts at the end of the great Gallery, but the Library-keeper knows little of them, a great many of them relate to their Saint *Charles*. I ſaw ſome fragments of *Latin* Bibles, but none ſeemed to be above Six Hundred Years old, there are alſo ſome fragments of Saint *Ambroſes* works, and of Saint *Jerom's rom*'s Epiftle that are of the fame antiquity. I was forry not to find St. *Ambrofe*'s Works intire, that I might have feen whether the Books of the Sacraments are afcribed to him in ancient Copies, for perhaps they belong to a more modern Author.

It is true, in thefe Books the Doctrine of a fort of a Corporal Prefence is afferted in very high expreffions; but there is one thing mentioned in them, which is ftronger againft it than all thofe citations can be for it; for the Author gives us the formal words of the Prayer of Confecration in his time, which he Prefaces with folemnity: Will you know how the change is wrought, hear the Heavenly words? For the Prieft faith, but whereas in the prefent Canon of the Mafs, the Prayer of Confecration is for a good part of it very near in the fame words with thofe which he mentions, there is one effential difference, for in the Canon they now pray that the Hofty may be to them the Body and Blood of *Chrift*, (which by the way doth not agree too well with the notion of Tranfubftantiation, and approacheth more to the Doctrine of the *Lutherians:*) whereas in the Prayer, cited by that Author, the Hofty is faid to be the figure of the Body and Blood of *Chrift:* here is the language of the whole Church of that time, and in the moft important part of the divine Office, which fignifieth more to me than a Thoufand Quotations out of particular Writers, which are but their private opinions: But this is the voice of the whole body in its addreffes to God: And it feems the Church of *Rome*, when the new Doctrine of the Corporal Prefence was received, faw that this Prayer of Confecration could not confift with it, which made her change fuch a main part of the Office. This gave me a curiofity every where to fearch for ancient Offices, but I found none in the Abbey of St. *Germains* that feemed older than the times of *Charles* the Great; fo I found none of any great Antiquity in all *Italy*:

Thofe

Those published by Cardinal *Bona*, and since by *P. Ma-billon*, that were brought from *Heidelberg*, are the most ancient that are in the *Vatican*; but these seem not to be above Eight hundred Years old: There are none of the ancient *Roman* Offices now to be seen in the *Vatican*. I was amazed to find none of any great Antiquity; which made me conclude that either they were destroyed, that so the difference between Ancient and Modern Rituals might not be turned against that Church, as an undeniable Evidence to prove the Changes that she hath made in divine matters, or that they were so well kept that Hereticks were not to be suffered to look into them. But to return to the *Ambrosian* Library, there is in it a Manuscript of great Antiquity, though not of such great consequence, which is *Ruffinus*'s Translation of *Josephus*, that is written in the old *Roman* hand, which is very hard to read. But there is a deed in the curious Collection that Count *Mascardo* hath made at *Verona*, which by the date appears to have been written in *Theodosius*'s time, which is the same sort of writing with the Manuscript of *Ruffinus*, so that it may be reckoned to have been writ in *Ruffinus*'s own time, and this is the most valuable, though the least known curiosity in the whole Library.

I need not say any thing of the curious Works in Crystal that are to be seen in *Milan*; the greatest quantities that are in *Europe*, are found in the *Alps*, and are wrought here; but this is too well known to need any further enlargement. It is certain, the *Alps* have much Wealth shut up in their Rocks, if the Inhabitants knew how to search for it: But I heard of no Mines that were wrought except Iron Mines; yet by the colourings, that in many places, the Fountains make, as they run along the Rocks, one sees cause to believe that there are Mines and Minerals shut up within them. Gold hath been often found in the River of *Arve*, that runs by *Geneva*.

The

The last Curiosity that I shall mention of the Town of *Milan*, is the Cabinet of the Chanoine *Settala* which is now in his Brothers hands, where there are a great many very valuable things, both of Art and Nature: there is a lump of Ore, in which there is both Gold, Silver, Emeralds, and Diamonds, which was brought from *Peru*. There are many curious motions where by an unseen Spring, a Ball, after it hath rowled down through many winding descents, is thrown up, and so it seems to be a perpetual motion. This is done in several forms, and is well enough disguised to deceive the vulgar. Many motions of little Animals that run about by Springs, are also very pretty. There is a Loadstone of a vast force that carries a great Chain: There is also a monstrous Child that was lately born in the Hospital, which is preserved in Spirit of Wine: It is double below, it hath one Breast and Neck, two pair of Ears, a vast Head, and but one Face. As for the Buildings in *Milan*, they are big and substantial, but they have not much regular or beautiful Architecture: The Governors Palace hath some noble apartments in it: The chief Place of the Town is that of the *Homodei*, which was built by a Bankier. There is one inconvenience in *Milan*, which throws down all the pleasure that one can find in it: they have no Glass Windows, so that one is either exposed to the Air, or shut up in a Dungeon: and this so universal, that there is not one house of ten that hath Glass in their Windows: The same defect is in *Florence*, besides all the small Towns of *Italy*, which is an effect of their poverty: For what by the oppression of the Government, what by the no less squeezing oppression of their Priests, who drain all the rest of their Wealth that is not eat up by the Prince, to inrich their Churches and Convents, the People here are reduced to a poverty, that cannot be easily believed by one that sees the Wealth that is in their Churches, and this is going on so constantly in *Milan*, that it is

scarce

scarce accountable from whence so vast a treasure can be found; but Purgatory is a fond not easily exhausted. The Wealth of the *Milanese* consists chiefly in their Silks, and that Trade falls so mightily by the vast Importations that the *East-India* Companies bring into *Europe*, that all *Italy* feels this very sensibly, and languishes extreamly by the great fall that is in the Silk-Trade: There is a great magnificence in *Milan*; the Nobility affect to make a noble appearance both in their Cloaths, their Coaches, and their Attendants; and the Women go abroad with more freedom here than in any Town of *Italy*. And thus I have told you all that hath hitherto occurred to me, that I thought worth your knowledge. I am

Yours,

Postscript.

IN the account that I gave you of *Geneva*, I forgot to mention a very extraordinary Person that is here, Mrs. *Walkier*; her Father is of *Shaff* House, she lost her sight when she was but a Year old, by being too near a Stove that was very hot: There rests in her Eye so much sight, that she distinguishes Day from Night; and when any Person stands between her and the light she will distinguish by the Head and its dress a Man from a Woman; but when she turns down her Eyes she sees nothing: she hath a vast memory; besides the *French* that is her natural language, she speakes both *High Dutch*, *Italian* and *Latine*: she hath all the Psalms by heart, in *French*, and many of them in *Dutch* and *Italian*: she understands the Old Philosophy well, and is now studying the New: she hath studied the body of Divinity well, and hath the Text of the Scriptures very ready: On all which matters I had long conversations with her; she not only sings well, but she plays rarely on the Organ; and I was told she played on the Violin, but her Violin was out of order. * But that which is most of all, is, she writes legibly: in order to her learning to write, her Father
who

who is a worthy Man, and hath such tenderness for her, that he furnisheth her with Masters of all sorts, ordered Letters to be carved in Wood, and she by feeling the Characters formed such an Idea of them, that she writes with a Crayon so distinctly, that her writing can be well read, of which I have several Essays. I saw her write, she doth it more nimbly than can be imagined; she hath a Machine that holds the Paper, and keeps her always in line. But that which is above all the rest, she is a person of extraordinary Devotion, great resignation to the Will of God, and a profound humility: The Preceptor that the Father kept in the house with her, hath likewise a wonderful faculty o acquiring Tongues. When he came first to *Geneva* (for he is of *Zurich*) he spoke not a word of *French* and within Thirteen months he Preacht in *Frencl* correctly, and with a good accent: He also began to study *Italian* in the month of *November*, and befor the end of the following *February* he preacht in *Italian*; his accent was good, and his stile was florid which was very extraordinary, for the *Italian* langu age is not spoken in *Geneva*, though the Race of th *Italians* do keep up still an *Italian* Church there.

THE THIRD LETTER.

Florence *the* 5*th. of* November.

I Have now another Month over my head since I writ last to you, and so I know you expect an account of the most considerable things that have occurred to me since my last from *Milan.* Twenty Miles from *Milan* we past through *Lodi* a miserable Garrison, though a Frontier Town; but indeed the Frontiers, both of the *Spaniards* and the *Venetians,* as well as those of other Princes of *Italy,* shew that they are not very apprehensive of one another; and when one passes through those places, which are represented in History as places of great strength, capable of resisting a long Siege, he must acknowledge that the sight of them, brings the *Idea* that he had conceived of them, a great many degrees lower. For *Lombardy,* which was so long the seat of War, could not stand out a good Army now for so many Days, as it did then for Years. The Garrison of *Crema,* which is the first of the *Venetian* Territory, is no better than that of *Lodi,* only the People in the *Venetian* Dominion are happier than under the *Spaniard.*

The Senate sends *Podesta*'s, much like the Bailiffs of the *Switzers,* who order the Justice and the Civil Government of the Jurisdiction assigned them: There is also a Captain General who hath the Military Authority in his hands; and these two are checks upon one another, as the *Bassa*'s and the *Cadi*'s are among the *Turks.* But here in *Crema* the Town is so small that

K

that both these are in one Person. We were there in the time of the Fair, Linnen Cloath and Cheese, which though it goes by the name of *Parmesan*, is made chiefly in *Lodi*, are the main Ingredients of the Fair. The magnificence of the *Podesta* appeared very extraordinary, for he went through the Fair with a great train of Coaches, all in his own Livery; and the two Coaches in which he and his Lady ride, were both extraordinary rich: his was a huge Bed-coach, all the out side black Velvet, and a mighty rich Gold fringe lined with black Damask, flowred with Gold. From *Crema* it is Thirty miles to *Brescia*, which is a great Town, and full of Trade and Wealth, here they make the best Barrils for Pistols and Muskets of all *Italy*: There are great Iron Works near it; but the War with the *Turk* had occasioned an Order that none be sold without a permission from *Venice*: They are building a Noble Dome at *Brescia*: I was shewed a Nunnery there, which is now under a great disgrace some years ago a new Bishop coming thither, began with the Visitation of that Nunnery: he discovered two Vaults, by one, Men came ordinarily into it: and by another the Nuns that were big went and lay-in of Child-bed: when he was examining the Nuns severel concerning those Vaults, some of them told him, that his own Priests did much worse: He shut up the Nuns, so that those who are professed live still there but none come to take the Vail: and by this means the House will soon come to an end: The Cittadel lies over the Town on a Rock, and commands it absolutely. Both here and in *Crema* the Towns have begun a Complement within these last Ten or Twelv Years to their *Podesta*'s, which is a matter of great Ornament to their Palaces, but will grow to a vast charge, for they erect Statues to their *Podesta*'s: and this being once begun, must be carried on: otherwise those, to whom the like Honour is not done, will resent it as a high affront, and the revenges of the

Noble

Noble *Venetians*, are dreadful things their to Subjects. This name of *Podesta* is very ancient, for in the Roman times, the chief Magistrates of the lesser Towns was called the *Potestas*, as appears by that of *Juveral-Fidenarum Gabiorumve esse potestas.*

From *Brescia* the beauty of *Lombardy* is a little interrupted; for as all the way from *Milan* to *Brescia* is as one Garden, so here on the one side we come under the Mountains, and we pass by the Lake of *Guarda*, which is Forty miles long, and where it is broadest, is Twenty miles broad: The miles indeed, all *Lombardy* over, are extream short, for I walkt often four or five miles in a walk, and I found a Thousand paces made their common mile; but in *Tuscany* and the Kingdom of *Naples*, the mile is Fifteen Hundred paces. We pass through a great Heath for Seven or Eight miles on this side of *Verona*, which begins to be cultivated. *Verona* is a vast Town, and much of it well built; there are many rich Churches in it; but there is so little Trade stirring, and so little money going, that it is not easie here to change a Pistol, without taking their coin of base alloy, which doth not pass out of the *Veronese*; for this seems a strange maxim of the *Venetians* to suffer those small states, to retain still a coin peculiar to them, which is extream inconvenient for Commerce. The known Antiquity of *Verona* is the Amphitheater, one of the least of all that the *Romans* built, but the best preserved, for though most of the great stones of the out-side are pickt out; yet the great flopping Vault on which the rows of the seats are also intire, they are four and forty rows, every row is a foot and half high, and as much in breadth, so that a Man sits conveniently in them, under the feet of those of the higher row: and allowing every Man a foot and a half, the whole Amphitheater can hold Twenty three thousand persons. In the Vaults, under the rows of seats, were the Stalls for the Beasts that were presented to enter-

K 2   tain

tain the Company: the thickneſs of the building, from the outward Wall to the loweſt row of ſeats, is ninety foot: But this Noble remnant of Antiquity is ſo often and ſo copiouſly deſcribed, that I will ſay no more of it. The next thing of value is the famous *Muſeum Calceolarium*, now in the hands of the Count *Maſcardo*, where there is a whole apartment of Rooms all furniſht with Antiquities and Rarities: There are ſome old Inſcriptions made by two Towns in *Africk*, to the Honour of *M. Craſſus*: There is a great collection of Medals and Medaillons, and of the *Roman* Weights and their Inſtruments for their Sacrifices, there are many Curioſities of Nature, and a great collection of Pictures, of which many are of *Paulo Veroneſe*'s hand. There is a noble Garden in *Verona* that riſeth up in Terraſſes the whole heigth of a Hill, in which there are many ancient Inſcriptions, which belongs to Count *Giuſto*. As we go from *Verona* to *Vincenza* which i thirty miles, we return to the beauty of *Lombardy*, for there is all the way as it were a ſucceſſion of Gardens the Ground is better cultivated here than I ſaw it in any other place of *Italy*: But the Wine is not good for at the roots of all their Trees they plant a Vine which grows up winding about the Tree to which i joins; but the Soil is too rich to produce a rich Wine, for that requires a dry ground: There is nea the Lake of *Guarda* a very extraordinary Wine which they call *Vino Santo*, which drinks like the beſt ſort of *Canary*, it is not made till *Chriſtmas*, and from thence it carries the name of *Holy Wine*, and it is not to be drunk till Midſummer, for it is ſo long before it i quite wrought clear, but I have not marked down how long it may be kept: We had it there for a groat an *Engliſh* quart, I wondred that they did no Trade with it. All the Cattle of *Italy* are gray or white, and all their Hogs are black, except in the *Bologneſe*, and there they are red. I will not inquire into the reaſons of theſe things: It is certain Hogs

Fleſh

Flesh in *Italy* is much better than it is in *France* and *England*, whether the truffs on which they feed much in Winter, occasion this or not, I know not, the musks of the pressed Grapes is also a mighty nourishment to them; but Cattel of that grayish colour are certainly weaker: The carriage of *Italy* is generally performed by them, and this is very hard work in *Lombardy* when it hath rained never so little, for the ground being quite level, and there being no raised High-ways or Cause-ways, the Carts go deep and are hardly drawn.

 Vincenza hath still more of its ancient liberty reserved than any of these Towns, as *Padua* hath less, for it delivered it self to the *Venetians*, whereas the other disputed long with it, and brought it often very low: one sees the marks of Liberty in *Vincenza* in the riches of their Palaces and Churches, of which many are newly built: They have a modern Theater made in imitation of the ancient *Roman* Theaters. Count *Valarano*'s Gardens at the Port of *Verona*, is the finest thing of the Town, there is in it a very noble Alley of Oranges and Citrons, some as big as a Mans body, but those are covered all the Winter long, for in this appears the sensible difference of *Lombardy* from those parts of *Italy*, that lies to the *South* of the *Apenins*, that here generally they keep their Oranges and Citrons in great Boxes as we do in *England*, that so they may be lodged in Winter, and defended from the breezes that blow sometimes so sharp from the *Alps*, that otherwise they would kill those delicate Plants: whereas in *Tuscany* they grow as other Trees in their Gardens, and in the Kingdom of *Naples* they grow wild without any care or cultivation. We were at *Vincenza* upon a Holy-day, and there I saw a preparation for a Procession that was to be in the afternoon: I did not wonder at what a *French* Papist said to me, that he could hardly bear the Religion of *Italy*, the Idolatry in it was so gross. The statue of the Virgin
was

was of Wood so finely painted, that I thought the Head was Wax, it was richly clad, and had a Crown on its Head, and was set full of Flowers: how they did when it was carried about, I do not know; but in the morning all People run to it and said their Prayers to it, ond kissed the ground before it with all the appearances of devotion.

From *Vincenza* it is Eighteen miles to *Padua* all like a Garden; here one sees the decays of a vast City, which was, once, one of the biggest of all *Italy*; the compass is the same that it was, but there is much uninhabited ground in it, and Houses there go almost for nothing, their Air is extream good, and there is so great a plenty of all things except money, that a little money goes a great way. The University here, though so much supported by the Venetians, that they pay fifty Professors, yet sinks extreamly: there are no Men of any great fame now in it: and the quarrels among the Students have driven away most of the strangers that used to come and study here, for it is not safe to stir abroad here after Sun set: The number of the Palaces here is incredible, and though the Nobility of *Padua* is almost quite ruined, yet the beauty of their ancient Palaces shews what they once were. The Venetians have been willing to let the ancient quarrels that were in all those conquered Cities continue still among them, for while one kills another, and the Children of the other take their revenges afterwards, both comes under the *bando* by this means, and the Confiscation goes to the Senate. At some times of grace when the Senate wants Money, and offers a Pardon to all that will compound for it, the numbers of the guilty Persons are incredible. In *Vincenza* and the Country that belongs to it, I was assured by Monsieur *Patin*, that learned Antiquary, that hath been many years a Professor in *Padua*, that there were Five and thirty thousand pardoned at the last Grace; this I could hardly believe, but he bid me

write

write it down upon his word. The Nobility of *Padua* and of the other Towns, seem not to see what a profit their quarrels bring to the *Venetians*, and how they eat out their Families: For one Family in the same Man's time, who was alive while I was there, was reduced from Fourteen thousand Ducats revenue to less than Three thousand, by its falling at several times under the *bando*: But their jealousies and their revenges are pursued by them with so much vigor, that when these are in their way, all other things are forgot by them. There is here the remnant of the Amphitheater, though nothing but the outward Wall stands: There is here, as well as in *Milan*, an inward Town, called the City, and an outward, without that, called the *Burgo*; but though there is a Ditch about the City, the great Ditch and Wall goeth about all and *Padua* is Eight miles in compass; it lies almost round: The publick Hall is the Noblest of *Italy*: the Dome is an ancient and mean Building; but the Church of St. *Anthony*, especially the Holy Chapel in it where the Saint lies, is one of the best pieces of modern Sculpture; for round the Chapel the chief Miracles in the legend of that Saint are represented in *Mezzo rilievo*, in a very surprizing manner: The devotion that is paid to this Saint, all *Lombardy* over, is amazing; he is called by way of excellence *il Santo*, and the Beggars generally ask Alms for his sake: But among the little Vows that hang without the Holy Chapel, there is one that is the highest pitch of Blasphemy that can be imagined *Exaudit*, speaking of the Saint *quos non audit & ipse Deus*, he hears those whom God himself doth not hear. St. *Justina* is a Church so well ordered within, the Architecture is so beautiful, it is so well inlightned, and the *Cupulo*'s are so advantagiously placed that if the outside answered the inside, it would be one of the best Churches of *Italy*, but the Building is of Brick, and it hath no Frontispiece, there are many new Altars

made

made as fine as they are Idolatrous, all full of Statues of Marble. This Abby hath a Hundred Thousand Ducats of Revenue, and so by its Wealth one may conclude that it belongs to the *Benedictine* Order. Cardinal *Barberigo* is Bishop here, he seems to set St. *Carlo* before him as his pattern; he hath founded a Noble Seminary for the secular Priests; he lives in a constant discipline himself, and endeavours to reform his Clergy all he can; but he is now in ill terms with his Canons, who are all Noble *Venetians*, and so allow themselves great liberties, of which they will not be willingly abridged; he is charitable to a high degree, and is in all respects a very extraordinary Man.

In the *Venetian* Territory, their subjects live easie and happy, if they could be so wise as to give over their quarrels, but though the taxes are not high, they oppress their Tenants so severely, that the Pesants live most miserably, yet on all hands round about them, the oppressions being more intollerable, they know not whither to go for ease, whereas on the contrary, the miseries under which their neighbours groan, chiefly those of the Ecclesiastical state, send in an increase of People among them, so that they are well stockt with People, but the *Venetians* are so jealous of their subjects understanding Military matters, which may dispose them to revolt, that they never make any Levies among them for their Wars, this jealousie is the true ground of that maxim, though another is pretended that is more plausible, which is their care of their own People, whom they study to preserve, and therefore they hire Strangers rather than expose their Subjects. It is certain a revolt here were no hard matter to effectuate, for the Garrisons and Fortifications are so slight, that those great Towns could easily shake off their yoke, if it were not for the factions that still reign among them, by which one party would chuse rather to expose the other to the rigor of the Inquisitors than concur with them in asserting

serting their liberty, and the Inquisitors in such cases proceed so secretly, and yet so effectually that none dares trust another with a secret of such consequence, and the oppressed Nobility of those States retain still so much of their old and unsubdued insolence, and treat such as are under them so cruelly, that the *Venetians* are as secure in those Conquests, as if they had many strong Cittadels and numerous Garrisons spread up and down among them. From *Padua* down to *Venice*, all along the River *Brent*, there are many Palaces of the Noble *Venetians* on both sides of the River, built with so great a variety of Architecture, that there is not one of them like another, there is also the like diversity in the laying out of their Gardens, and here they retire during the hot months, and some allow themselves all the excesses of dissolute liberty that can possibly be imagined. From *Lizza Fucina* which is at the mouth of the *Brent*, we pass for Five or Six miles on the *Lagunes* or shallows to *Venice*, these shallows sink of late so much that the preserving *Venice* still an Island, is like to become as great a charge to the *Venetians*, as the keeping out the Sea is to the Dutch; for they use all possible industry to cleanse the Channels of their *lagunes*, and to keep them full of water; and yet many think that the water hath failed so much in this last age, that if it continues to abate at the same rate, within an age or two more, *Venice* may become a part of the *Terra firma*. It is certainly the most surprizing sight in the whole World, to see so vast a city, scituated thus in the Sea, and such a number of Islands so united together by Bridges brought to such a regular figure, the Pilotty supplying the want of earth to build on, and all so nobly built, which is of all the things that one can see the most amazing. And though this Republick is much sunk from what it was, both by the great losses they have suffered in their Wars with the *Turks*, and by the great decay of Trade, yet there

there is an incredible Wealth, and a vast plenty of all things in this place. I will not offer to describe neither the Church nor the Palace of S. *Mark*, which are too well known to need a long digression to be made for them. The painting of the Walls and the roofs of the Halls, and publick Rooms in the Palace are of vast value: Here I saw that Story of Pope *Alexander* the III. treading on the neck of the Emperor *Frederick Barbarossa*. The nobleness of the stair-cases, the riches of the Halls, and the beauty of the whole building, are much prejudiced by the beastliness of those that walk along, and that leave their marks behind them, as if this were rather a common house of Office, than so Noble a Palace: And the great Hall, where the whole body of the Nobility meet, in the Great Council, hath nothing but the roof and walls that answers to such an Assembly; for the seats are liker the benches of an Auditory of Schollars, than of so glorious a body. When the two sides of this Palace are built as the third, which is the most hid, it will be one of the gloriousest Palaces that the World can shew. The two sides that are most seen, the one facing the square of St. *Mark*, and the other the great *Canale*, are only of Brick, the third being all of Marble, but the War of *Candy* put a stop to the building. St. *Mark*'s Church hath nothing to recommend it, but its great antiquity, and the vast riches of the building, it is dark and low, but the pavement is so rich a Mosaick, and the whole roof is also Mosaick, the outside, and inside are of such excellent Marble, the frontispiece is adorned with so many Pillars of Porphiry and Jasp, and above all with the four Horses of Corinthian Brass, that *Tiridates* brought to *Tiberius*, which were carried afterwards to *Constantinople*, and were brought from thence to *Venice*, and in which the gilding is still very bright, that when all this is considered one doth no where see so much cost brought together. I did not see the

Gospel

Gospel of St. *Mark*, which is one of the valuablest things of the Treasure; but they do not now open it to strangers, yet Doctor *Grandi*, a famous Physitian here, told me that, by a particular order, he was suffered to open it; he told me it was all writ in Capital Letters, but the characters were so worn out, that though he could discern the ends of some Letters, he could not see enough to help him to distinguish them or to know whether the M. S. was in *Greek* or *Latin*. I will not say one word of the Arsenal, for as I saw it in its worst state, the War that is now on foot having disfurnished a great deal of it, so it hath been often described, and it is known to be the Noblest Magazine, the best ordered, and of the greatest variety that is in the whole World; its true it is all that this State hath, so that if the Magazines of other Princes, which lie spread up and down in the different places of their dominions were gathered together, they would make a much greater shew. The Noblest Convent of *Venice* is that of the *Dominicans*, called *St. John*, and *S. Paul*, the Church, and Chapels are vastly rich; there is one of *St. Luke*'s *Madona*'s here as they pretend; the Dormitory is very great; the Room for the Library, and every thing in it, except the Books, is extream fine. But St. *George*, which is a Convent of the *Benedictines* in an Isle intirely possessed by them over against the St. *Mark*'s square is much the richest; the Church is well contrived and well adorned; and not only the whole building is very magnificent, but which is more extraordinary at *Venice* they have a large Garden, and noble walks in it. The *Redemptore*, and the *Salute* are two Noble Churches that are the effects of Vows that the Senate made when they were afflicted with the Plague, the latter is much the finer, it is to the *Virgin*, and the other is only to our *Saviour*; so naturally doth the devotion of that Church carry it higher for the Mother than the Son: It is true the *Salute* is later than the other, so

no

no wonder if the Architecture, and the riches exceed that which is more ancient. The School of St. *Roch,* and the Chapel, and Hall are full of great pieces of *Tintorets*; a *Cena* of *Paulo Veronese* in the Refectory of St. *George*, and the Picture of St. *Peter* the Martyr of *Titians* are the most celebrated pieces of V*enice* : Duke *Pefaro*'s Tomb in the Frairy is the Noblest I ever saw. But if the riches of all the Convents, and the Parish Churches of V*enice* amazed me, the fronts especially, many of which are of white Marble, beautified with several Statues; the meanness of the Library of St. *Mark* did no less surprize me. There are in the Antichamber to it, Statues of vast value, and the whole roof of the Library is composed of several pieces of the greatest Masters put in several frames; but the Library hath nothing answerable to the riches of the case, for the *Greek* Manuscripts are all modern, I turned over a great many, and saw none above Five Hundred Years old : I was indeed told that the last Library-keeper was accused for having conveyed away many of their Manuscripts; and that Four Years ago being clapt in Prison for this by the Inquisitors he, to prevent further severities, poysoned himself. I went to the Convent of the *Servi*, but I found Father *Paul* was not in such consideration there, as he is elsewhere: I asked for his Tomb, but they made no account of him, and seemed not to know where it was it is true the Person to whom I was recommended was not in V*enice*, so perhaps they refined too much in this matter: I had great discourse with some at V*enice* concerning the memorials out of which F *Paul* drew his History, which are no doubt all preserved with great care in their Archives, and since the transactions of the Council of *Trent*, as they are o great importance, so they are become now much controverted by the different relations that *F. Paul*, and Cardinal *Pallavicini* have given the World of tha matter ; the only way to put an end to all dispute n matter of fact, is to print the Originals themselves: A Person of great credit at *Venice* promised to me to do his utmost, to get that proposition set on foot, tho the great exactness that the Government there hath always affected as to the matter of their Archives, is held so sacred that this made him apprehend they would not give way to any such search. The affinity of the matter brings into my mind a long Conversation that I had with a Person of great Eminence at *Venice*, that as he was long at *Constantinople*, so was learned far beyond what is to be met with in *Italy*, he told me he was at *Constantinople* when the Inquiry into the Doctrine of the *Greek* Church was set on foot, occasioned by the famous Dispute between Mr. *Arnaud* and Mr. *Claude*, he being a zealous Roman Catholick, was dealt with to assist in that business; but being a Man of great Honour and Sincerity, he excused himself, and said he could not meddle in it: He hath a very low and bad opinion of the *Greeks*, and he told me that none of their Priests were more inveterate enemies to the Church of *Rome*, than those that were bred up at *Rome*; for they to free themselves of the prejudices that their Countrey-men are apt to conceive against them, because of their education among the *Latines* do affect to shew an opposition to the *Latin* Church beyond any other *Greeks*. He told me that he knew the ignorance and corruption of the *Greeks* was such, that as they did not know the Doctrines of their own Church, so a very little Money, or the hope of Protection from any of the Ambassadors that come from the *West*, would prevail with them to sign any that that could be desired of them : He added one thing, that though he firmly believed Transubstantiation himself, he did not think they believed it; let them say what they pleased themselves, he took his measures of the Doctrine of their Church, rather from what they did, than from what they said:

L   For

For their Rites not being changed now for a great many ages were the true Indications of the doctrine received among them; whereas they were both ignorant of the tradition of their doctrine, and very apt to prevaricate when they saw advantages or protection set before them, therefore he concluded that since they did not adore the Sacrament after the Consecration, that was an evident sign that they did not believe the corporal presence, and was of a force were able to balance all their subscriptions: He told me he was often scandalized to see them open the bag in which the Sacrament was preserved, and shew it with no sort of respect no more than when they shewed any Manuscript, and he looked on adoration as such a necessary consequence of Transubstantiation, that he could not imagine that the latter was received in Church that did not practice the former. To this I will add what an eminent *Catholick* at *Paris* told me he said the Originals of those attestations were in too exact and too correct a stile to have been formed in *Greece*, he assured me they were penned at *Paris* by one that was a Master of the purity of the *Greek* tongue. I do not name those Persons because they are yet alive, and this might be a prejudice to them. One of the chief Ornaments of *Venice* was the famous young Woman that spake five Tongues well, of which the *Latin* and *Greek* were two; she passed Doctor of Physick at *Padua* according to the ordinary forms; but which was beyond all, she was a Person of such extraordinary vertue and piety, that she is spoken of as a Saint, she died some months before I came to *Venice*: she was of the noble Family of the *Cornara* though not of the three chief branches, which are *Saint Maurice*, *Saint Paul* and *Calle*, who are descended from the three Brothers of the renowned Queen of *Cyprus*, but the distinction of her Family was *Piscopia*. Her extraordinary merit made all People willi willing to remember the blemish of her descent of the one side, for though the *Cornara*'s reckon themselves size of Nobility beyond all the other Families of *Venice*, yet her Father having entertained a *Gondalier*'s Daughter so long that he had some Children by her, at last for their sakes Married the Mother, and payed considerable fine to save the forfeiture of Nobility, which his Children must have undergone, by reason of the meanness of the Mothers birth. The *Cornara*'s carry it so high that many of the Daughters of that Family have made themselves Nuns, because they thought their own name was so Noble that they could not induce themselves to change it with any other, and when lately one of that Family married the Heir of the *Sagredo*, which is also one of the ancientest Families that was extream rich, and she had scarce any portion at all, for the *Cornara*'s are now very low, some of their Friends came to wish them joy of so advantagious a match; but they very coldly rejected the complement, and bid the others go and wish the *Sagredo* joy, since they thought the advantage was wholly of their side.

There are of the truly ancient Noble Families of *Venice* Four and Twenty yet remaining, and even among these there are twelve that are thought superior to the rest in rank; since the first formation of their Senate they have created many Senators. In their Wars with *Genua* they conferred that honour on Thirty Families; several of their Generals have had that honour given them as a reward of their service: they have also offered this honour to some Royal Families: for both the Families of *Valois* and *Bourbon* were nobles of *Venice*, and *Henry* the III. when he came through *Venice* from *Poland* to take possession of the Crown of *France*, went and sate among them, and drew his ballot as a Noble *Venetian*; many Popes have procured this honour for their Nephews: Only the

L. 2. Bar-

Barberines would have the *Venetians* offer it to them without their asking it, and the *Venetians* would not give it without the others asked it, and so it stuck at this. But during the War of *Candy* Cardinal *Francis Barberin* gave Twelve Thousand Crowns a Year towards the War, and the temper found for making them Noble *Venetians* was, that the Queen Mother of *France* moved the Senate to grant it. In all the Creations of Senators before the last War of *Candy*, they were free; and the considerations were either great services, or the great dignity of those on whom they bestowed this Honour. Those new Families are divided into those that are called Ducal Families, and those that were called simply new Families, the reason of the former designation is not rightly understood; but one that knew all that related to that constitution particularly well gave me a good account of it: That which naturally occurs as the reason of it, is, that all those Families that are called Ducal, have had the Dukedom in their house: But as all the old Families have had the same honour, though they carry not that Title, so some of the new Families have also had it, that yet are not called Ducal. Others say that those Families that have had branches who have been made Dukes, without their being first Procurators of S. *Mark*, or that have been chosen to that honour, without their pretending to it, are called Ducal: But the true account of this is, that from the Year 1450. to the Year 1620. for a Hundred and Seventy Years there was a combination made among those new Families to preserve the Dukedom still among them: For the old Families carrying it high and excluding the new Families from the chief Honours, Nineteen of the new Families entred into mutual engagements to exclude the ancient Nobility It is true they made the Dukedom sometimes fall on some of the new Families that were not of this Association

ciation; but this was more indifferent to them, as long as the ancient Families were shut out, and that it appeared that they bore the chief sway in the Election. This Combination was a thing known to the very People, though the Inquisitors did all they could to break it, and at least to hide it, so that I never met with it in any of their Authors: But this failed in the Year 1620. when *Memmio* was chosen Duke, who was descended of one of the ancient Nobility, which was so great a mortification to the case Ducale that one of them (*Venniero*) hanged himself, by the rage to which that disgrace drove him, yet his Man came into the room in time before he was dead, and cut him down, and he lived long after that in a better mind. Since that time one of the *Bembo*'s, two of the *Cornaro*'s, and one of the *Contrarini*'s, and the present Prince of the *Justiniani*, the first of that Family that hath had that honour, have been Dukes, who are all of the ancient Families: So that this Faction is now so intirely buried, that it is not generally known, even in *Venice* it self, that it was ever amongst them; and thus time and other accidents bring about happy events, which no care nor industry could produce: For that which all the endeavours of the Inquisitors could not compass, was brought about of it self.

It is true, the Factions in *Venice*, though violent enough in the persons of those who manage them, yet are not derived by them as an inheritance to their Posterity, as it was among the *Florentines*; who though they value themselves as a size of Men much above the *Venetians*, whom they despise as a phlegmatick and dull race of People, yet shewed how little they understood with all their vivacity, to conduct their state, since by their domestick heats they lost their liberty, which the *Venetians* have had the wisdom still to preserve. This Faction of the Case Du-

cale was perhaps willing to let the matter fall, for they loſt more than they got by it; for the ancient Families in revenge ſet themſelves againſt them, and excluded them from all the other advantagious imployments of the State. For the others being only united in that ſingle point relating to the Dukedom the ancient Families let them carry it, but in all other Competitions they ſet up always ſuch Competitors againſt the pretenders that were of the Ducal Families, that were much more eſteemed than theſe were; ſo that they ſhut them out of all the beſt Offices of the *Republick*. Such a Faction as this was, if it had been ſtill kept up, might in concluſion have proved fatal to their Liberty. It is indeed a wonder to ſee, the Dignity of the Duke ſo much courted, for he is only a priſoner of ſtate, tied up to ſuch rules, ſo ſeverely reſtrained and ſhut up as it were in an apartment of the Palace of St. *Mark*, that it is not ſtrange to ſee ſome of the greateſt Families, in particular the *Cornaro*'s, decline it. All the Family, if ever ſo numerous, muſt retire out of the Senate, when a Duke is choſen out of it, only one that is next to him of kin ſits ſtill, but without a Vote: And the only real Priviledge that the Duke hath, is, that he can of himſelf, without communicating with the *Savii*, propoſe matters, either to the Council of Ten, to the Senate, or to the Great Council; whereas all other propoſitions muſt be firſt offered to the *Savii*, and examined by them, who have a ſort of *Tribunitian* power to reject what they diſlike, and though they cannot hinder the Duke to make a propoſition, yet they can mortifie him when he hath made it: They can hinder it to be voted, and after it is voted they can ſuſpend the execution of it till it is examined over again: And a Duke that is of an active Spirit muſt reſolve to endure many of theſe afflictions, and it is certain that the *Savii* do ſometimes

times affect to shew the greatness of their Authority, and exercise a sort of Tyranny in the rejecting of Propositions when they intend to humble those that make them. Yet the greatest part of the best Families court this Honour of Dukedom extreamly; when *Segrado* was upon the point of being chosen Duke, there was so violent an outcry against it over all *Venice*, because of the disgrace, that they thought would come on the *Republick*, if they had a Prince whose Note had miscarried in some unfortunate disorders, the Senate complyed so far with this Aversion, that the People testified, That though the Inquisitors took care to hang or drown many of the chief of the Mutineers, yet they let the design for *Sagredo* fall: Upon which he was so much disgusted that he retired to a house he had in the *Terra firma*, and never appeared more at *Venice*: During which time of his retirement, he writ two Books, the one *Memorie Ottomaniche*, which is Printed, and he is accounted the best of all the Modern Authors: The other was Memoires of the Government, and History of *Venice*, which hath never been Printed; and some say it is too sincere, and too particular, so that it is thought it will be reserved among their Archives. It hath been a sort of maxim now for some time, not to chuse a married Man to be Duke, for the Coronation of a Dutchess goes high, and hath cost above Hundred thousand Ducats. Some of the ancient Families have affected the Title of Prince, and have called their branches Princes of the Blood, and though the *Cornara*'s have done this more than any other, yet others upon the account of some Principalities, that their Ancestors had in the Islands of the *Archipelago*, have also affected those vain Titles: But the Inquisitors have long ago obliged them to lay aside all those high Titles,

and

and such of them that boast too much of their Blood, find the dislike which that brings on them very sensibly; for whensoever they pretend to any great Employments, they find themselves always excluded. When an Election of Ambassadors was proposed, or of any of the chief Offices, it was wont to be made in those terms, that the Council must chuse one of its principal Members for such an Employment: But because this lookt like a term of distinction, among the Nobility, they changed it Five and twenty Years ago; and instead of Principal, they use now the term Honourable, which comprehends the whole body of the Nobility, without any distinction. It is at V*enice* in the Church, as well as in the State, that the Head of the Body hath a great Title, and particular Honours done him; whereas in the mean while this is a meer Pageantry, and under these big words there is lodged only a light shadow of Authority; for their Bishop has the glorious Title of Patriark, as well as the Duke is called their Prince, and his serenity, and hath his name stampt upon their Coin so the Patriark with all his high Title hath really no Authority: For not only St. *Mark*'s Church is intirely exempted from his jurisdiction, and is immediately subject to the Duke, but his Authority is in all other things so subject to the Senate and so regulated by them, that he hath no more power than they are pleased to allow him: So that the Senate is as really the supream Governor over all Persons, and in all Causes as the King of *England* have pretended to be in their own Dominions since the Rrformation: But besides all this the Clergy of V*enice* have a very extraordinary sort of exemption, and are a sort of a Body like a Presbytery independent of the Bishop: The Curats are chosen by the Inhabitants of every Parish, and

thi

this makes that no Noble *Venetian* is suffered to pretend to any Curacy, for they think it below that Dignity to suffer one of their Body to engage in a Competition with one of a lower Order, and to run the hazard of being rejected.

I was told the manner of those Elections was the most scandalous thing possible, for the several Candidates appear on the day of election, and set out their own merits, and defame the other pretenders in the foulest language, and in the most scurrilous manner imaginable; the secrets of all their lives are publisht in most reproachful terms, and nothing is so abject and ridiculous that is not put in practice on those occasions: There is a sort of an Association among the Curats for judging of their common concerns, and some of the Laity of the several Parishes assist in those Courts, so that here is a real *Presbytery*. The great libertinage that is so undecently practised by most sorts of people at *Venice*, extends it self to the Clergy to such a degree, that though ignorance and vice seem the only indelible characters that they carry generally over all *Italy*, yet those appear here in a much more conspicuous manner than elsewhere, and upon those popular elections all comes out. The Nuns of *Venice* have been under much scandal for a great while; there are some Monasteries that are as famous for their strictness and exactness to their rules, as others are for the liberties they take; chiefly those of St. *Zachary* and St. *Lawrence*, where none but Noble *Venetians* are admitted, and where it is not so much as pretended that they have retired for devotion; but it is owned to be done meerly that they might not be too great a charge to their Family: They are not vailed, their neck and breast is bare, and they receive much company: but that which I saw was in a publick Room, in which there were many grills for several Parlors, so that the conversation

tion is very confused, for there being a different company at every grill, and the *Italians* speaking generally very loud, the noise of so many loud talkers is very disagreeable. The Nuns talk much and very ungracefully, and allow themselves a liberty in rallying that other places could not bear. About four years ago the Patriark intended to bring in a reform into those Houses, but the Nuns of St. *Lawrence* with whom he began, told him plainly they were Noble *Venetians*, who had chosen that way of life as more convenient for them, but they would not subject themselves to his regulations, yet he came and would shut up their house, so they went to set fire to it; upon which the Senate interposed and ordered the Patriark to desist. There is no Christian State in the World that hath expressed a jealousie of Churchmens getting into the publick Councels so much as the *Venetians*, for as a Noble *Venetian* that goes into Orders, looses thereby his right of going to vote in the great Councel, so when any of them are promoted to be Cardinals, the whole kindred and family must during their lives, withdraw from the great Councel, and are also incapable of all imployments: And by a clause which they added when they received the Inquisition, which seemed of no great consequence, they have made it to become a Court absolutely subject to them; for it being provided that the Inquisitors should do nothing but in the presence of such as should be Deputed by the Senate to be the witnesses of their proceedings; those Deputies either will not come but when they think fit, or will not stay longer than they are pleased with their proceedings; so that either their absence or their withdrawing dissolves the Court: for a citation cannot be made, a witness cannot be examined, nor the least point of form carried on if the Deputies of the Senate are not present: and thus it is,

*that

that though there is a Court of Inquisition at *Venice*, yet there is scarce any person brought into trouble by it, and there are many of the *Protestant* Religion that live there without any trouble ; and though there is a Congregation of them there that hath their exercises of Religion very regularly, yet the Senate gives them no trouble. It is true, the Hosty's not being carried about in Procession, but secretly by the Priest to the Sick, makes that this uneasie discrimination of *Protestant* and *Papist* doth not offer it self here as in other places, for the straitness of the Streets and the Channels through which one must go almost every foot, makes that this could not be done in *Venice* as it is elsewhere, and from *Venice* this rule is carried over their whole Territory, tho the like reason doth not hold in the *Terra Firma* The *Venetians* are generally ignorant of the matters of Religion to a scandal, and they are as unconcerned in them as they are strangers to them, so that all that vast pomp in their Ceremonies and wealth in their Churches is affected rather as a point of magnificence, or a matter of emulation among families, then that superstition hath here such a power over the Spirits of the people as it hath elsewhere : for the Atheism that is received by many here is the dullest and cursest thing that can be imagined. The young Nobility are so generally corrupted in their Morals, and so given up to a most supine ignorance of all sort of knowledge, that a man cannot easily imagine to what a height this is grown, and for Military Courage there is scarce so much as the ambition of being thought brave remaining among the greater part of them. It seemed to me a strange thing to see the *Broglio* so full of graceful young Senators and Nobles, when there was so glorious a War on foot with the *Turks*, but instead of being heated in point of honour to hazard their lives, they rather

think

think it an extravagant piece of folly for them to g
and hazard it when a little money can hire ſtrange
that do it on ſuch eaſie terms ; and thus their Arn
are in the hands of ſtrangers, while they ſtay ;
home managing their intrigues in the *Broglio*, ar
diſſolving their ſpirits among their Courtiſan
And the reputation of their ſervice is of late years (
much ſunk, that it is very ſtrange to ſee ſo man
come to a ſervice ſo decried, where there is ſo li
tle care had of the Souldiers, and ſo little regar
had to the Officers ; the arrears are ſo ſlowl
paid, and the rewards are ſo ſcantly diſtributec
that if they do not change their maxims the
may come to feel this very ſenſibly ; for as the
Subjects are not acquainted with Warlike matter
ſo their Nobility have no ſort of ambition tha
way, and ſtrangers are extreamly diſguſted. .
is chiefly to the conjecture of affairs that the
owe their ſafety, for the feebleneſs of all thei
Neighbours, the *Turk*, the *Emperour*, the King of *Spai*
the Pope, and the Duke of *Mantua*, preſerve
them from the apprehenſion of an Invaſion, an
the quarrels, and the degeneracy of their Sub
jects, ſave them from the fears of a Revolt
but a formidable Neighbour would put them har
to it. One great occaſion of the degeneracy of th
Italians, and in particular of the *Venetian* Nob
lity, is a maxim that hath been taken up fo
ſome conſiderable time, that for the preſervatio
of their Families, it is fit than only one of a Fa
mily ſhould marry; to which I will not ad
that it is generally believed that the Wife is i
common to the whole Family: By this mean
the younger Brothers that have appointmen
for life, and that have no Families that com
from them, are not ſtirred up by any ambition to ſig
nalize themſelves or to make Families, and ſo the
give way to all the lazineſs of luxury, and are quit
enervated by it.   Wherea

Whereas the best services done in other States flows [fr]om the necessities as well as the aspirings of younger [b]rothers or their Families, whose blood qualifies [th]em to pretend, as well as their pride and necessi[ti]es push them on, to acquire first a reputation, and [th]en a fortune: But all this is a mystery to the *Ve[ne]tians*, who apprehend so much from the active Spi[ri]ts of a necessitous Nobility, that to lay those to [sle]ep, they incourage them in all those things that [m]ay blunt and deprefs their minds, and youth natu[ra]lly hates Letters as much as it loves pleasure, when [it] is so far from being restrained, that it is rather [pu]shed on to all the licentiousness of unlimited dis[or]ders.

Yet I must add one thing, that though *Venice*, is [th]e place in the whole World where pleasure is [m]ost studied, and where the youth have both the [gr]eatest Wealth, and the most leisure to pursue it: [ye]t it is the place that I ever saw where true and in[no]cent pleasure is the least understood, in which I [w]ill make a little digression that perhaps will not be [un]pleasant. As for the pleasures of friendship or [ma]rriage they are strangers to them, for the horri[bl]e distrust, in which they all live, of one another, [ma]kes that it is very rare to find a friend in *Italy*, [bu]t most of all in *Venice*: and though we have been [to]ld of several stories of celebrated friendships there, [ye]t these are now very rare. As for their Wives [th]ey are bred to so much ignorance, they converse so [litt]le, that they know nothing but the dull superst[iti]on on Holy-days in which they stay in the Church[es] as long as they can, and so prolong the little li[be]rty they have of going abroad on those days as [ch]ildren do their hours of play: They are not im[pl]oyed in their domestick affairs, and generally they [un]derstand no sort of work, so that I was told that [the]y were the insipidest creatures imaginable; they [are], perhaps, as vitious as in other places; but it is

M among

among them down-right lewdness, for they are not drawn into it by the intranglements of amour that inveigle and lead many persons much farther than they imagined or intended at first, but in them the first step without any preamble or preparative, is down-right beastliness. And an *Italian* that knew the World well, said upon this matter a very lively thing to me, he said their jealousie made them restrain their Daughters, and their Wives so much, that they could have none of those domestick entertainments of Wit, Conversation, and Friendship, that the *French* or *English* have at home: It is true those he said hazard a little the honour of their Families by that liberty, but the *Italians* by their excessive caution, made that they had none of the true delights of a Married State; and notwithstanding all their uneasie jealousie, they were still in danger of a contraband Nobility, therefore he thought they would do much better to hazard a little, when it would produce a certain satisfaction, then to watch so anxiously, and thereby have an insipid companion instead of a lively Friend, though she might, perhaps, have some ill moments. As for their houses they have nothing convenient at *Venice*, for the Architecture is almost all the same, one stair-case, a Hall that runs along the body of the house, and chambers on both hands, but there are no apartments, no Closets or Back-stairs; so that in house that are of an excessive wealth, they have yet no sort of convenience; Their Bedsteads are of Iron because of the Vermin that their moisture produces, the bottoms are of boards, upon which they lay so many quilts that it is a huge step to get up to them, their great Chairs are all upright without a stop in the back, hard in the bottom, and the wood of the arms is not covered; they mix water with their wine in their Hogsheads, so that for above half the year the wine is either dead or sour, they do not leaven

their

their Bread, so that it is extream heavy, and the Oven is too much heated, so that the crum is as Dough, when the crust is hard as a stone, in all Inns they boil Meat first before it is roasted, and thus, as indeed they make it tender, so it is quite tastless and insipid: And as for their Land-carriage all *Lombardy* over, it is extream inconvenient, for their Coaches are fastned to the pearch, which makes them as uneasie as a Cart: It it true, they begin to have at *Rome*, and *Naples*, Coaches that are fastned to a sort of double pearch, that runs round the bottom of the Coach of both sides, which are thin that they ply to the motion of the Coach, and are extream easie, but those are not known in *Lombardy*, and besides this, their Caleshes are open, so that one is exposed to the Sun, and dust in Summer, and to the Weather in Winter: But though they are covered as ours are, on the other side of the *Appenins*, yet I saw none that were covered in *Lombardy*: And thus by an enumeration of many of the innocent pleasures, and conveniences of life, it appears that the *Venetians* pursue so violently forbidden pleasures, that they know not how to find out that which is allowable. Their constant practices in the *Broglio* is their chief business, where those that are necessitous are pursuing for Employments of advantage, and those that are full of wealth take a sort of pleasure in crossing their pretentions, and in embroiling matters. The walk in which the Nobility tread is left to them, for no others dare walk among them, and they change the side of the square of St. *Mark* as the Sun, and the Weather directs them. Perhaps a derivation that Mr. *Patin* gave me of *Brolio* from the Greek *Peribolâion*, a little corrupted is not forced; and since they make all their parties, and manage all their intreague in those Walks, I am apt to think that broils, brovillons and imbroilments are derived from the

M 2 agitations

agitations that are managed in those walks.

As for the laſt created Nobility of *Venice*, I cam to know some particulars that I have not yet seen i any books, which I ſuppoſe will not be unacceptabl. to you. It is certain that if the *Venetians* could hav foreſeen at the beginning of the War of *Candy*, th vaſt expence in which the length of it engaged then they would have abandoned the Iſle, rather than hav waſted their Treaſure, and debaſed their Nobility This laſt was extream ſenſible to them; for as th dignity of the rank they hold is ſo much the more e minent as it is reſtrained to a ſmall number, ſo a the beſt Imployments and Honours of the State be longing to this body, the admitting ſuch a numbe into it, as muſt riſe out of Seventy Eight Familie was in effect the ſharing their Inheritance among ſ many adopted Brothers. This had been leſs Infa mous if they had communicated that Honour onl to the ancient Citizens of *Venice*, or to the Nobilit of thoſe States that they have ſubdued in the *Terr firma*; for as there are many Citizens who are as an cient as the Nobility, only their Anceſtors not hap ning to be of that Council that aſſumed the Govern ment about Four Hundred Years ago, they have no been raiſed to that Honour, ſo there had been no In famy in creating ſome of them to be of the Nobility. It had been alſo brought under conſultation long ago, upon the reduction of thoſe States in the *Terra firma*, whether it was not adviſable according to the maxims of the ancient *Romans* to communicate that dignity to ſome of their chief Families, as being the ſureſt way to give ſome contentment to thoſe States, it being al ſo a real as well as a cheap ſecurity, when the chief Families in thoſe Cities, were admitted to a Share in all the Honours of the Republick. It is true ſome of the Nobility of thoſe States thought they had Honour enough by their birth, and ſo *Zambara* of *Breſcia* re fuſed to accept an Honour from thoſe that had robbed

his

his Country of its liberty, yet his posterity are now of another mind, for they came and bought in this last sale of honour that which was freely offered to their Ancestor, and was rejected by him. When the Senate found it self extreamly pressed for money during the war it was at first proposed that some Families, to the number of Five, might be enobled; they offering Sixty Thousand Ducats if they were *Venetians*, and Seventy Thousand if they were Strangers: There was but one Person that opposed this in the Senate, so it being passed there, was presented to the great Council; and there it was like to have passed without any difficulty, but one Person opposed it with so much vigor, that though the Duke desired him to give over his opposition, since the necessities of the War required a great supply, yet he persisted still; and though one of the *Savii* set forth with tears the extremities to which the State was reduced, he still insisted and fell upon one conceit that turned the whole Council, he said they were not sure if Five Persons could be found that would purchase that honour at such a rate, and then it would be a vast disgrace, to expose the offer of Nobility first to sale, and then to the affront of finding no buyers when it was offered to be sold, and by this means he put by the resolution for that time: But then another method was taken that was more honourable, and was of a more extended consequence. *Labia* was the first that presented a Petition to the great Council, setting forth his merits towards the Republick, and desiring that he might be thought worthy to offer a Hundred Thousand Ducats towards the service of the State; this was understood to be the asking to be made noble at that price. *Delfino* said he thought every Man might be well judged worthy to offer such an assistance to the Publick, and that such as brought that supply might expect a suitable acknowledgment from the Senate, who might afterwards of their own ac-

M 3 cord

cord bestow that honour on those that expressed so much zeal for the Publick; and this would be too much debased if it were thus bought and sold; but it seems the purchasers had no mind to part with their money, and to leave the reward to the gratitude of the Council, so the Petition was granted in plain terms; and the Nobility so acquired was not only to descend to the Children of him that was enobled, but to his Brothers and the whole Family to such a degree. After *Labia* a great many more came with the like Petitions, and it was not unpleasant to see in what terms Merchants, that came to buy this Honour set forth their merits, which were that they had taken care to furnish the Republick with such things as were necessary for its preservation. There was a sort of a Triumvirat formed of a *Jew*, a *Greek* and an *Italian*, who were the Brokers, and found out the Merchants; and at last brought down the price from a Hundred Thousand to Sixty Thousand Ducats, and no other qualifications were required if they had money enough: For when *Correge* said to the Duke that he was afraid to ask that honour for want of merit, the Duke asked him if he had a Hundred Thousand Ducats, and when the other answered the Summ was ready, the Duke told him that was a great merit. At last Seventy Eight purchased this honour to the great regret of *Labia*; who said that if he had imagined that so many would have followed him in that demand, he would have bid so high for it that it should have been out of their power to have done it. It is true many of the Purchasers were Ancient and Noble Families, but many other were not only Merchants, but were of the lower sort of them; who as they had inriched themselves by Trade, did then impoverish themselves by the acquisition of an honour that as it obliged them to give over their Trade, and put them in a higher way of living, so it hath not brought them

yet

yet in any advantage to ballance that loss; for they are so much despised, that they are generally excluded when they compete with the ancient Nobility, though this is done with that discretion, that the old Families do not declare always against the new, for that would throw the new into a faction against them, which might be a great prejudice to them, for the new are much more numerous than the old.

Another great prejudice that the *Republick* feels by this great Promotion, is that the chief Families of the Citizens of *Venice*, who had been long practised in the affairs of State, and out of whom the Envoyes, the Secretaries of State, and the Chancellour that is the head of the Citizens, as well as the Duke is the head of the Nobility, are to be chosen, having purchased the chief Honour of the State there is not now a sufficient number of capable Citizens, left for serving the State in those Employments; but this defect will be redrest with the help of a little time. But if this increase of the Nobility hath lessened the Dignity of the ancient Families, there is a regulation made in this Age that still preserves a considerable distinction of Authority in their hands. Crimes against the State, when committed by any of the Nobility, were always judged by the Inquisitors, and the Council of Ten, but all other Crimes were judged by the Council of Forty. But in the Year 1624. one of the Nobles was accused of Peculat committed in one of their Governments, and the *Avogadore* in the pleading, as he set forth his Crime, called him a Rogue and a Robber: yet though his crimes were manifest, there being but Six and twenty Judges present, Twelve only condemned him, and Fourteen acquitted him; this gave great offence, for though he was acquitted by his Judges, his Crimes were evident; so that his Fame could not be restored: for the Depositions of the Witnesses, and the *Avogadores* (or the Attorney Gene-

Generals) Charge were heard by the People; so it was proposed to make a difference between the Nobility and the other Subjects: and since all Trials before the Forty were publick, and the Trials before the Ten were in secret, it seemed fit to remit the Nobility to be tried by the Ten: Some foresaw that this would tend to a Tyranny, and raise the Dignity of the ancient Families, of whom the Council of Ten is always composed, too high: Therefore they opposed it upon this ground, That since the Council of Forty sent out many Orders to the Governors, it would very much lessen their Authority, if they were not to be the Judges of those who obliged to receive their Orders: But to qualify this Opposition, a Proviso was made that reserved to the Council of Forty, a power to Judge of the Obedience that was given to their Orders, but all other Accusations of the Nobility were remitted to the Council of Ten: and the body of the Nobility were so pleased with this Distinction that was put between them and the other Subjects, that they did not see that this did really enslave them so much the more, and brought them under more danger: since those who judge in secret have a freer scope to their passions, than those whose proceedings are publick, and so are in effect judged by the Publick, which is often a very effectual restraint upon the Judges themselves. But the Council of Ten being generally in the hands of the great Families: Whereas those of all sorts are of the Council of Forty, which was the chief Judicatory of the State, and is much Ancienter than that of Ten: It had been much more wisely done of them to have been still Judged by the Forty: And if they had thought it for their Honour to have a difference made in the way of judging the Nobility, and the other Subjects, it had been more for their security to have brought their Trials to this, That

whereas

whereas the Forty Judge all other offenders with open doors, the Nobility should be judged the doors being shut, which is a thing they very much desire now, but without any hope of ever obtaining it: For this power of Judging the Nobility is now considered as Right of the Ten, and if any Man would go about to change it, the Inquisitors would be perhaps, very quick with him, as a mover of Sedition, and be, in that case, both Judge, and Party; Yet the Inquisitors being apprehensive of the distaste that this might breed in the body of the Nobility, have made a sort of regulation, though it doth not amount to much; which is, that the Nobility shall be Judged before the Council of Ten for atrocious cases, such as matter of State, the robbing the Publick, and other enormous Crimes; but that for all other matters they are to be Judged by the Forty: yet the Council of Ten draws all cases before them, and none dare dispute with them.

But this leads me to say a little to you of that part of this Constitution, which is so much censured by strangers: but is really both the greatest glory, and the chief security of this Republick, which is the unlimited power of Inquisitors, that extends not only to the chief of the Nobility, but to the Duke himself, who is so subject to them, that they may not only give him severe reprimands, but search his Papers, make his Process, and in conclusion, put him to death without being bound to give an account of their Proceedings, except to the Council of Ten. This is the dread not only of all the Subjects, but of the whole Nobility, and of all that bear Office in the Republick, and makes the greatest among them tremble, and so obligeth them to an exact conduct. But though it is not to be denied that upon some occasions they may have been a little too sudden, particularly in the known story of *Foscarini*, yet such unjustifiable

se-

severities have occurred so seldom, that as the wi[s]-
dom of this Body in making and preserving such [an]
Institution, cannot be enough admired, so the dextrous conduct of those who mannage this vast tru[st]
so as not to force the Body to take it out of the[ir]
hands, is likewise highly to be wondered at. [In]
short, the insolence, the factions, the revenges, t[he]
necessities and ambition that must needs possess
great many Members of so vast a Body as is the N[o]-
bility of *Venice*, must have thrown them often in[to]
many fatal Convulsions, if it were not for t[he]
dread in which they all stand of this Court: whi[ch]
hath so many spies abroad, chiefly among the *G[on]-
daliers*, who cannot fail to discover all the [se]-
cret Commerce of *Venice*, besides the secret a[d]-
vices that are thrown in at so many of those L[i]-
ons mouths that are in several places of St. *Mar[ks]*
Palace, within which there are boxes that are und[er]
the Keys of the Inquisitors, so that it is scarce p[os]-
sible for a Man to be long in any design against t[he]
State, and not to be discovered by them. A[nd]
when they find any in fault, they are so inexorab[le]
and so quick, as well as severe in their Justice, t[hat]
the very fear of this is so effectual a restraint, t[hat]
perhaps the long preservation of *Venice*, and of [its]
Liberty, is owing to this single piece of their con[sti]-
tution: and the Inquisitors are Persons generally
distinguished for their merit who must be all of d[if]-
ferent Families; and their Authority lasts so shor[t a]
while, that the advantages of this vast Authority t[hat]
is lodged with them, are constant and visible; wher[e]
the unhappy instances of their being imposed on, a[nd]
carrying their suspicions too far, are so few, that wh[en]-
ever the Nobility grows weary of his yoke, and thro[ws]
it off, one may reckon the Glory and Prosperity of [Ve]-
nice at an end. It was terribly attackt not long ag[o by]
Cornaro, when *Jerom Cornaro* was put to death, [for]
his correspondence with *Spain*; he was not near

into the great Family of that name, yet the Family thought their Honour was so much toucht when one of its remotest branches was condemned of Treason, that they offered a Hundred thousand Crowns to have saved him, and by consequence to have preserved the Family from that Infamy; but though this was not accepted, for he suffered as he well deserved, yet it was so visible that none of the Family were concerned in his Crimes, that it did not at all turn to their prejudice. But upon the first occasion that offered it self after that, to quarrel with the proceeding of the Inquisitors, they laid hold on it, and aggravated the matter extreamly, and moved for the limiting of their Authority, but the Great Council was wiser than to touch so sacred a part of the Government, so they retained their power very entire, but they manage it with all possible caution; A Forreigner that hath been many years in their Service, told me that the Stories with which strangers were frighted at the Arbitrary power that was rested in those Inquisitors were slight things, in comparison of the advantages that they found from it: And after Eleven Years spent in their Service, he said, he never was so much as once sent for to receive a reprimand from them. And if the Nobility, that have any Commerce with strangers, confess it sincerely to the Inquisitors, they are in danger by it; but if they conceal it, or any main circumstances of it, their Process will be soon dispatched. These are the most remarkable things that I could pick up, during my stay at *Venice*. I have avoided to say any thing relating to their several Councels, Officers, and Judicatories, or to the other parts of their Government, which are to be found in all Books; and the Forms, by which they give Votes by Ballot, are so well known, that it were an abusing of your time to enlarge my self concerning them; nor was I sufficiently informed concerning

cerning the particulars of the Sale of Nobility that is now on foot since this last War with the *Turks*, which hath made them willing to take up once again this easie way of raising of Money: Nor could I give credit to that of which a Person of great Eminence there assured me, that there was a poysoner general in *Venice*, that had a Salary, and was employed by the Inquisitors to dispatch those against whom a publick proceeding would make too great a noise; this I could not believe, though my Author protested, that the Brother of one that was solicited to accept of the Employment, discovered it to him. There is no place in the World where strangers live with more freedom and I was amazed to see so little exactness among the Searchers of the Custom-house; for though we had a Mullets load of Trunks and Portmantles, yet none offered to ask us either coming or going, what we were, or what we carried with us. But the best and Noblest Entertainment that *Venice* afforded while I was there, was the company of Mr. *dela Haye* the *French* Ambassadour, who as he hath spent his whole life in publick Embassies, so he hath acquired so great a knowledge of the World, with so true a Judgment, and so obliging a civility, that he may well pass for a Pattern; and it is no wonder to see him still engaged in a constant succession of publick Employments; and his Lady is so wonderful a Person, that I pay them both but a very small part of what I owe them in this acknowledgement, which I judge my self bound to make of their extraordinary civilities to me: and indeed without the advantage of such a rendezvous as I had there, a fortnights stay at *Venice* had been a very tedious matter: From *Venice* we went again to *Padua*; From thence to *Rovigo* which is but a small Town, and so to the *Po* which divides the Territory of the *Republick*, from the *Ferrarese*, which is now the *Popes* Country, and

here

here one sees what a difference a good and a bad Government makes in a Countrey; for though the Soil is the same on both sides of the River, and the *Ferrarese* was once one of the beautifullest spots of all *Italy*, as *Ferrara* was one of its best Towns, while they had Princes of their own, who for a course of some Ages were Princes of such Eminent virtue, and of so Heroical a Nobleness, that they were really the Fathers of their Country, nothing can be imagined more changed than all this is now. The Soil is abandoned, and uncultivated, nor were there hands enough so much as to mow their Grass, which we saw withering in their Meadows to our no small wonder. We were amazed to see so rich a Soil thus forsaken of its Inhabitants, and much more when we passed through that vast Town, which by its extent shews what it was about an Age ago, and is now so much deserted, that there are whole sides of Streets without Inhabitants, and the poverty of the place appears signally in the Churches, which are mean and poorly adorned, for the superstition of *Italy* is so ravenous, and makes such progress in this Age, that one may justly take the measures of the Wealth of any place from the Churches. The Superstition or Vanity of this Age, is so much beyond that of the past, though the contrary to this is commonly believed, that all the vast buildings of great Churches or rich Convents, and the surprizing Wealth that appears in them on Festival days are the donatives of the present Age; so that it is a vulgar error that some have taken up, who fancy that Superstition is at a stand, if not in a decay, unless it be acknowledged that the craft of the Priests hath opened to them a new method to support their riches, when the old ones of Purgatory, and Indulgences were become less effectual in an Age of more knowledge, and better enlightned, and that is to engage Men to an emulation and a

N   vanity

vanity in enriching their Churches, as much as other *Italians* have in the inriching ther Palaces, so that as they have a pleasure as well as a vanity in seeing so much dead Wealth in their houses, they have translated the same humour to their Churches: And the vanity of the present Age that believes little or nothing of those contrivances, of Purgatory, or the like, produceth the same, if not greater effects, in the building and inriching their Churches, and so carries it in expence and prodigality from the Superstition of the former Ages that believed every thing. But to return to *Ferrara*, I could not but ask all I saw, how it came, that so rich a Soil was so strangely abandoned, some said the Air was become so unhealthy, that those who stay in it were very short lived; but it is well known that Fourscore Years ago it was well peopled; and the ill Air is occasioned by the want of Inhabitants; for there not being people to drain the ground and to keep the Ditches clean, this makes that there is a great deal of Water that lies on the ground and rots, which infects the Air in the same manner as is observed in that vast and rich, but uninhabited Champaign of *Rome*, so that the ill Air is the effect rather than the cause of the dispeopling of the *Popes* Dominions. The true cause is the severity of the Government, and the heavy Taxes, and frequent Confiscations, by which the Nephews of several *Popes*, as they have devoured many of the Families of *Ferrara*, so they have driven away many more. And this appears more visibly by the different state, as well as the Constitution of *Bologna*, which is full of People that abound in Wealth, and as the Soil is extream rich, so it is cultivated with all due care. For *Bologna* delivered it self to the Popedom upon a capitulation, by which there are many Priviledges reserved to it: Crimes there are only punished in the Persons of those

those who commit them, but there are no confiscations of Estates; and though the Authority, in Criminal matters, belongs to the *Pope*, and is managed by a Legate and his Officers, yet the Civil Government, the Magistracy, and the power of Judicature in Civil matters, is entirely in the hands of the State: And by this regulation it is, that as the riches of *Bologna* amaze a stranger, it neither being on a Navigable River, by which it is not capable of much Trade, nor being the Center of a Soveraignty where a Court is kept; so the Taxes that the *Popes* fetch from thence, are so considerable, that he draws much more from this place of Liberty, than from those where his Authority is unlimited and absolute, but that are by those means almost quite abandoned; for the greatness of a Prince or State rising from the numbers of the Subjects, those maxims that retain the Subjects, and that draw strangers to come among them, are certainly the truest maxims for advancing the greatness of the Master. And I could not but with much scorn, observe the folly of some *Frenchmen*, who made use of this argument to shew the greatness of their Nation, that one found many *Frenchmen* in all places to which one could come, whereas there were no *English* nor *Dutch*, nor *Switzers*, and very few *Germans*: But is just contrary to the right consequence that ought to be drawn from this observation. It is certain, that few leave their Country, and go to settle elsewhere, if they are not pressed with so much uneasiness at home that they cannot well live among their Friends and Kinred; so that a mild Government drives out no swarms: Whereas it is the sure mark of a severe Government that weakens it self, when many of the Subjects find it so hard to subsist at home, that they are forced to seek that abroad, which they would much rather do in their own Country, if Impositions, and other severities did not force them to change their habitations.

But to return to the wealth of *Bologna*, it appears in every corner of the Town, and all round it, though its scituation is not very favourable, for it lies at the foot of the *Appenins* on the *North-side*, and is extream cold in Winter. The houses are built as at *Padua* and *Bern*, so that one walks all the Town over covered under *Piazza's*; but the walks here are both higher and larger than any where else, there are many Nobl. Palaces all over the Town, and the Churches, and Convents are incredibly rich; within the Town the richest are the *Dominicans*, which is the chief house of the Order, where their Founders body is laid in one of the best Chapels of *Italy*; and next to them are the *Franciscans*, the *Servites*, the *Jesuites*, and the Canons Regular of St. *Salvator*. In this last there is a scrowl of the *Hebrew* Bible, which though it is not the tenth part of the Bible, they fancy to be the whole Bible; and they were made believe by some *Jew*, that hath no doubt sold it at a high rate, that it was written by *Ezrah's* own hand, and this hath past long for current; but the Manuscript is only a fine Copy like those that the *Jews* use in their Synagogues, that may be, perhaps, Three or Four Hundred Years old; that part of it on which I cast my eye was the book of *Esther*, so by the bulk of the scrowl, I judged it to be the collection of those small books of the Old Testament that the *Jews* set after the Law; but those of the house fancy they have a great treasure in it, and perhaps such *Jews* as have seen it are willing to laugh at their ignorance, and so suffer them to go on in their error. The chief Church in the Town is St. *Petrone's*, and there one sees the curious and exact *Meridional-line*, which that rare Astronomer *Cassini* laid along a great part of the pavement in a brass Circle; it marks the true point of midday from *June* to *January*, and is one of the best performances that perhaps the World ever saw. In the great square before

before the Church, on the one side of which is the Legates Palace, among other Statues one surprized me much, it was Pope *Joans*, which is so named by the People of the Town, it is true the Learned Men say it is the Statue of Pope *Nicolas* the IV. who had indeed a youthly and womanish face. But as I looked at this Statue very attentively, through a little prospect that I carried with me, it appeared plainly to have the face of a young Woman, and was very unlike that of Pope *Nicolas* the IV. which is in *St. Maria Maggiore* at *Rome*: For the Statue of that Pope, though it hath no beard, yet hath an age in it that is very much different from the Statue at *Bologna*. I do not build any thing on this Statue, for I do not believe that Story at all, and I my self saw in *England* a Manuscript of *Martinus Polonus*, who is one of the ancient Authors of this matter, which did not seem to be written long after the Author's time; In it this Story is not in the Text, but is added on the margin by another hand. On the Hill above *Bologna* stands the Monastery of St. *Michael in Bosco*, which hath a most charming scituation, and prospect, and is one of the best Monasteries in *Italy*; it hath many Courts, and one that is Cloistered, and is *Octangular*; which is so nobly painted *in Fresco*, that it is great pity to see such work exposed to the Air: All was retouched by the famous *Guido Reni*, yet it is now again much decayed: The *Dormitory* is very Magnificent; the Chappel is little but very fine, and the Stalls are richly carved. On the other-side of *Bologna*, in the Bottom, the *Carthusians* have also a very rich Monastery: Four miles from *Bologna* there is a *Madona* of St. *Lukes*, and because many go thither in great devotion, there is a *portico* a building, which is already carried on almost half way; it is walled towards the *North*, but stands on Pillars to the *South*, and is about Twelve Foot broad, and Fifteen Foot high, which is carried on very vigoroufly, for in Eight

N 3 or

or Ten Years the half is built, so that in a little time, the whole will be very probably finished, and this may prove the beginning of many such like *Portico*'s in *Italy*, for things of this kind want only a beginning, and when they are once set on foot they do quickly spread themselves in a Country that is so intirely subdued by superstition and the artifices of their Priests. In *Bologna* they reckon there are Seventy Thousand Persons. I saw not one of the chief glories of this place for the famous *Malpighi* was out of Town while I was there. I saw a Play there, but the Poesie was so bad, the Farces so rude, and all was so ill acted, that I was not a little amazed to see the Company express so great a satisfaction in that which would have been hiss'd off the Stage either in *England* or *France*. From *Bologna* we go Eight miles in a Plain, and then we engage into that range of Hills that carry the name of *Apenins*, though that is strictly given only to one that is the highest: All the way to *Florence* this track of Hills continues, though there are several bottoms, and some considerable little Towns in them; but all is up-hill and down-hill, and *Florence* it self is just at the bottom of the last Hill. The high-ways all along these Hills are kept in so very good case, that in few of the best Inhabited Countries doth one find the high-ways so well maintained as in those forsaken Mountains; but this is so great a passage that all that are concerned in it find their account in the expence they lay out upon it. On the last of these Hills, though in a little bottom, in the midst of a Hill, stands *Pratolino*, one of the great Dukes Palaces, where the retreat in summer must be very agreeable, for the Air of those Mountains is extream thin and pure. The Gardens in *Italy* are made at a great cost, the Statues and Fountains are very rich and noble, the Grounds are well laid out, and the Walks are long and even: But as they have no Gravel to give them those firm and beautiful walks that we have in *England*, so the constant green-

greenness of the Box doth so much please them, that they preferring the sight to the smell, have their Gardens so high sented by plots made within them, that there is no pleasure to walk in them; they also lay their walks so between hedges, that one is much confined in them. I saw first in a Garden at *Vincenza*, that which I found afterwards in many Gardens in *Italy*, which was extream convenient, there went a course of Water round about the Walls, about a foot from the ground in a channel of stone that went along the side of the Wall; and in this there were holes so made, that a pipe of white Iron or Wood put to them, conveyed the Water to such plants, as in dry season, needed watering; and a cock, set the Water a running in this course, so that without the trouble of carrying Water, one Person could easily manage the watring of a great Garden. *Florence* is a beautiful and noble Town, full of great Palaces, rich Churches, and stately Convents. The streets are paved in imitation of the old *Roman* highways, with great Stone bigger than our common pavement Stone, but much thicker, which are so hollowed in their joinings to one another, that horses find fastning enough to their feet: There are many Statues and Fountains in the streets, so that in every corner one meets with many agreeable objects. I will not entertain you with a description of the great Dukes Palace and Gardens, or of the old Palace and the Gallery that joins to it, and of the vast Collection of Pictures, Statues, Cabinets, and other curiosities that must needs amaze every one that sees them; the Plate, and in particular the Gold Plate, and the great Coach, are all such extraordinary things that they would require a very copious description; if that had not been done so often, that it were to very little purpose to Copy what others have said; and these things are so exactly seen by every traveller, that I can say nothing that is more particular of these subjects then you will find in

in the common Itineraries of all Travellers. Th[e]
great Dome is a magnificent building, but the Fron[-]
tifpiece to the great Gate is not yet made. Th[e]
Cupulo, is after S. *Peters*, the greateft and higheft tha[t]
I faw in *Italy*; it is Three Hundred foot high, and o[f]
a vaft compafs, and the whole Architecture of thi[s]
Fabrick is very fingular as well as regular. Onl[y]
that which was intended to add to its beauty, leffne[d]
it very much in my thoughts; for the Walls that ar[e]
all of Marble being of white and black Marble lai[d]
in different figures and orders, looked too like a livery, and had not that air of noblenefs which in m[y]
opinion becomes fo glorious a Fabrick. The *Bapti-
ftery* that ftands before it was a Noble *Heathen* Temple; its Gates of brafs are the beft of that fort that
are in the World: There are fo many Hiftories fo
well reprefented in *bas reliefs* in them, with fo much
exactnefs, the work is fo natural and yet fo fine,
that a curious Man could find entertainment for many days, if he would examine the three Gates of this
Temple, with a critical exactnefs. The *Annunciata*,
S. *Marks*, S. *Croce*, and S. *Maria Novella*, are Churches of great beauty and vaft riches; but the Church
and Chappel of S. *Laurence* exceeds them all as much
in the riches within, as it is inferior to them in the
out-fide which is quite flea'd, if I may fo fpeak, but
on defign to give it a rich out-fide of Marble. In a
Chappel within this Church, the Bodies of the great
Dukes lie depofited, till the famous Chappel is finifhed. But I was much fcandalized to fee Statues
with nudities here, which I do not remember to have
feen any where elfe in Churches. I will not offer at
a defcription of the Glorious Chappel, which as it
is without doubt the richeft piece of building that
perhaps the World ever faw, fo it goes on fo flow-
ly, that though there are always many at work, yet
it doth not feem to advance proportionably to the
number of the hands that are imployed in it. A-
mong

Among the Statues that are to be in it, there is one of the Virgins made by *Michael Angelo*, which represents her grief at the Passion of her Blessed Son, that hath the most life in it of all the Statues I ever saw.

But the famous Library that belongs to this Convent, took up more of my time than all the other Curiosities of *Florence*; for here is a collection of many Manuscripts, most of them are *Greek*, that were gathered together by Pope *Clement* the VII. and given to his Country: There are very few Printed Books mixed with them; and those Books that are there, are so rare, that they are almost as curious as Manuscripts. I saw some of *Virgils* Poems in old Capitals. There is a Manuscript in which some parts both of *Tacitus* and *Apuleius* are written, and in one place, one in a different hand hath writ, that he had compared those Manuscripts: and he adds a date to this in *Olibrius*'s time, which is above Twelve hundred years ago. I found some Dipthongs in it cast into one Letter, which surprized me, for I thought that way of writing of them had not been so ancient: but that which pleased me most, was, that the Library-keeper assured me, that one had lately found the famous Epistle of St. *Chrisostomes* to *Cesarius* in *Greek*, in the end of a Volume full of other things, and not among the Manuscripts of that Fathers Books of which they have a great many. He thought he remembred well the place where the Book stood; so we turned over all the Books that stood near it, but found it not: He promised to look it out for me, if I came back that way. But I changing my design, and going back another way, could not see the bottom of this. It is true, the Famous *Magliabecchi*, who is the Great Dukes Library-keeper, and is a Person of most wonderful civility and full of candour, as well as he is learned beyond imagination, assured me that this could be no other than a mistake of the Library-keepers; he said such a discovery could not have been

made

made without making so much noise that he mu[st]
have heard of it. He added there was not one Ma[n]
in *Florence* that either understood *Greek*, or that exa[-]
mined Manuscripts, so that he assured me I could n[ot]
build on what an Ignorant Library-keeper had tol[d]
me: So I set down this matter as I found it withou[t]
building much on it. *Florence* is much sunk fro[m]
what it was, for they do not reckon that there are [a-]
bove Fifty thousand Souls in it: and the other Stat[es]
that were once great Republicks, such as *Siena* an[d]
Pisa, while they retained their liberty, are no[w]
shrunk almost into nothing: It is certain that a[ll]
three together are now not so numerous, as any o[ne]
of them was Two hundred Years ago. *Legorn* [is]
full of People; and all round *Florence* there are
great many Villages; but as one goes over *Tuscany* it a[p-]
pears so dispeopled, that one cannot wonder to find [a]
Country that hath been a Scene of so much action an[d]
so many Wars, now so forsaken and so poor, an[d]
that in many places the Soil is quite neglected for war[nt]
of hands to cultivate it: and in other places wher[e]
there are more People, they look so poor, and the[ir]
houses are such miserable ruines, that it is scarce ac[-]
countable how there should be so much poverty in [so]
rich a Country, which is all over full of beggars: an[d]
here the style of begging was a little altered fro[m]
what I found in *Lombardy*; for whereas there the[y]
begged for the sake of S. *Anthony*, here all begge[d]
for the Souls that were in Purgatory, and this w[as]
the stile in all the other parts of *Italy* through whic[h]
I passed. In short, the dispeopling of *Tuscany*, an[d]
most of the Principalities of *Italy*, but chiefly of t[he]
Popes Dominions, which are more abandoned tha[n]
any other part of *Italy*, seemed to flow from nothin[g]
but the severity of the Government and the great d[e-]
cay of Trade: for the greatest Trade of *Italy* bein[g]
in Silk, the vast importation of Silks that the *East*
India Companies bring into *Europe*, hath quite ruined a
tho[se]

...se that deal in this manufacture: Yet this is not the ...ef cause of the dispeopling of those rich Coun-...ies, the severity of the Taxes is the true reason: not-...ithstanding all that decay of Trade, the Taxes are ...ll kept up. Besides this, the vast Wealth of the ...onvents, where the only People of *Italy* are to be ...und, that live not only at their ease, but in great ...enty and luxury, makes many forsake all sort of In-...stry, and seek for a retreation of those seats of ...easure; so that the People do not encrease fast e-...ugh to make a new Race to come instead of those ...hom a hard Government drives away. It must ...eds surprize an unattentive Traveller to see, not on-... the *Venetian* Territory; which is indeed a rich ...ountry, but the Baliages of the *Switzers*, and the ...oast of *Genoa* so full of People, when *Tuscany*, the ...trimony, and the Kingdom of *Naples* have so few ... habitants. In the Coast of *Genoua*, there is for ...any miles as it were a constant tract of Towns and ...illages, and all those are well peopled, though they ...ve scarce any Soil at all, lying under the Moun-...ins that are very barren, and that exposed them ... a most uneasie Sun; and that they lie upon a boi-...ous Sea that is almost always in a storm, and that ...fords very few Fish: and yet the gentleness of the ...overnment draws such multitudes thither, and those ...e so full of Wealth, that Money goes at Two *per* ...nt. But on the other hand to ballance this a little, ...strange and wild a thing is the nature of Man, at ...ast of *Italians*, that I was told that the worst People ...all *Italy*, are the *Genoeses*, and the most generally ...rrupted in their Morals, as to all sorts of Vice, so ...at though a severe Government and Slavery are con-...ary to the nature of Man, and to human Society, to ...stice and Equity; and to that essential equality ...at Nature hath made among Men: yet on the other ...nd, all Men cannot bear that ease and liberty that ...cometh human Nature. The superstition of *Italy*,

and

and the great waft of Wealth that one fees in their Churches, particularly thofe prodigious maffes of Plate with which their Altars are covered on Holydays, doth alfo fink their Trade extreamly; for Silver being in Commerce, what blood is in the Body, when fo much of that is dead and circulates no more, it is no wonder if fuch extravafation (if I may ufe fo long and hard a word) of Silver, occafions a great deadnefs in Trade. I had almoft forgot one Remark that I made in the Hill of the *Appennins*, juft above *Florence*, that I never faw fuch tall and big Cypreffe as grew over all that Hill, which feemed a little ftrange that Tree being apt to be ftarved by a cold Winter among us, and there the Winters are fevere. All the way in *Tufcany* is very rugged, except on the fides of the *Arne*. But the uneafinefs of the Road is much qualified by the great care that is had of the Highways, which are all in very good cafe: The Inns are wretched and ill furnifhed both for Lodging and Diet. This is the plague of all *Italy*, when once one hath paffed the *Appennins*: for, except in the great Towns one really fuffers fo much that way, that the pleafure of Travelling is much abated by the inconvenience that one meets in every Stage through which he paffes. I am

S I R,

Yours.

BOOK II.

The Fourth Letter.

From Rome *the Eight of* December.
1685.

I *Am now in my last stage of my Voyage over* Italy; *for since my last from* Florence, *I have not only got hither, but have been in* Naples; *and have now satisfied my Curiosity so fully, that I intend to leave this Place within a day or two, and go to* Civita-vecchia, *and from thence by Sea to* Marseilles, *and to avoid an unpleasant Winters Journey over the* Alps. *It is true I close the sight of* Turin, Genoa, *and some other Courts: but tho' I am told these deserve well the pains of the Journey; yet when one rises from a great Meal, no Delicacies, how much soever they might tempt him at another time can provoke his appetite: so I confess freely that the sight of* Naples *and* Rome, *have so fil'd my stomack that way, that the Curiosity of seeing new Places is now very low with me, and indeed these that I have of last seen are such, that Places which at an other time wou'd please me much, would now make but a slight and cold Impression.*

All the way from *Florence*, through the Great Duke's Country looked so sad, that I concluded it

A must

must be the most dispeopled of all *Italy*: but indeed, I changed my Note, when I came into the *Popes* Territories at *Pont Centino*, where there was a rich bottom all uncultivated, and not so much as stocked with Cattle: But as I passed from M. *Fiascone* to *Viterbo*, this appeared yet more amazing, for a vast Champion Country lay almost quite deserted. And that wide Town which is of so great a compass, hath yet so few Inhabitants, and those look so poor and miserable, that the people in the Ordinary Towns in *Scotland*, and in its worst places make a better appearance. When I was within a days Journey of *Rome*, I fancied that the Neighbourhood of so great a City must mend the matter: but I was much disappointed, for a soil that was so Rich, and lay so sweetly, that it far exceeded any thing I ever saw out of *Italy*, had neither Inhabitants in it, nor Cattle upon it, to the tenth part of what it could bear: The surprize that this gave me, encreased upon me as I went out of *Rome* on its other side, chiefly all the way to *Naples*, and on the way to *Civita-vecchia*, for that vast and rich Champion Countrey that runs all along to *Terracina*, which from *Civita-vecchia* is above a hundred miles long, and is in many places twelve or twenty miles broad, is abandoned to such a degree, that as far as ones eye can carry one, there is often not so much as a House to be seen; but on the Hills that are on the North side of this Valley, and by this dispeopling of the Country, the Air is now become so unwholesome, that it is not safe to be a night in it all the Summer long, for the Water that lies upon many places not being drained, it rots: and in the Summer this produces so many noisom steams, that it is felt even in *Rome* it self; and if it were not for the breeses that come from the Mountains, the Air would be intollerable: When one sees all this large but vast Countrey from the Hill of *Marino* twelve miles beyond *Rome*, he cannot
wonder

wonder enough at it. In a word, it is the rigour of the Government, that hath driven away the Inhabitants, and their being driven away, hath now reduced it to such a pass, that it is hardly possible to people it: for such as would come to drain and cultivate it, must run a great hazard, and few can resolve on that, when they can hope for no other reward of their Industry, but an uneasie Government. It is the greatest solœcism in Goverument for the Prince to be Elective, and yet Absolute; for an Hereditary Prince is induced to consider his posterity, and to maintain his people, so that those that come after him may still support the rank which they hold in the World: But an Elective Prince hath nothing of that in his eye, unless he hath a pitch of generosity which is not ordinary among men, and least of all among *Italians*, who have a passion for their Families, which is not known in other places: and thus a *Pope*, who comes in late to this dignity, which by consequence he cannot hope to hold long, doth very naturally turn to those Councels, by which his Family may make all the Hay they can during this Sun-shine: And tho anciently the *Cardinals* were a check upon the *Pope*, and a sort of Councel without whom he could do nothing even in Temporals; yet now they have quite lost that; and they have no other share in affairs than that to which the *Pope* thinks fit to admit them, so that he is the most absolute Prince in *Europe*. It is true as to Spirituals they retain still a large share, so that in censures and definitions, the *Pope* can do nothing regularly, without their concurrence; tho it is certain that they have not so good a Title to pretend to that, as to share in the Temporal Principality. For if the *Pope* drives any thing from St. *Peter*, all that, is singly in himself, and it is free to him to proceed by what method he thinks best; since the Infallibility, according to their pretensions, rests singly in him: Yet because their was not so

A a 2 much

much to be got by acting Arbitrarily in those matters, and a Summary way of exercising this Authority, might have tempted the World to have enquired too much into the grounds on which it is built; Therefore the *Popes* have let the *Cardinals* retain still a share in this Supremacy over the Church, tho they have no claim to it, neither by any Divine nor Ecclesiastical warrants: But as for the endowments of the See of *Rome*, to which they may justly lay claim, as being in a manner the Chapter of that See; there is so much to be got by this, that the *Popes* have engrossed it wholly to themselves: and thus it is that the Government of this Principality is very unsteady. Sometimes the *Pope*'s Family are extreamly glorious, and magnificent, at other times, they think of nothing but of establishing their house: Sometimes the *Pope* is a man of sense himself; Sometimes he is quite sunk, and as the last *Pope* was, he become a Child again through old age: Sometimes he hath a particular stifness of temper, with a great slowness of understanding, and an insatiable desire of heaping up wealth, which is the character of him that now Reigns. By this diversity which appears eminently in every new Pontificate that commonly avoids those excesses that made the former Reign odious, the Councels of the *Popedom* are weak and disjointed. But if this is sensible to all *Europe*, with relation to the general concerns of that Body, it is much more visible in the Principality if self, that is subject to so variable a head. There hath been in this Age a succession of four ravenous Reigns, and tho there was a short interruption in the Reign of the *Rospigliosi*, that coming after the *Barberins*, the *Pamphili*, and the *Ghigi*'s, did inrich it self: and yet, it disordered the Revenue by the vast magnificence in which he Reigned, more in twenty nine months time, than any other had done in so many years. The *Altieri* did, in a most scandalous manner, raise themselves

in

In a very short and difpifed Reign, and built one of the Nobleft Palaces in *Rome*. He that Reigns now doth not indeed raife his Family avowedly, but he doth not eafe the people of their Taxes: and as there is no magnificence in his Court, nor any publick buildings now carrying on at *Rome*, fo the many vacant Caps, occafion many empty Palaces: and by this means there is fo little expence now made at *Rome*, that it is not poffible for the people to live and pay the Taxes, which hath driven, as is believed, almoft a fourth part of the Inhabitants out of *Rome*, during this Pontificate. And as the pre-emption of the Corn makes that there is no profit made by the Owners, out of the cultivation of the Soil, all that going wholly to the *Pope*, fo there are no ways left here of employing one's Mony to any confiderable advantage: For the publick Banks, which are all in the *Pope*'s hand, do not pay in effect three *per cent* tho they pretend to give four *per cent* of intereft. The fettlement is indeed four *per cent*, and this was thought fo great an advantage, that actions on the *Pope*'s Bank were bought at a hundred and Sixteen the hundred. But this *Pope* broke through all this, and declared he would give all men their Money again, unlefs they would pay him thirty *per cent* for the continuing of this Intereft; and thus for a hundred Crowns Principal, one not only paid at firft one hundred and fixteen; but afterwards thirty, in all one hundred fix and forty for the hundred which is almoft the ha'f loft: For whenfoever the *Pope* will pay them back their Money, all the reft is loft: And while I am here there is a report that the *Pope* is Treating with the *Genoefes* for Money at two *per cent* and if he gets it on thofe Terms, then he will pay his Debts; and the Subjects that have put in Money in this Bank, will, by this means lofe fix and forty *per cent*, which is almoft the half of their Stock. A man of quality at *Rome*, and an eminent Church-man,

man, who took me likewife for one of their Clergy; becaufe I wore the habit of a Church-man, faid that it was a horrible fcandal to the whole *Chriftian* World, and made one doubt of the Truth of the *Chriftian* Religion, to fee more oppreffion and cruelty in their Territory, then was to be found even in *Turkey:* tho it being in the hands of *Chrift's* Vicar, one fhould expect to find there the pattern of a mild and gentle Government: and how, faid he can a man expect to find his Religion here, where the common maxims of Juftice and Mercy were not fo much as known: And I can never forget the lively reflection that a *Roman* Prince made to me upon the folly of all thofe fevere Oppreffions, which as they drive away the Inhabitants, fo they reduce thofe that are left to fuch a degeneracy of Spirit by their neceffities, that the *Spaniards*, whofe Dominions look fo big in the Map, are now brought fo low: and if they had kept ftill the poffeffion they once had of the *United-Netherlands*, they would fignifie no more towards their prefervation, than their other Provinces did: which, by their unskilful conduct they have both difpeopled and exhaufted: Whereas by their lofing thofe feven Provinces, thofe States have fallen upon fuch wife Notions of Government, and have drawn fo much Wealth, and fuch numbers of people together, that *Spain* it felf was now preferved by them, and was faved in this Age by the lofs it made of thofe Provinces in the laft: and thofe States that if they had remained fubject to *Spain*, would have fignified little to its fupport, did that now much more confiderably by being *Allies*, then they could have done if they had fhaken off their Yoak.

Indeed if *Spain* had been fo happy as to have fuch Viceroys and Governors, as it has now in *Naples*, their affairs could not have declined fo faft as they have done. The Marquis of *Carpi*, in his youth intended to have taken fo fevere a revenge of an injury that

that he thought the late King of *Spain* did him in an amour, that he designed the blowing him up by Gunpowder, when he was in the Council Chamber: but that crime was discovered in time: and was not only forgiven him in consideration of the greatness of his Family, he being the Son of *Don Lewis de Haro*: but after that he was made for several years Ambassador in *Rome*: He is now Viceroy of *Naples*, and is the only Governor of all the places through which I passed, that is, without exception beloved and esteemed by all sorts of people: for during the few years of his Ministry, he hath redressed such abuses that seemed past cure, and that required an Age to correct them: He hath repressed the insolence of the *Spaniards* so much at *Naples*, that the Natives have no occasion to complain of the haughtiness of their Masters: for he proceeds against the *Spaniards* with no less severity, when they give cause for it, than against the *Neapolitans*: He hath taken the pay of the Souldiers so immediately into his own care, that they, who before his coming, were half naked, and robbed, such as passed on the streets of *Naples* in day light, are now exactly payed, well disciplined, and so decently cloathed, that it is a pleasure to see them: He examines their Musters also so exactly, that he is sure not to be cheated by false lists: He hath brought the Markets and Weights of *Naples* to a true exactness: And whereas the Bread was generally too light, he has sent for Loaves out of the several places of the Markets and weighed them himself: And by some severe punishment on those that sold the Bread too light, he hath brought this matter to a just regulation: He hath also brought the Courts of Judicature, that were thought generally very corrupt, to reputation again, and it is believed he hath Spies to Watch in case the Trade of Bribes is found to be still going on: He hath fortified the Palace which was before his time, so much exposed,

that

that it would have been no hard thing to have made a defcent upon it: But the two things that raife his reputation moft, are his Extirpating of the *Banditi*, and the regulation of the Coin, which he hath taken in hand. It is well enough known what a Plague the *Banditi* have been to the Kingdom, for they going in Troops, not only robbed the Country, but were able to refift an ordinary Body of Souldiers, if they had fet on them: Thefe travelled about, feeking for Spoyl all the Summer long, but in Winter they were harboured by fome of the *Neapolitan* Barrons, who gave them Quarters: And thereby did not only protect their own Lands, but had them as fo many Inftruments ready to execute their Revenges on their Enemies. This was well known at *Naples*, and there was a Councel that had the care of the reducing the *Banditi* committed to them, who as they catched fome few, and hanged them, fo they fined fuch Barrons as gave them harbour; and it was believed that thofe Fines amounted to near a hundred and fifty thoufand Crowns a year: And thus the Difeafe went on; only now and then there was a little Blood let, which never went to the bottom of the Diftemper. But when the prefent Viceroy entred upon the Government, he refolved to extirpate all the *Banditi*, and he firft let all the Barons underftand, that if they harboured them any more, a little Fine would not fave them: but that he would proceed againft them with the utmoft feverity, and by this means the *Banditi* could find no Winter Quarters: So they betook themfelves to fome faftneffes among the Hills, and refolved to make good the Paffes, and to accommodate themfelves the beft they could amidft the Mountains. The *Viceroy* fent a great Body againft them. but they defended themfelves for fome time vigbroufly, and in one Sally they killed five hundred men: but at laft, feeing that they were like to be hard preft; and that the *Viceroy*
in-

intended to come againſt them in Perſon, they accepted of the Terms that he offered them, which was a Pardon for what was paſt, both as to Life and Gallies, and ſix pence a day for their entertainment in Priſon during Life, or the *Viceroys* pleaſure; and ſo they rendred themſelves. They are kept in a large Priſon, and now and then as he ſees cauſe for it, he ſends ſome few of them up and down to ſerve in Garriſons. And thus, beyond all mens expectation, he finiſhed this matter in a very few months; and the Kingdom of *Naples* that hath been ſo long a ſcene of Pillage and Robbery, is now ſo much changed, that in no place of *Europe* do the Subjects enjoy a more entire ſecurity. As for the Coin, it, as all the other *Spaniſh* money, is ſo ſubject to clipping, that the whole money of *Naples* is now light, and far below the true Value, ſo the *Viceroy* hath reſolved to redreſs this: He conſiders that the crying down of money, that paſſeth upon the Publick credit, is a robbing of thoſe in whoſe hands the money happens to be when ſuch Proclamations are put out, and therefore he takes a method that is more general, in which every one will bear his ſhare, ſo that none will be cruſhed by it. He hath laid ſome Taxes on the whole Kingdom, and hath got a great many to bring in ſome Plate to be Coined: And when he hath thus prepared ſuch a quantity, as may ſerve for the circulation that is neceſſary, he intends to call in all the old money, and to give out new money for it. Thus doth this *Viceroy*, ſet ſuch a Pattern to the other Miniſters of the Crown of *Spain*, that if many would follow it, the State of their affairs would be ſoon altered.

 The Kingdom of *Naples* is the richeſt part of all *Italy*: for the very Mountains that are near the half of the Soil, are fruitful, and produce either Wine or Oyl in great abundance. *Apulia* is a great Corn Countrey, but is exceſſive hot, and in ſome years all

is

is burnt up. The *Jesuits* are the Proprietors of near the half of *Apulia*, and they treat their Tenants with the same rigour that the Barons of this Kingdom do generally use towards their Farmers; for the Commons here are so miserably oppressed, that in many places they die of hunger, even amidst the great plenty of their best years, for the Corn is exported to *Spain*: but neither the *Spaniards* nor the *Neapolitans* understand Trade so well as to be their own Merchants or Carriers, so that the *English* do generally carry away the profit of this Trade. The Oyl of this Kingdom is still a vast Trade, and the Manufacture of the Wool and Soap of *England*, consumes yearly some thousands of Tuns. The Silk Trade is so low that it only serves themselves, but the exportation is inconsiderable: the sloth and laziness of this people renders them incapable of making those advantages of so rich a Soil, that a more industrious sort of people would find out: For it amazes a Stranger to see in their little Towns, the whole men of the Town walking in the Market places in their torn Cloaks, and doing nothing; and tho in some big Towns, such as *Capua*, there is but one Inn, yet even that is so miserable, that the best Room and Bed in it, is so bad, that our Footmen in *England* would make a grievous out-cry if they were no better lodged: nor is there any thing to be had in them; the Wine is intollerable, the Bread ill baked, no Victuals, except Pigeons, and the Oyl is rotten. In short, except one carries his whole provision from *Rome* or *Naples*, he must resolve to endure a good deal of misery in the four days journey that is between those two places. And this is what a Traveller, that sees the riches of the soil, cannot comprehend: but as they have not hands enough for their Soil, so those they have are generally too little employed, that it is no wonder to see their Soil produce so little, that in the midst of all that abundance that

Nature

Nature hath set before them, they are one of the poorest Nations of *Europe*. But besides this, which I have named, the vast and dead wealth that is in the hands of the Churchmen, is another evident cause of their misery. One that knew the State of this Kingdom well, assured me, that if it were divided into five parts, upon a strict Survey, it would be found that the Churchmen had four parts of the five; which he made out thus, they have in Soil above the half of the whole, which is two and a half: and in Tithes and Gifts and Legacies they have one and a half more: for no man dieth without leaving a considerable Legacy to some Church or some Convent. The Wealth that one sees in the City of *Naples* alone, passeth imagination; there are four and twenty Houses of the Order of the *Dominicans*, of both Sexes, and two and twenty of the *Franciscans*, seven of the *Jesuites*, besides the Convents of the *Olivitanes*, the *Theatines*, the *Carmelites*, the *Benedictines*, and above all, for scituation and riches, the *Carthusians* on the top of the Hill that lyeth over the Town. The riches of the *Annunciata* are prodigious: It is the greatest Hospital in the World, the Revenue is said to be four hundred thousand Crowns a year: the number of the Sick is not so great as at *Milan*: Yet one convenience for their Sick I observed in their Galleries, which was considerable, that every Bed stood as in an *Alcove*, and had a Wall on both sides separating it from the Beds on both hands, and as much void space of both sides of the Bed, that the Bed it self took up but half the Room. The young Children that they maintain are so many, that one can hardly believe the numbers that they boast of: for they talk of many thousands that are not seen, but are at Nurse: a great part of the Wealth of this House goeth to the enriching their Church, which will be all over within crusted with inlayings of lovely Marble, in a great variety and beauty of colours:

The

The Plate that is in the Treasure here and in the Dome (which is but a mean building, because it is ancient, but hath a Noble Chappel, and a vast Treasure) and in a great many other Churches are so prodigious, that upon the modest estimate, the Plate of the Churches of *Naples* amounts to eight millions of Crowns. The new Church of the *Jesuits*, that of S. *John* the Apostle, and that of S. *Paul* are surprizingly rich; the Gilding and Painting that is on the Roofs of those Churches have cost millions: And as there are about a hundred Convents in *Naples*, so every one of these, if it were in another place, would be thought well worth, seeing, tho the riches of the greater Convents here, make many of them to be less visited. Every year there is a new Governour of the *Annunciata*, who perhaps puts in his own Pocket twenty thousand Crowns; and to make some compensation when he goeth out of Office, he giveth a vast piece of Plate to the House, a Statue for a Saint in Silver, or some Coloss of a Candlestick; for several of those Pieces of Plate, are said to be worth ten thousand Crowns; and thus all the Silver of *Naples* becomes dead and useless: The *Jesuits* are great Merchants here: their Wine Cellar is a vast Vault, and holds above a thousand Hogsheads, and the best Wine of *Naples* is sold by them, yet they do not retail it out so scandalously as the *Minims*, who live on the great Square before the Viceroys Palace, and sell out their Wine by retail: They pay no duty, and have extraordinary good Wine, and are in the best place of the Town for this retail. It is true the *Neapolitans* are no great Drinkers, so the profits of this Tavern are not so great as they would be in colder Countries: for here men go only in for a draught in the mornings, or when they are a thirst. Yet the House groweth extream rich, and hath one of the finest Chappels that is in all *Naples*; but the Trade seems very unbecoming men of that Profession,

and

and of so strict an Order. The Convents have a very particular Priviledge in this Town: for they may buy all the Houses that lye on either side, till the first Street that discontinueth the Houses; and there being scarce a Street in *Naples* in which there is not a Convent; by this means, they may come to buy in the whole Town: And the progress that the wealth of the Clergy makes in this Kingdom, is so visible, that, if there is not some stop put to it, within an Age, they will make themselves Masters of the whole Kingdom: It is an amazing thing to see so profound an ignorance, as Reigns among the Clergy, prevail so effectually, for tho all the Secular Persons here speak of them with all possible scorn, yet they are the Masters of the Spirits of the people. The Women are infinitely superstitious, and give their Husbands no rest, but as they draw from them great presents to the Church. It is true, there are Societies of men at *Naples* of freer thoughts than can be found in any other place of *Italy*: The *Greek* learning begins to flourish there, and the new Philosophy is much Studied; and there is an Assembly that is held in D. *Joseph Valleta*'s Library (where there is a vast Collection of well chosen Books) composed by men that have a right taste of true learning and good sense: They are ill looked on by the Clergy, and represented as a set of Atheists, and as the Spawn of *Pomponitius*'s School: But I found no such thing among them, for I had the Honour to meet twice or thrice with a considerable number of them, during the short stay that I made among them: There is a learned Lawyer *Francisco Andria* that is considered as one of the most inquisitive men of the Assembly: There is also a Grand-child of the Great *Alciat*, who is very curious as well as learned. Few Churchmen come in to this attempt for the reviving of Learning among them: On the contrary, it is plain, that they dread it above all things. Only one Eminent Preacher

B b   *Rinaldi*

Rinaldi, that is Arch-deacon of *Capua*, Associate himself with them: He was once of the *Jesuites* Order, but left it; and as that alone served to give a good character of him to me, so upon a long conversation with him, I found a great many other things that possessed me with a high value for him. Some Phylitians in *Naples* are brought under the scandal of Atheism, and it is certain, that in *Italy*, men of searching understandings, who have no other Idea of the *Christian* Religion, but that which they see received among them, are very naturally tempted to disbelieve it quite; for they believing it all alike in gross without distinction, and finding such notorious cheats as appear in many parts of their Religion, are upon that induced to disbelieve the whole. The Preachings of the Monks in *Naples* are terrible things. I saw a *Jesuite* go in a sort of a Procession, with a great company about him, and calling upon all that he saw, to follow him to a place where a Mountebank was selling his Medicines, near whom he took his Room, and entertained the people with a sort of a Farce, till the Mountebank got him to give over fearing least his action should grow tedious, and did perse the company that was brought together. There are no famous Preachers, nor men of any reputation nor learning among the *Jesuites*: I was told they had not men capable to teach their Schools, and that they were forced to hire Strangers: The Order of the Oratory hath not that reputation in *Italy*, that it hath gained in *France*, and the little Learning that is among the Clergy in *Naples*, is among some few Secular Priests.

The new method of *Molinos* doth so much prevail in *Naples*, that it is believed he hath above twenty thousand followers in this City: And since this hath made some noise in the World, and yet is generally but little understood, I will give you some account of him: He is a *Spanish* Priest that seems to be but

at

an ordinary Divine, and is certainly a very ill Reasoner when he undertakes to prove his opinions: He hath writ a Book, which is intituled, *Il Guida Spirituale*, which is a short abstract of the Mystical Divinity; the substance of the whole, is reduced to this, that in our Prayers and other Devotions, the best methods are to retire the mind from all gross Images, and so to form an act of Faith, and thereby to present our selves before God, and then to sink into a silence and cessation of new acts, and to let God act upon us, and so to follow his conduct: This way he prefers to the multiplication of many new acts, and different forms of Devotion; and he makes small account of corporal austerities, and reduces all the exercises of Religion to this simplicity of mind: He thinks this is not only to be proposed to such as live in Religious Houses, but even to secular persons, and by this he hath proposed a great Reformation of mens minds and manners: He hath many Priests in *Italy*, but chiefly in *Naples*, that dispose those who confess themselves to them, to follow his methods: The *Jesuits* have set themselves much against this conduct, as foreseeing that it may much weaken the Empire that Superstition hath over the minds of people, that it may make Religion become a more plain and simple thing, and may also open a door to *Enthusiasms*: They also pretend, that his conduct is factious and seditious, that this may breed a Schism in the Church. And because he saith in some places of his Book, *That the mind may rise up to such a simplicity in its acts, that it may rise in some of its Devotions to God immediately, without contemplating the Humanity* of Christ: they have accused him, as intending to lay aside the Doctrine of *Christ*'s Humanity, tho it is plain that he speaks only of the purity of some single acts: Upon all those heads they have set themselves much against *Molinos*; and they have also pretended that some of his Disciples, have infused it into their Penitents, that they may go and Communicate as they find themselves disposed, without going first to Confession, which they thought weakned much the Yoke, by which the Priests subdue the Consciences of the people to their Conduct: Yet he was much supported both in the Kingdom of *Naples* and in *Sicily*; He had also many friends and followers at *Rome*. So the *Jesuites*, as a Provincial of the Order assured me, finding they could not ruine him by their own force, got a great King, that is now extreamly in the Interests of their Order to interpose, and to represent to the Pope the danger of such innovations. It is certain the Pope understands the matter very little, and that he is possessed with a great opinion of *Molino*'s sanctity, yet upon the complaints of some Cardinals, that seconded the zeal of that King, he and some of his followers were clapt in the Inquisition, where they have been now for some months, but they are still well used, which is believed to flow from the good opinion that the Pope hath of him, who saith still, that tho he may have erred, yet he is certainly a good man: Upon this imprisonment, *Pasquin* said a pleasant thing in one week, one man had been condemned to the Gallies for somewhat he had said, another had been hanged for somewhat he had writ, and *Molinos* was clapt in Prison, whose Doctrine consisted chiefly in this, that men ought to bring their minds to a state of inward quietness, from which the name of *Quietists* was given to all his followers: The *Pasquinade* upon all this, was, *Si parliamo, in Galere, si scrivemmo Impiccati, si stiamo in quiete all' Saint' Officio, e che bisogna fare:* If we speak, we are sent to the Gallies; if we write, we are hanged: if we stand quiet, we are clapt up in the Inquisition: what must we do then? Yet his Followers at *Naples* are not daunted, but they believe he will come out of this Trial victorious.

The

The City of *Naples*, as it is the best scituated, and in the best climate, so it is one of the Noblest Cities of *Europe*, and if it is not above half as big as *Paris* or *London*, yet it hath much more beauty then either of them: the Streets are large and broad, the pavement is great and Noble, the Stones being generally above a foot square: and it is full of Palaces and great Buildings: The Town is well supplied by daily Markets, so that provisions are ever fresh and in great plenty, the Wine is the best of Europe, and both the Fish and Flesh is extream good: it is scarce ever cold in Winter, and there is a fresh Air comes both from the Sea and the Mountains in Summer. The Viceroys Palace is no extraordinary Building, only the Stair-case is great: But it is now very richly furnished within, in Pictures and Statues: there are in it some Statues of the *Egyptian* Deities of Touchstone, that are of great value: There are no great Antiquities here, only there is an ancient *Roman Portico* that is very Noble, before St. *Pauls* Church: But without the City near the Church and Hospital of St. *Gennaro*, that is without the Gates, are the Noble *Catacombs*; which because they were beyond any thing I saw in *Italy*, and to which the *Catacombs* of *Rome* are not to be compared, and since I do nor find any account of them, in all the Books that I have yet seen concerning *Naples*, I shall describe them more particularly.

They are vast and long Galleries cut out of the Rock: there are three Stories of them one above another. I was in two of them, but the Rock is fallen in the lowest, so that one cannot go in to it, but I saw the passage to it: These Galleries are generally about twenty foot broad, and about fifteen foot high: so that they are Noble and spacious places, and not little and narrow as the *Catacombs* at *Rome*, which are only three or four foot broad, and five or six foot high. I was made believ that

these

these *Catacombs* of *Naples*, went into the Rock nine mile long; but for that I have it only by report: yet if that be true, they may perhaps run towards *Puzzolo*, and so they may have been the burial places of the Towns on that Bay; but of this I have no certainty. I walked indeed a great way, and found Galleries going off in all hands without end, and whereas in the *Roman Catacombs* there are not above three or four rows of niches that are cut out in the Rock one over another, into which the dead bodies were laid; Here there are generally six or seven rows of those niches, and they are both larger and higher; some niches are for Childrens bodies, and in many places there are in the Floors, as it were great Chests hewn out of the Rock, to lay the bones of the dead as they dried, in them; but I could see no marks either of a cover for these holes that looked like the bellies of Chests, or of a facing to shut up the niches when a dead body was laid in them; so that it seems they were monstrous unwholesome and stinking places, where some thousands of bodies lay rotting, without any thing to shut in so loathsome a sight, and so odious a smell: For the niches shew plainly that the Bodies were laid in them only wrapt in the dead cloaths, they being too low for Coffins. In some places of the Rock there is as it were a little Chappel hewen out in the Rock, that goes off from the common Gallery, and there are niches all round about; but I saw no marks of any Wall that shut in such places, tho I am apt to think these might be burying places appropriated to particular families. There is in some places on the Walls and Arch, Old *Mosaick* work, and some Painting, the Colours are fresh, and the manner and Characters are *Gothick*, which made me conclude that this might have been done by the *Normans* about six hundred years ago, after they drove out the *Saracens*: In some places there are Palm-trees painted, and Vines in other

places.

places. The freshness of the Colours shews these could not have been done while this place was imployed for burying, for the steams and rottenness of the Air, occasioned by so much corruption, must have dissolved both Plaister and Colours. In one place there is a man Painted with a little beard, and *Paulus* is written by his head: there is another reaching him a Garland, and by his head *Laud* is written, and this is repeated in another place right over against it. In another place I found a cross Painted, and about the upper part of it these Letters J. C. X. O. and in the lower part N J K A. are Painted: A learned Antiquary that went with me, agreed with me that the manner of the Painting and Characters did not seem to be above six hundred years old, but neither of us knew what to make of these Letters: The lower seemed to relate to the last word of the Vision, which it is said that *Constantine* saw with the Cross that appeared to him: But tho the first two Letters might be for *Jesus*, it being ordinary in old Coins and Inscriptions to put a C. for an S. and X. stands for *Christ*, yet we knew not what to make of the O. unless it were for the Greek *Theta*, and that the little line in the bosom of the *Theta* was worn out, and then it stands for *Theos*; and thus the whole Inscription is, *Jesus Christ, God overcometh*. Another Picture in the Wall had written over it S. *Johannes*, which was a clear sign of a barbarous Age: In another place there is a Picture high in the Wall, and three Pictures under it, that at top had no Inscription; those below it had these Inscriptions, S. *Katharina*, S. *Agape*, and S. *Margarita*; these Letters are clearly modern, besides that, *Margaret* and *Katherine* are modern names, and the addition of *ta* a little above the S. were manifest Evidences that the highest Antiquity that can be ascribed to this Painting is six hundred years. I saw no more Painting, and I began to grow weary of the dark, darkness, and the thick Air of the place, so I staid not above an hour in the *Catacombs*. This made me reflect more particularly on the *Catacombs* of *Rome* than I had done, I could imagine no reason why so little mention is made of those of *Naples*, when there is so much said concerning those of *Rome*; and could give my self no other account of the matter, but that it being a maxim to keep up the reputation of the *Roman Catacombs*, as the Repositories of the Reliques of the primitive *Christians*, it would have much lessened their credit, if it had been thought that there were *Catacombs* far beyond them in all respects, that yet cannot be supposed to have been the work of the primitive *Christians*; and indeed, nothing seems more evident than that these were the common burying places of the ancient *Heathens*. One enters into them without the Walls of the Towns, according to the Laws of the twelve Tables, and such are the *Catacombs* of *Rome* that I saw, which were those of *S. Agnes* and *S. Sebastian*, the entry into them being without the Town; this answers the Law, tho in effect they run under it, for in those days when they had not the use of the needle, they could not know which way they carried on those works when they were once so far ingaged under ground as to lose themselves. It is a vain imagination to think that the *Christians*, in the primitive times, were able to carry on such a work; for as this prodigious digging into such Rocks, must have been a very visible thing by the Mountaines of Rubbish that must have been brought out, and by the vast number of hands that must have been employed in it; so it is absurd to think that they could ho'd their *Assemblies* amidst the annoyance of so much corruption. I found the steams so strong, that tho I am as little subject to vapours as most men, yet I had all the day long after I was in them, (which was not near an hour) a confusion, and as it were a boiling

ing in my head, that difordered me extreamly; and if there is now fo much ftagnating Air there, this muft have been fenfible in a more eminent and infufferable manner, while there were vaft numbers of bodies rotting in thofe niches. But befides this improbability that prefents it felf from the nature of the thing, I called to mind a paffage of a Letter of *Cornelius* that was Bifhop of *Rome*, after the middle of the third *Century*, which is preferved by *Eufebius* in his fixth Book, *Chapter* 43. in which we have the State of the Church of *Rome* at that time fet forth. There were forty fix *Presbiters*, feven *Deacons*, as many *Sub-deacons*, and ninety four of the Inferiour Orders of the Clergy among them: there were alfo fifteen hundred Widows, and other poor maintained out of the publick Charities. It may be reafonably fuppofed that the numbers of the *Chriftians* were as great when this Epiftle was writ, as they were at any time before *Conftantine's* dayes; for as this was writ at the end of that long peace, of which both *S. Cyprian* and *Lactantius* fpeak, that had continued above a hundred years; fo after this time, there was fuch a fucceffion of Perfecutions that came fo thick one upon another, after fhort intervals of quiet, that we cannot think the numbers of the *Chriftians* increafed much beyond what they were at this time. Now there are two particulars in this State of the Clergy, upon which one may make a probable eftimate of the numbers of the *Chriftians*, the one is their poor, which were but fifteen hundred, now upon an exact furvey, it will be found that where the poor are well looked to, their number rifes generally to be the thirtieth or fortieth part of mankind; and this may be well believed to be the proportion of the poor among the *Chriftians* of that Age: For as their Charity was vigorous and tender, fo we find *Celfus*, *Julian*, *Lucian*, *Porphiry*, and others, object this to the *Chriftians* of that time, that
- their

their Charities to the poor drew vast numbers of the lower sort among them, who made themselves *Christians* that they might be supplied by their Brethren: So that this being the State of the *Christians* then, we may reckon the poor the thirtieth part, and so fifteen hundred multiplied by thirty, produce five and forty thousand: And I am the more inclined to think that this rises up near to the full sum of their numbers, by the other Character of the numbers of the Clergy, for as there were forty six *Presbyters*, so there were ninety four of the inferior Orders, who were by two more then the double of the number of the Priests; and this was in a time in which the care of Souls was more exactly looked after, then it has been in the more corrupted Ages, the Clergy having then really more work on their hands, the instructing of their *Catechumenes*, the visiting their Sick, and the supporting and comforting the weak, being tasks that required so much application, that in so vast a City as *Rome* was in those dayes, in which it is probable the *Christians* were scattered over the City, and mixed in all the parts of it, we make a conjecture that is not ill grounded, when we reckon that every *Presbyter* had perhaps about a thousand Souls committed to his care, so this rises to six and forty thousand, which comes very near the sum that may be gathered from the other hint, taken from the number of their poor. So that about fifty thousand is the highest account to which we can reasonably raise the numbers of the *Christians* of *Rome* in that time; and of so many persons, the old, the young, and the women, make more then three fourth parts, so that men that were in condition to work were not above twelve thousand, and by consequence, they were in no condition to undertake and carry on so vast a work. If *Cornelius* in that *Letter* speaks of the numbers of the *Christians* in excessive Terms, and if *Tertullian* in his *Apologetick* hath also set out the numbers of the

Chri-

Christians of his time, in a very high strain, that is only to be ascribed to a pompous Eloquence, which disposeth people to magnifie their own party; and we must allow a good deal to a hyperbole that is very natural to all that set forth their forces in general Terms. It is true, it is not so clear when those vast cavities were dug out of the Rocks. We know that when the Laws of the twelve Tables were made, sepulture was then in use: and *Rome* being then grown to a vast bigness, no doubt they had repositories for their dead; so that since none of the *Roman* Authors mention any such work, it may not be unreasonable to Imagine that these Vaults had been wrought and cut out from the first beginnings of the City, and so the latter Authors had no occasion to take notice of it. It is also certain, that the burning came to be in use among the *Romans*, yet they returned back to their first customs of burying bodies long before *Constantines* time; so that it was not the *Christian* Religion that produced this change: All our modern Writers take it for granted that the change was made in the times of the *Antonines*; yet there being no Law made concerning it, and no mention being made in an Age, full of Writers, of any orders that were given for burying places, *Velserus*'s opinion seems more probable, that the custome of burning wore out by degrees, and since we are sure that they once buryed, it is more natural to think that the slaves and the meaner sort of people were still buried, that being a less expence, and a more simple way of bestowing their bodies than burning, which was both pompous and chargeable, and (if there were already burying places prepared) it is much easier to Imagine how the custome of burying grew Universal, without any Law made concerning it.

I could not for some time find out upon what grounds the Modern Criticks take it for granted, that burying began in the times of the *Antonines*, till I
had

had the happiness to talk of this matter with the learned *Gronovius*, who seems to be such a Master of all the Antient learning, as if he had the Authors lying alwayes open before him: He told me, that it was certain the change from burning to burying was not made by the *Christian* Emperours, for *Macrobius*, (lib. 7. chap. 7.) sayes, in plain terms, that the Custome of burning the Bodies of the Dead was quite worn out in that Age, which is a clear Intimation that it was not laid aside so late as by *Constantine*, and as there was no Law made by him on that head, so he, and the succeeding Emperours, gave such an entire tolleration to *Paganism*, admitting those of that Religion to the greatest Imployments, that it is not to be imagined that there was any order given against burning; so that it is clear the *Heathens* had changed it of their own accord, otherwayes we should have found that among the complaints that they made of the grievances, under which they lay from the *Christians*; but it is more difficult to fix the time when this change was made. *Gronovius* shewed me a passage of *Phlegons*, that mentions the Bodies that were laid in the ground, yet he did not build on that, for it may have relation to the customs of burying that might be elsewhere. And so *Petronius* gives the account of the burial of the *Ephesian* Matrons Husband: but he made it apparent to me, that burying was commonly practised in *Commodus*'s time; for *Xiphilinus* tells us, that in *Pertinax*'s time the friends of those whom *Commodus* had ordered to be put to Death, had dug up their Bodies, some bringing out only some parts of them, and others raising their entire Bodies. The same Author also tells us, that *Pertinax* buried *Commodus*'s Body, and so saved it from the rage of the people, and here is a positive Evidence, that burying was the common practise of that time. It is true, it is very probable that as we see some of the *Roman* Families continued

to

to bury their dead, ev'n when burning was the more common custome, so, perhaps, others continued after this to burn their dead, the thing being Indifferent, and no Law being made about it, and therefore it was particularly objected to the *Christians* after this time, that they abhorred the custome of burning the Bodies of the Dead, which is mentioned by *Minutius Felix*, but this, or any other evidences, that may be brought from Medals of Consecrations after this time, will only prove that some were still burnt, and that the *Christians* practised burying Universally, as expressing their belief of the Resurrection; whereas the *Heathens* held the thing indifferent. It is also clear from the many genuine Inscriptions that have been found in the *Catacombs*, which bear the dates of the Consuls, that these were the common Burial places of all the *Christians* of the fourth and fifth *Century*; for I do not remember that there is any one date that is Antienter, and yet not one of the Writers of those Ages speak of them as the work of the Primitive *Christians*. They speak indeed of the Burial places of the Martyrs, but that will prove no more but that the *Christians* might have had their Quarters, and their Walks in those common Burial places where they laid their Dead, and which might have been known among them, tho it is not likely that they would in times of persecutions make such Inscriptions as might have exposed the Bodies of their dead Friends to the rage of their Enemies. And the Spurious acts of some Saints and Martyrs are of too little credit to give any support to the common Opinion. *Damasus*'s Poetry is of no better authority. And tho those Ages were inclined enough to give credit to Fables, yet it seems this of those *Catacombs* having been the work of the Primitive Christians, was too gross a thing to have been so early imposed on the World. And this silence in an Age, in which Superstition was going on at so great a

C c rate

rate, has much force in it, for so vast a Work, as those *Catacombs* are, must have been well known to all the *Romans*. It were easie to carry this much further, and to shew that the bas relicts that have been found in some of those *Catacombs*, have nothing of the beauty of the Ancient and *Roman* time. This is also more discernable in many Inscriptions that are more *Gothick* then *Roman*, and there are so many Inscriptions relating to Fables, that it is plain these were of later times, and we see by St *Jerom*, that the Monks began, even in his time, to drive a Trade of Reliques; so it is no wonder, that to raise the credit of such a heap as was never to be exhausted, they made some miserable Sculptures, and some Inscriptions; and perhaps, shut up the entries into them with much care and secresy, intending to open them upon some dream or other Artifice, to give them the more reputation, which was often practised in order to the drawing much Wealth and great Devotion, even to some single Relique; and a few being upon this Secret, either those might have died, or by the many revolutions that hapned in *Rome*, they might have been dispersed before they made the discovery: And thus the knowledge of those places was lost, and came to be discovered by accident in the last Age, and hath ever since supplied them with an inexhaustible Magazine of Bones, which by all appearance are no other then the Bones of the *Pagan Romans*; which are now sent over the World to feed a Superstition that is as blind as it proves expensive. And thus the Bones of the *Roman* Slaves, or at least those of the meaner sort, are now set in Silver and Gold with a great deal of other costly garniture, and entertain the superstition of those who are willing to be deceived, as well as they serve the ends of those that seek to deceive the World. But because it cannot be pretended that there was such a number of *Christians* at *Naples* as could have wrought

such

such *Catacombs*, and if it had been once thought that those were the common Burial places of the ancient Heathens, that might have induced the World to think that the *Roman Catacombs* were no other; therefore there hath been no care taken to examine these. I thought this deserved a large Discourse, and therefore I have dwelt perhaps a little too long on this Subject. I will not enter upon a long Description of that which is so well known as Mount *Vesuvio*, it had roared so loud about a month before I came to *Naples*, that at *Naples* they could hardly sleep in the Nights, and some old Houses were so shaken by the Earthquake that was occasioned by this convulsion of the Hill, that they fell to the ground: And the last eruption, above fifty years ago, was so terrible, that there was no small fear in *Naples*, tho it lies at the distance of seven miles from the Hill, yet the Storm was choaked under ground; for tho it smoakt much more than ordinary, yet there was no eruption: It was, indeed, smoaking not only in the mouth of the little Mount that is formed within the great waste that the Fire hath made, but also all along the bottom, that is between the outward mouth of this Mountain, which is four miles in compass; and that inward Hill. When one sees the mouth of this Fire, and so great a part of the Hill, which is covered some foot deep with Ashes and Stones of a metallick composition, that the Fire throws out, he cannot but stand amazed, and wonder what can be the fuel of so lasting a burning, that hath calcined so much matter, and spewed out such prodigious quantities. It is plain there are vast Veins of Sulphur all along in this Soil, and it seems in this Mountain they run along through some Mines and Rocks, and as their slow consumption, produceth a perpetual smoke, so when the Air within is so much rarified, that it must open it self, it throws up those masses of Mettle and Rock that shut it in;

but how this Fire draws in Air to nourish its Flame, is not so easily apprehended, unless there is either a conveyance of Air under ground, by some undiscovered vacuity, or a more insensible transmission of Air, through the pores of the Earth. The heat of this Hill operates so much upon the Soil that lies upon it toward the foot of it, that it produceth the richest Wine about *Naples*, and it also purifieth the Air so much, that the Village at bottom is thought the best Air of the Countrey, so that many come from *Naples* thither for their health. *Ischia*, that is an Island not far from *Naples*, doth also sometimes spew out fire.

On the other side of *Naples* to the *West*, one passeth through the Cave that pierceth the *Pausalippe*, and is four hundred and forty paces long, for I walked it on foot to take its true measure, it is twenty foot broad, and at first forty foot high; but afterwards it is but twenty foot high; the Stone cut out here is good for building, so that as this opened the way from *Puzzoli* to *Naples*, it was also a Quarry for the building of the Town: All along the way here one discovers a strange boiling within the ground, for a little beyond this grot of *Pausalippe*, as we come near the lake of *Aniano*, there is of the one hand, a bath occasioned by a steam that riseth so hot out of the ground, that as soon as one goeth a little into it, he finds himself all over in a sweat, which is very proper for some Diseases, especially that which carries its name from *Naples*: And about twenty paces from thence, there is another little grot, that sends out a poisonous steam, that as it puts out a Candle, as soon as it cometh near it, so it infallibly killeth any living Creature within a minute of time; for in half that time a Dog, upon which the experiment is commonly tryed, the grot being from thence called *Grotto di Cane*, fell in a convulsion. From that one goeth to see the poor rests of *Puzzoli*, and of all that Bay that was once

all

all about a tract of Towns, it having been the retreat of the *Romans*, during the heats of the Summer. All the rarities here, have been so often, and so copiously described, that I am sensible I can add nothing to what is so well known. I will say nothing of the *Amphitheather*, or of *Cicero* and *Virgils* Houses, for which there is nothing but a dubious Tradition; they are ancient Brick buildings of the *Roman* way, and the Vaults of *Virgil's* House are still intire; The *Sulfatara* is a surprizing thing; here is a bottom out of which the force of the Fire, that breaks out still in many places, in a thick steaming smoke, that is full of Brimstone, did throw up about a hundred and fifty years ago, a vast quantity of Earth which was carried above three miles thence, and formed the Hill, called *Monte Novo* upon the ruines of a Town, that was overwhelmed with this eruption, which is of a very considerable heigth; they told me that there was before that time a Channel that went from the Bay into the Lake of *Averno*, of which one sees the beginnings in the Bay at some distance from the Shore; it carrieth still the name of *Julio's Mole*, and is believed to have been made by *Julius Cæsar*: But by the swelling of the ground upon the eruption of the *Sulfatara*, this passage is stopt, and the *Averno* is now fresh water, it is eighteen fathom deep. On the side of it is that amazing Cave, where the *Sibil* is said to have given out her inspirations: the hewing it out of the Rock, hath been a prodigious work, for the Rock is one of the hardest Stones in the World, and the Cave goeth in seven hundred foot long, twenty foot broad, and as I could guess eighteen foot high; And from the end of this great Gallery, there is a narrow passage of three foot broad, two hundred foot long, and seven high, to a little apartment, to which we go in a constant sloping descent from the great Cave; Here are three little Rooms, in one of them there are some rests of an old

Cc 3 *Mosaick*.

Mosaick, with which the Walls and Roof were laid over; there is also a spring of Water, and a Bath in which it is supposed the *Sibil* bathed her self; and from this Cave it is said that there runs a Cave all along to *Cuma*, which is three long miles, but the passages is now choakt by the fal'ing in of the Rock in several places: This piece of work amazed me. I did not much mind the popular opinion that is easily received there, that all this was done by the Devil; the marks of the chizzel in all the parts of the Rock sheweth that this is not a work of Nature. Certainly they had both much leisure, and many hands at their command who set about it, and it seems to have been wrought out with no other design but to subdue the people more intirely to the conduct of the Priests that managed this Imposture, so busie and industrious hath the ambition and fraud of the Priests been in all Ages and in all corrupt Religions. But of all the Scenes of Noble objects that present it self in the Bay of *Puzzoli*, the rests of *Caligula*'s Bridge are the most amazing, for there are yet standing eight or ten of the Pillars that supported the Arches, and of some of the Arches the half is yet intire. I had not a line with me to examine the depth of the Water where the furthest of those Pillars is built, but my Water-man assured me it was fifty cubits. + This I cannot believe, but it is certainly so deep that one can scarce imagine how it was possible to build in such a depth, and for the carrying off the Sea, that seems yet more impossible. It is a Noble Monument of the profuse and extravagant expence of a Brutal Tyrant, who made one of the vastest Bridges that ever was attempted over three or four miles of Sea, meerly to Sacrifice so great a Treasure to his vanity: As for *Agripina*'s Tomb, it is no great matter, only the bas reliefs are yet en ire. The marvellous Fish-Pond is a great Basin of Water wrought like a huge Temple, standing upon eight

and

and forty great Pillars, all hewed out of the Rock; and they are laid over with four crufts of the old Plaifter, which is now as hard as Stone; this is believed to be a work of *Nero*'s: and about a quarter of a mile from thence there is another vaft work which goeth into a Rock; but at the entrance there is a noble *Portico* built of Pillars of Brick, and as one enters into the Rock he finds a great many Rooms regularly fhaped, hewed out of the Rock, and all covered over with Plaifter, which is ftill intire, and fo white that one can hardly think that it hath not been wafhed over fince it was firft made: there are a vaft number of thofe Rooms, they are faid to be a hundred, from whence this Cave carrieth the name of the *Centum Cameræ*: This hath been as expenfive a work as it is ufelefs, it is intituled to *Nero*, and here they fay he kept his Prifoners But there is nothing in all this bay that is both fo curious and fo ufeful as the Baths, which feems to flow from the fame reafon, that is the caufe of thofe eruptions in the *Vefuvis* and *Sulfatara*, and the *Grottos* formerly mentioned; that as this heat makes fome Fountains there to be boiling hot, fo it fends up a fteam through the Rock that doth not break through the pores of the Stone where it is hard, but where the Rock is foft and fpungy, there the fteams come through with fo melting a heat that a man is foon, at it were, diffo'ved in fweat; but if he ftoops low in the paffages that are cut in the Rock he finds no heat, becaufe there the Rock is hard. Thofe fteams, as they are all hot, fo they are impregnated with fuch Minerals, as they find in their way through the Rock; and near this Bath there are Galleries hewed out of the Rock and faced with a building; in which there are, as it were, Bedfteads made in the Walls, upon which, thofe that come thither, to fweat for their health, lay their Quilts and Bed-cloaths, and fo come regularly out of their fweats.

It

It is certain that a man can no where pass a day of his life both with so much pleasure, and with such advantage, as he finds in this journey to *Puzzoli* and all along the Bay: but tho anciently this was all so well built, so peopled, and so beautifully laid out, yet no where doth one see more visibly what a change time brings upon all places: for *Naples* hath so intirely eat out this place, and drawn its Inhabitants to it, that as *Puzzoli* it self is but a small Village, so there is now no other in all this Bay, which was anciently built almost all round, for there were seven big Towns upon it. Having thus told you what I found most considerable in *Naples*, I cannot pass by that Noble remnant of the *Via Appia* that runs along thirty miles of the way between it and *Rome*, without making some mention of it: this high-way is twelve foot broad, all made of huge stones, most of them blew, and they are generally a foot and half large on all sides: the strength of this cause-way appears in its long duration, for it hath lasted above eighteen hundred Years; and is in most places for several miles together, as intire as when it was first made: and the botches that have been made for mending such places, that have been worn out by time, shews a very visible difference between the Ancient and the Modern way of Paving. One thing seems strange, that the way is level with the Earth on both sides: whereas so much weight as those Stones carry should have sunk the ground under them by its pressure: Besides that the Earth, especially in low grounds, receives a constant increase chiefly by the dust which the Winds or Brooks carry down from the Hills, both which reasons should make a more sensible difference between those wayes and the soil on both sides: and this makes me apt to believe, that anciently those wayes were a little raised above the level of the ground, and that a course of so many Ages hath now brought them to an equality: Those wayes were

chiefly

chiefly made for such as go on foot: for as nothing is more pleasant then to walk along them, so nothing is more inconvenient for Horses and all sorts of carriage, and indeed Mulets are the only beasts of burthen that can hold out long in this Road, which beats all Horses after they have gone it a little while. There are several rests of *Roman* Antiquities at the Mole of *Cajeta*; but the Isle of *Caprea*, now called *Crapa*, which is a little way into the Sea off from *Naples*, gave me a strange Idea of *Tiberius's* Reign, since it is hard to tell whether it was more extraordinary to see a Prince abandon the best Seats and Palaces of *Italy*, and shut himself up in a little Island, in which I was told there was a Tradition of seven little Palaces that he built in it; or to see so vast a body as the *Roman* Empire so governed by such a Tyrannical Prince, at such a distance from the chief Scene, so that all might have been reversed long before that the news of it could have been brought to him. And as there is nothing more wonderfull in Story then to see so vast a State that had so great a sense of liberty, subdued by so brutal and so voluptuous a man as *Antony*, and so raw a youth as *Augustus*; so the wonder is much improved when we see a Prince at a hundred and fifty miles distance, shut up in an Island, carry the Reins of so great a body in his hand, and turn it which way he pleased.

But now I come to *Rome*, which as it was once the Empress of the World in a succession of many Ages, so hath in it at present more curious things to entertain the attention of a *Traveller*, then any other place in *Europe*. On the side of *Tuscany*, the entry into *Rome* is very surprizing to strangers, for one cometh along for a great many miles, upon the remains of the *Via Flamminia*, which is not indeed so entire as the *Via Appia*; yet there is enough left to raise a just Idea of the *Roman* greatness, who laid

such

such cause-ways all *Italy* over. And within the Gate of the *Porta di Populo*, there is a Noble *Obelisk*, a vast Fountain, two fine little Churches, like two Twins resembling one another, as well as placed near one another, and on several hands one sees a long *Vista* of streets. There is not a Town in these parts of the World, where the Churches, Convents, and Palaces are so Noble, and where the other Buildings are so mean, which indeed, discovers very visibly the misery under which the *Romans* groan. The Churches of *Rome* are so well known, that I will not adventure on any description of them, and indeed, I had too Transient a view of them to make it with that degree of exactness which the subject requires. *St. Peters* alone wou'd make a big Book, not to say a long *Letter*. Its length, heighth and breadth are all so exactly proportioned, and the eye is so equally possessed with all these, that the whole, upon the first view, doth not appear so vast as it is found to be upon a more particular attention: and as the four Pillars upon which the *Cupulo* rises, are of such a prodigious bigness, that one would think they were strong enough to bear any superstructure whatsoever; so when one climbs up to the top of that vast heighth, he wonders what Foundation can bear so huge a weight; for as the Church is of a vast heighth, so the *Cupulo* rises four hundred and fifteen big steps above the Roof of the Church. In the heighth of the Concave of this *Cupulo*, there is a representation, that tho it can hardly be seen from the floor below, unless one hath a good sight, and so it doth not, perhaps, give much scandal, yet it is a gross indication of the Idolatry of that Church; for the Divinity is there pictured as an ancient man compass'd about with Angels. I will say nothing of the great Altar, of the Chair of *S. Peter*, of the great Tombs; of which the three chief are *Paul* the III. *Urban* the VIII. and *Alexander* the VII. nor of the vaſt Vaults under this Church, and the remains of Antiquity that are reſerved in them: nor will I undertake a deſcription of the adjoining Palace, where the Painting of the *Corridori*, and of many of the Rooms by *Raphael* and *Michael Angelo* are ſo rich, that one is ſorry to ſee work of that value laid on *Freſco*, and which muſt by conſequence ware out too ſoon, as in ſeveral places it is almoſt quite loſt already. I could not but obſerve in the *Sala Regia* that is before the famous Chappel of *Siſto V.* and that is all Painted in *Freſco*, one corner that repreſents the murther of the renowned Admiral *Chaſtilion*, and that hath written under it theſe words, *Rex Colinii necem probat:* The vaſt length of the Gallery on one ſide, and of the Library in another do ſurprize one; the Gardens have many Statues of a moſt exceſſive value, and ſome good Fountains; but the Gardens are ill entertained both here and in the Palace on the *Quirinal*. And, indeed, in moſt of the Palaces of *Rome*, if there were but a ſmall coſt laid out to keep all in good caſe that is brought together at ſo vaſt a charge, they would make another ſort of ſhew, and be looked at with much more pleaſure: In the apartments of *Rome* there are a great many things that offend the ſight: The Doors are generally mean, and the Locks meaner, except in the Palace of Prince *Borgheſe*, where, as there is the vaſteſt Collection of the beſt pieces, and of the hands of the greateſt Maſters that is in all *Europe*, ſo the Doors and Locks give not that diſtaſt to the eye, that one finds elſewhere. The Flooring of the Palaces is all of Brick; which is ſo very mean, that one ſees the diſproportion that is between the Floors and the reſt of the Room, not without a ſenſible preception and diſlike. It is true, they ſay, their Air is ſo cold and moiſt in Winter that they cannot pave with Marble; and the heat is ſometimes ſo great in Summer, that Flooring of Wood would crack

with

with heat, as well as be eat up by the vermin that would neſtle in it. But if they kept in their great Palaces ſervants to waſh their Floors, with that care that is u'ed in *Holland*, where the Air is moiſter, and the climate is more productive of Vermine, they would not find ſuch effects from wooden Floors, as they pretend. In a word, there are none that lay out ſo much wealth all at once, as the *Italians* do upon the Building and Finiſhing of their Palaces and Gardens, and that afterwards, beſtow ſo little on the preſerving of them: another thing I obſerved in their Palaces, there is, indeed, a great ſeries of Noble rooms one within another, of which their apartments are compoſed, but I did not find, at the end of the apartments, where the Bed Chamber is, ſuch a diſpoſition of rooms for back-ſtairs, dreſſing-rooms, cloſets, ſervants rooms, and other conveniences as are neceſſary for accommodating the Apartment. It is true, this is not ſo neceſſary for an apartment of State, in which Magnificence is more conſidered then convenience; but I found the ſame want in thoſe apartments in which they lodged; ſo that notwithſtanding all the riches of their Palaces, it can not be ſaid that they are well lodged in them, and their Gardens are yet leſs underſtood, and worſe kept then their Palaces. It is true, the *Villa Borgheſe* ought to be excepted, where as there is a prodigious collection of *bas reliefs*, with which the Walls are, as it were, covered all over, that are of a vaſt value; ſo the ſtatues within, of which ſome are of Porphiry, and others of Touchſtone, are amazing things: The whole grounds of this Park, which is about three miles in compaſs, and in which there are ſix or ſeven lodges, are laid out ſo ſweetly, that I thought I was in an *Engliſh* Park when I walked over it. The *Villa Pamphilia* is better ſcituated upon a higher ground, and hath more Water-works, and twice the extent of the other in Soil, but neither doth the

Houſe

House nor Statues approach to the riches of the [...]
nor are the grounds so well laid out and [...]
But for the Furniture of the Palaces of R[...]
publick apartments are all covered over with [...]
and for those apartments in which they l[...]
are general'y furnish'd eith[er] with red velvet or red
Damask, with a broad g[ol]d Galloon at every breadth
of the stuff, and a good Fringe at top and bottom, but
there is very little Tapistry in *Italy*.

I have been carried into all this disgression, from
the general view, that I was giving you of the *Popes*
Palace. I named one part of it which well ingage
me into new digression, as it well deserves one, and
that is the Library of the *Vatican*: The Case is
great, but that which is lodged in it is much greater;
for here is a collection of Books that filleth a mans
eye: There is first a great Hall, and at the end of it
there runs out on both sides, two Galleries of so vast
a length, that tho the half of them is already furnished with Books, yet one would hope that there is
room left for more new Books then the World will
ever produce. The *Heidelberg* Library stands by it
self, and filleth the one side of the Galery, as the
Duke of *Urbins* Library of Manuscripts filleth the
other. But tho these last are very fair and beautiful,
yet they are not of such Antiquity as those of *Heidelberg:* When it appeared that I was come from
England, King *Henry* the VIIIs. Book of the
seven Sacraments, with an inscription writ upon it
with his own hand to *Pope Leo* the X. was shewed
me; together with a collection of some *Letters* that
he writ to *Ann Bulen* of which some are in *English*,
and some in *French*. I that knew his hand well saw
clearly that they were no forgeries. There are not
many *Latin* Manuscripts of great Antiquity in this
Library; some few of *Virgils* I saw writ in Capitals.
But that which took up almost half of one day that
I spent at one time in this place, related to the present

D d   dispute

dispute that is on foot between *Mr. Schelstrate* the Library-keeper, and *Mr. Maimbourg*, concerning the Council of *Constance*. The two points in debate are the words of the decree made in the fourth Session, and the *Popes* confirmation. In the fourth Session, according to the *French* Manuscripts, a Decree was made, subjecting the *Pope*, and all other persons whatsoever, to the Authority of the Council, and to the Decrees it was to make, and to the Reformation it intended to establish both in the Head and the Members: which as it implies that the Head was corrupted and needed to be reformed, so it sets the Council so directly above the *Pope*, that this Session being confirmed by the *Pope*, putteth those who assert the *Popes* infallibility to no small straits: For if *Pope Martin*, that approved this Decree was infallible, then this Decree is good still; and if he was not infallible, no other *Pope* was infallible: To all this *Schelstrate* answers from his Manuscripts, that the words of a Reformation, in Head and Members, are not in the Decree of that Session; and he did shew me several Manuscripts, of which two were evidently writ during the sitting of the Council, and were not at all dashed, in which these words were not. I know the hand and way of writing of that Age too well to be easily mistaken in my judgement concerning those Manuscripts; but if those words are wanting, there are other words in them that seem to be much stronger for the superiority of the Council above that *Pope*. For it is Decreed, that *Popes*, and all other persons, were bound to submit to the decisions of the Council, as to Faith: which words are not in the *French* Manuscripts: Upon this I told *M. Schelstrate* that I thought the words in these Manuscripts were stronger then the other, since the word Reformation, as it was used in the time of that Council, belonged chiefly to the cor-

recting

resting of abuses, it being often applied to the regulations that were made in the *Monastick Orders*, when they were brought to a more exact observation of the rule of their Order: So tho the Council had decreed a Reformation both of Head and Members, I do not see that this would import more than that the *Papacy* had fallen into some disorders that needed a Reformation: and this is not denied even by those who assert the *Pope's* infallibility: but a submission to points of Faith, that is expresly asserted in the *Roman* Manuscripts, is a much more positive evidence against the *Pope's* Infallibility; and the word Faith is not capable of so large a sense as may be justly ascribed to Reformation. But this difference, in so main a point between Manuscripts concerning so late a Transaction, gave me an occasion to reflect on the vast uncertainty of Tradition, especially of matters that are at a great distance from us; when those that were so lately Transacted, are so differently represented in Manuscripts, and in which, both those of *Paris* and *Rome* seem to carry all possible evidences of sincerity. As for the *Popes* confirmation of that Decree, it is true by a General Bull, *Pope Martin* confirmed the Council of *Constance* to such a period; but besides that, he made a particular Bull, as *Schelstrat* assured me, in which he enumerated all the Decrees that he confirmed, and among tho'e, this Decree concerning the Superiority of the Council is not named; this seemed to be of much more importance, and therefore I desired to see the Original of the Bull: for their seem to be just reasons to apprehend a forgery here: He promised to do his endeavours, tho he told me that would not be easie, for the Bulls were strictly kept; and the next day when I came, hoping to see it, I could not be admitted: but he assured me that if that had not been the last day of my stay at *Rome*, he would have procured a

D d 2 Warrant

Warrant for my seeing the Original: so this is all I can say as to the Authenticalness of that Bull: But supposing it to be genuine, I could not agree to *M. Schelstrate* that the General Bull of Confirmation, ought to be limited to the other that enumerates the particular Decrees: but since that particular Bull was never discovered till he hath found it out, it seems it was secretly made, and did not pass according to the forms of the Consistory: and was a fraudulent thing of which no noise was to be made in that Age, and therefore in all the dispute that followed in the Concel of *Basil* between the *Pope* and the Council, upon this very point, no mention was ever made of it by either side: and thus it can have no force, unless it be to discover the Artifices and fraud of that Court: that at the same time in which the necessity of their affairs obliged the *Pope* to confirm the Decrees of the Council, he contrived a secret Bull, which in another Age might be made use of, to weaken the Authority of the General Confirmation that he gave: and therefore a Bull that doth not pass in due form and is not promulgated, is of no Authority: and so this Pretended Bull cannot limit the other Bull. There were some other things, relating to this debate, that were shewed me by *M. Schelstrate*, but these being the most important, I mention them only. I will not give you here a large account of the learned men at *Rome*, *Bellori* is deserved'y Famous for his knowledge of the *Greek* and *Ægyptian* Antiquities, and for all that belongs to the Mythologies and superstitions of the *Heathens*, and hath a Closet richly furnished with things relating to those matters. *Fabretti* is justly celebrated for his Understanding of the Old *Roman* Architecture and Fabricks. *Padre Fabri* is the chief Honour of the *Jesuit's* Colledge, and is much above the common rate, both for Philosophy, Mathematicks, and
Church

Church History. And he to whom I was the most obliged, Abbot *Nazari* hath so general a view of the several parts of learning, tho he hath chiefly applied himself to Philosophy and Mathematicks, and is a man of so ingaging a civility, and used my self in so particular a manner, that I owe him, as well as those others, whom I have mentioned, and whom I had the Honour to see, all the acknowledgments of esteem and gratitude that I can possibly make them.

One sees in Cardinal *d'Estrees* all the advantages of a high birth, great parts, a generous civility, and a measure of knowledge farre above what can be expected from a person of his rank; but as he gave a noble protection to one of the leardnest men that this Age hath produced, Mr. *Launnoy*, who lived many years with him, so it is visible, that he made a great progress by the conversation of so extraordinary a person; and as for Theological learning, there is now none of the Colledge equal to him. Cardinal *Howard* is too well known in *England* to need any character from me. The Elevation of his present condition hath not in the least changed him; he hath all the sweetness and Gentleness of temper that we saw in him in *England*, and he retains the unaffected simplicity and humility of a Frier amidst all the dignity of the Purple, and as he sheweth all the generous care and concern for his Countreymen that they can expect from him; so I met with so much of it, in so many obliging marks of his goodness for my self, that went far beyond a common civility, that I cannot enough acknowledge it. I was told the Popes Confessor was a very extraordinary man for the Oriental Learning, which is but little known in *Rome*: He is a Master of the *Arabick* Tongue, and hath writ, as Abbot *Nazari* told me, the learned a Book against the *Mahumetan* Religion, that the World hath yet seen, but it is not yet Printed. He is not so much esteemed in Rome as he would be elsewhere; for his Learning is not in vogue, and the School Divinity and Casuistical Learning, being that for which Divines are most esteemed there; He whose Studies lead him another way, is not so much valued as he ought to be; and perhaps, the small account that the Pope makes of learned men, turns somewhat upon the Confessor, for it is certain, that this is a Reign in which Learning is very little encouraged.

Upon the general contempt that all the Romans have, for the present Pontificate, one made a pleasant reflection to me, he said those Popes that intended to raise their Families, as they saw the censure that this brought upon them, so they studied to lessen it by other things that might soften the Spirits of the people. No man did more for beautifying Rome, for finishing St. Peters, and the Library, and for furnishing Rome with water, then Pope Paul the V. tho. at the same time he did not forget his Family; and tho the other Popes that have raised great Families, have not done this to so eminent a degree as he did, yet there are many remains of their Magnificence, whereas those Popes that have not raised Families, have it seems thought that alone was enough to maintain their reputation, and so they have not done much either to recommend their Government to their Subjects, or their Reign to posterity; and it is very plain, that the present Pope taketh no great care of this. His life hath been certainly very innocent, and free of all those publick scandals that make a noise in the World, and there is at present a regularity in Rome, that deserveth great commendation, for publick Vices are not to be seen there: His personal sobriety is also singular. One assured me that the expence of his Table did not amount

amount to a Crown a day, tho this is, indeed, short of *Sisto* V. who gave order to his Steward never to exceed five and twenty *Bajokes*, that is eighteen pence a day for his Diet. The Pope is very careful of his health, and doth never expose it, for upon the least disorder he shuts himself up in his Chamber, and often keepeth his Bed for the least indisposition many dayes; but his Government is severe, and his Subjects are ruined.

And here one thing cometh into my mind, which perhaps is not ill grounded, that the poverty of a Nation, not only dispeoples it, by driving the people out of it, but by weakning the natural fertility of the Subjects; for as men and women well cloathed, and well fed, that are not exhausted with perpetual labour, and with the tearing anxieties that want brings with it, must be much more lively, then those that are pressed with want; so it is very likely that the one must be much more disposed to propagate then the other: and this appeared more evident to me, when I compared the fruitfulness of *Geneva* and *Switzerland*, with the barrenness that reigns over all *Italy*. I saw two extraordinary instances of the copious production of *Geneva*: Mr. *Tronchin* that was Professor of Divinity, and Father to the judicious and worthy Professor of the same name, that is now there, died at the age of seventy six years, and had a hundred and fifteen persons all alive, that had either descended from him, called him Father. And Mr. *Calendrin* a pious and laborious Preacher of that Town, that is descended from the Family of the *Calendrini*; who receiving the Reformation about a hundred and fifty years ago, left *Lucca* their Native City with the *Turretini*, the *Diodati*, and the *Bourlamacchi*, and some others that came and settled at *Geneva*: He is now but seven and forty years old, and yet

he

he hath a hundred and five perſons that are deſcended of his Brothers and Siſters, or married to them; ſo that if he liveth but to eighty, and the Family multiplieth as it hath done; he may ſee ſome hundreds that will be in the ſame relation to him; but ſuch things as theſe are not to be found in *Italy*.

There is nothing that delights a Stranger more in *Rome*, then to ſee the great Fountains of Water that are almoſt in all the corners of it: That o'd *Aquaduct* which *Paul* the V. reſtored, cometh from a collection of Sources, five and thirty miles diſtant from *Rome*, that runs all the way upon an *Aquaduct* in a Channel that is vaulted, and is liker a River then a Fountain: It breaketh out in five ſeveral Fountains, of which ſome give water about a foot ſquare. That of *Sixtus* the V. the great Fountain of *Aqua Travi*, hath yet no decoration, but diſchargeth a prodigious quantity of Water. The glorious Fountain in the *Piazza Navona*, that hath an air of greatneſs in it that ſurprizeth one, the Fountain in the *Piazza de Spagna*, thoſe before St. *Peters*: and the *Palazzo Farneſe*, with many others, furniſh *Rome* ſo plentifully, that almoſt every private Houſe hath a Fountain that runs continually: All theſe I ſay are noble decorations, that carry an uſefulneſs with them that cannot be enough commended: and gives a much greater *Idea* of thoſe who have taken care to ſupply this City, with one of the chief pleaſures and conveniences of life, then of others who have laid out millions, meerly to bring quantities of Water to give the eye a little diverſion, which would have been laid out much more nobly and uſefully, and would have more effectually eternized their Fame, if they had been imployed as the *Romans* did their Treaſure, in furniſhing great Towns with Water.

There

There is an universal Civility that reigns among all sorts of people at *Rome*, which in a great measure flows from their Government, for every man, being capable of all the advancements of that State, since a simple Ecclesiastick may become one of the *Monsignori*: and of these may be a Cardinal, and one of these may be chosen Pope, this makes every man behave himself towards all other persons with an exactness of respect: for no man knows what any other may grow to. But this makes professions of esteem and kindness go so promiscuously to all sorts of persons, that one ought not to build too much on them. The conversation of *Rome* is generally upon news, for tho there is no news Printed there, yet in the several Antichambers of the Cardinals (where if they make any considerable figure, there are Assemblies of tho'e that make their Court to them) one is sure to hear all the news of *Europe* together with many speculations upon what passeth. At the Queen of *Swedens* all that relateth to *Germany* or the *North* is ever to be found, and that Princess that must ever reign among all that have a true taft, either of wit or learning, hath still in her drawing Rooms the best Court of the Strangers, and her civility together, with the vast variety with which she furnisheth her conversation, maketh her to be the Chief of all the living rarities that one sees in *Rome*: I will not use her own word to my self, which was, that she new grew to be one of the Antiquities of *Rome*. The Ambassadors of Crowns, who live here in another form than in any other Court, and the Cardinals and Prelates of the several Nations, that do all meet and center here, maketh that there is more news in *Rome* than any where: For Priests and the men of Religious Orders, write larger and more particular Letters, than any other sort of men. But such as apply themselves to make

their

their Court here, are condemned to a loss of time that had need be well recompenced, for it is very great. As for one that Studies Antiquities, Pictures, Statues, or Musick, there is more entertainment for him at *Rome*, than in all the rest of *Europe*, but if he hath not a taft of these things, he will soon be weary of a place where the Conversation is alwayes general, and where there is little sincerity or openness practised, and by consequence, where friendship is little understood. The Women here begin to be a little more conversable, tho a Nation naturally jealous, will hardly allow a great liberty in a City that is composed of Ecclefiasticks; who being denied the priviledge of Wives of their own, are suspected of being sometimes too bold with the Wives of others: The liberties that were taken in the Constable of *Naples*'s Palace, had indeed digufted the *Romans* much at that freedom, which had no bounds. But the Dutchess of *Bracciano*, that is a *French* Woman, hath by the exactness of her deportment, amidst all the innocents Freedoms of a Noble conversation, recovered in a great measure, the credit of those liberties, that Ladies beyond the Mountains, practise with all the strictness of Virtue: For she receiveth visits at publick hours, and in Publick Rooms, and by the liveliness of her conversation, maketh that her Court is the pleasantest Assembly of Strangers, that is to be found in any of the Palaces of the *Italians* at *Rome*.

I will not engage in a description of *Rome*, either ancient or modern, this hath been done so oft, and with such exactness, that nothing can be added to what hath been already published. It is certain that when one is in the Capitol, and sees those poor rests of what once it was, he is surprized to see a building of so great a fame sunk so low, that one can scarce imagine that it was once a Castle, scituated

ated upon a Hill able to hold out against a Siege of the *Gauls:* The *Tarpeian* Rock is now of so small a fall, that a man would think it no great matter, for his diversion, to leap over it and the shape of the ground hath not been so much altered on one side, as to make us think it is very much changed on the other. For *Severus*'s Triumphal Arch, which is at the foot of the Hill on the other side, is not now buried above two foot within the ground, as the vast *Amphitheater* of *Titus* is not above three foot sunk under the level of the ground. Within the Capitol one sees many Noble remnants of Antiquity, but none is more glorious, as well as more useful, then the Tables of their Consuls which are upon the Walls: and the Inscription on the Columna *Rostrola*, in the time of the first *Punick War*, is without doubt the most valuable Antiquity in *Rome*. From this all along the sacred way, one findeth such remnants of Old *Rome* in the ruines of the Temples, if the *Triumphal Arches*, in the *Portico's*, and other remains of that Glorious Body, that as one cannot see these too often, so every time one sees them, they kindle in him vast Idea's of that Republick, and make him reflect on that which he learned in his youth with great pleasure. From the heigth of the Convent of *Araceli*, a man hath a full view of all the extent of *Rome*, but literally, it is now, *seges ubi Roma fuit;* for the parts of the City, that were most inhabited anciently, are those that are now laid in great Gardens; or, as they call them, Vineyards, of which some are half a mile in compass: The vastness of the *Roman* magnificence and luxury, is that which passeth imagination; the prodigious *Amphitheater* of *Titus*, that could conveniently receive eighty five thousand spectators; the great extent of the *Circus maximus;* the Vaults where the Waters were received that furnished

nished *Titus*'s baths, and above all *Dioclesian*'s baths, tho bui't when the Empire was in it's decay, are so far above all modern buildings, that there is not so much as room for a comparison. The extent of these baths is above half a mile in compass: the vastness of the rooms in which the Bathers might swim, of which the *Carthusian*'s Church, that yet remains entire, is one, and the many great Pillars all of one Stone of Marble, beautifully spotted, are things of which these latter Ages are not capable. The beauty of their Temples, and of the *Portico*'s before them is amazing, chiefly that of the *Rotunda*, where the Fabrick without looketh as mean, being only Brick, as the Architecture is bold: for it riseth up in a Vault, and yet at the Top there is an open left of thirty foot in Diameter, which, as it is the only Window of the Church, so it filleth it with light, and is the hardiest piece of Architecture that ever was made.

The Pillars of the *Portico* are also the noblest in *Rome*, they are the highest and biggest that one can see any where all of one Stone: and the numbers of those Ancient Pillars with which, not only many of the Churches are beautified, chiefly *St. Mary Maggiore*, and *St. John* in the *Lateran*, but with which even private Houses are adorned, and of the fragments of which there are such multitudes in all the streets of *Rome*, giveth a great Idea of the expencefulness of the Old *Romans* in their buildings: for the hewing and fetching a few of those Pillars, must have Cost more than whole Palaces do now: since most of them were brought from *Greece*: Many of these Pillars are of *Porphiry*, others of *Jasp*, others of *Granated* Marble, but the greatest number is of white Marble: The two Columns *Trajans* and *Antonins*: the two Horses that are in the Mount *Cavallo*, and the other two Horses in the Capitol, which have not indeed the postures and

motion

motion of the other, The brass Horse that as is believed, carrieth *Marcus Aurelius*; the remains of *Nero's Colossus*, the Temple of *Bacchus* near the *Catacomb* of *S. Agnus*, which is the entirest and the least altered of all the Ancient Temples: The great Temple of Peace; those of the Sun and Moon: that of *Romulus* and *Remus*, (which I considered as the ancientest Fabrick that is now left, for it is little and simple, and standeth in such a place, that when *Rome* grew so costly, it could not have been let alone unchanged, if it had not been that it was reverenced for its Antiquity) the many other *Portico's*, the Arches of *Severus*, of *Titus*, and *Constantine*, in the last of which, one sees that the Sculpture of his age, was much sunck from what it had been, only in the Top there are some *bas reliefs* that are clearly of a much ancienter time, and of a better manner. And that which exceedeth all the rest, the many great *Aqueducts* that come from all hands and run over a vast distance, are things which a man cannot see oft enough, if he would form in himself a just *Idea* of the vastness of that Republick, or rather Empire: There are many Statues and Pillars, and other Antiquities of great value dug up in all the quarters of *Rome* these last hundred and fourscore years, since Pope L▓▓▓▓s. time; who as he was the greatest Patron ▓▓▓▓▓ing and Arts, that perhaps, ever was, so was the ▓enerousest Prince that ever Reigned; and it was he that first set on foot the inquiring into the Riches of Old *Rome*, that lay till his time, for the most part, hid under ground; and indeed if he had been less scandalous in his Impiety and Atheism, of which neither he nor his Court were so much as ashamed, he had been one of the most celebrated persons of any Age. Soon after him *Pope Paul* the III. gave the ground of the *Monte Palatino* to his Family: But I was told that this large piece of ground, in which one should look for the greatest Collection of the Antiquities of the highest value, since this is the ruin of the Palace of the *Roman* Emperors, hath never been yet searched into with any exactness : So that when a curious Prince cometh that is willing to employ many hands in digging up and down this Hill, we may expect new Scenes of *Roman* Antiquities. But all this matter would require Volumes, and therefore I have only named these things, because I can add nothing to those copious descriptions that have been so oft made of them. Nor will I say any thing of the modern Palaces or the Ornaments of them, either in Pictures or Statues, which are things that carry one so far, that it is not easie to give bounds to the discriptions into which one findeth himself carried, when he once enters upon so fruitful a subject. The number of the Palaces is great, and every one of them hath enough to fix the attention of a Traveller, till a new one drives the former out of his thoughts: It is true, the *Palestrina*, the *Borghese*, and the *Farnese*, have somewhat in them that leave an impression which no new objects can wear out: and as the last hath a Noble square before it with two great Fountains in it, so the Statue of *Hercules* and the *Bull* that are below, and the Gallery above Stairs are unvaluable, the Roof of the Gallery is one of the ⬛ Pieces of Painting that is extant, being all ⬛ *arrachio's* hand, and there are in that Gallery the greatest number of Heads of the *Greek* Philosophers and Poets that I ever saw together: That of *Homer*, and that of *Socrates*, were the two that struck me most, chiefly the latter, which as it is, without dispute, a true Antick, so it carrieth in it all the characters that *Plato* and *Xenophon* give us of *Socrates*; the flat Nose, the broad Face, the simplicity of Look, and the mean appearance which that great Philosopher

pher made, so that I could not return oft enough to look upon it, and was delighted with this more then with all the wonders of the *Bull*, which is indeed a Rock of Marble cut out into a whole Scene of Statues; but as the History of it is not well known, so there are such Faults in the Sculpture, that tho it is all extream fine, yet one seeth it hath not the exactness of the best times. As for the Churches and Convents of *Rome*, as the number, the vastness, the riches, both of Fabrick, Furniture, Painting and other Ornaments amaze one, so here again a Stranger is lost, and the Convent that one seeth last, is alwayes the most admired: I confess the *Minerva*, which is the *Dominicans*, where the Inquisition sitteth, is that which maketh the most sensible Impression upon one that passeth at *Rome* for an Heretick, tho except one committeth great follies, he is in no danger there, and the poverty that reigns in that City maketh them find their interest so much in using Strangers well, whatsoever their Religion may be, that no man needs be affraid there: And I have more then ordinary reason to ackowledge this who having ventured to go thither, after all the liberty that I had taken to write my thoughts freely both of the Church and See of *Rome*, and was known by all with whom I conversed there, yet met with the highest civilities possible among all sorts of people, and in particular, both among the *English* and *Scottish Jesuites*, tho they knew well enough that I was no friend to their Order.

In the Gallery of the *English Jesuites*, among the Pictures of their Martyrs, I did not meet with *Garnet*; for perhaps that name is so well known, that they would not expose a Picture, with such a name on it, to all Strangers, yet *Oldcorn*, being a name less known, is hung there among their Martyrs, tho he was as clearly convicted of the Gun-powder Treason,

Treason, as the other was: and it seemed a little strange to me, to see that at a time in which, for other reasons, the Writers of that Communion have not thought fit, to deny the truth of that Conspiracy, a *Jesuit* convicted of the blackest crime that ever was projected, should be reckoned among their Martyrs. I saw likewise there the Original of these Emblematical Prophecies, relating to *England*, that the *Jesuits* have had at *Rome* near sixty years, and of which I had some time ago procured a Copy, so I found my Copy was true. I hapned to be at *Rome*, during St. *Gregory*'s Fair and Feast, which lasted several dayes. In his Church the *Hosty* was exposed: and from that, all that came thither, went to the Chappel that was once his House, in which his Statue and the Table where he served the poor, are preserved: I saw such vast numbers of people there, that one would have thought all *Rome* was got together. They all kneeled down to his Statue, and after a prayer said to it, they kissed his feet, and every one touched the Table with his Beads, as hoping to draw some vertue from it. I will add nothing of the several Obelisks and Pillars that are in *Rome*, of the celebrated Chappels that are in some of the great Churches, in particular those of *Sixtus* the V. and *Paul* the V. in *Santa Maria Maggiore*, of the Water works in the *Quirinal*, the *Vatican*, and in many of the Vineyards: Nor will I go out of *Rome* to describe *Frescati*, (for *Tivoly* I did not see) The young Prince *Borgese*, who is indeed one of the glories of *Rome*, as well for his Learning as for his Virtue, did me the Honour to carry me thither with those two learned Abbots *Fabretti* and *Nazari*, and entertained me with a magnificence that became him better to give, than me to receive. The Water-works in the *Aldobrandin* Palace have a magnificence in them beyond all that
I ever

I ever saw in *France*, the mixture of Wind with the Water, and the Thunders and Storms that this maketh is noble: The Water works of the *Ludovisio*, and the *Monte Dragone*, have likewise a greatness in them that is natural; and indeed the riches that one meets with in all places within Doors in *Italy*, and the poverty that one seeth every where abroad, are the most unsuitable things imaginable: but it is very likely that a great part of their moveable Wealth will be ere long carried into *France*; for as soon as any Picture or Statue of great value is offered to be sold, those that are imployed by the King of *France*, do presently buy it up, so that as that King hath already, the greatest collection of Pictures that is in *Europe*, he will very probably in a few years more, bring together the chief […] of *Italy*.

I have now given you an account of [what ap-]peared most remarkable to me in *Rome* […] to this add a very extraordinary piece of […] History, that fell out there within these two […] which I had first from those two learned A[bbots] *bretti* and *Nazari*, and that was afterwards […] authentically confirmed to me by Cardinal *H[owar]*, who was one of the Congregation of Cardinals that examined and judged the matter. There were two Nuns near *Rome*, one as I remember was in the City, and the other not far from it, who, after they had been for some years in a Nunnery, perceived a very strange change in Nature, and that their Sex was altered, which grew by some degrees a total alteration in one: and tho the other was not so entire a change, yet it was visible she was more Man than Woman; upon this the matter was looked into: That which naturally offereth it self here, is that these two had been alwayes what they then appeared to be; but that they had gone into a Nun-

Ee 3 nery,

nery in a difguife to gratifie a brutal appetite. But to this, when I propofed it, anfwer was made, that as the breafts of a Woman that remained ftill, did in a great meafure fhake off that objection, fo the proofs were given fo fully of their having been real females, that there was no doubt left of that, nor had they given any fort of fcandal in the change of their Sex; And if there had been any room left to fufpect a cheat or difguife, the proceedings would have been both more fevere and more fecret: and thefe perfons would have been burnt, or at leaft put to death in fome terrible manner. Some Phyfitians and Chyrurgions were appointed to examine the matter, and at laft, after a long and exact enquiry, they were judged to be abfolved from their vows, and were difmiffed from the obligation of a Religious life, and required to go in mens habit. One of them was a Valet de Chambre to a *Roman* Marquefs, when I was there: I heard of this matter only two dayes before I left *Rome*, fo that I had not time to enquire after it more particularly; but I judged it fo extraordinary, that I thought it was worth communicating it to fo curious an Inquirer into nature.

And fince I am upon the fubject of the changes that have been made in nature, I fhall add one of another fort that I examined while I was at *Geneva*: There is a Minifter of S. *Gervais*, Mr. *Gody*, who hath a Daughter, that is now Sixteen years old: Her Nurfe had an extraordinary thicknefs of hearing, at a year old, the Child fpoke all thofe little words that Children begin ufually to learn at that age, but fhe made no progrefs; yet this was not obferved, till it was too late, and as fhe grew to be two years old, they perceived there that fhe had loft her hearing, and was fo deaf that ever fince tho fhe hears great noifes, yet fhe hears nothing that one can
fpeak

speak to her. It seems while the milk of her Nurse, was more abundant, and that the Child sucks more moderately the first year, those humors in the blood and milk had not that effect on her, that appeared after she came to suck more violently: and that her Nurses milk being in less quantity, was thicker, and more charged with that vapour that occasioned the deafness. But this Child hath by observing the motions of the mouths and lips of others, acquired so many words, that out of these she hath formed a sort of *jargon*, in which she can hold conversation whole days with those that can speak her own Language. I could understand some of her words, but could not comprehend a period, for it seemed to be a confused noise: She knows nothing that is said to her, unless she seeth the motion of their mouths that speak to her; so that in the night, when it is necessary to speak to her, they must light a Candle: Only one thing appeared the strangest part of the whole narration: She hath a Sister with whom she has practised her Language more than with any other: and in the night by laying her hand on her Sisters mouth, she can perceive by that, what she sayes, and so can discourse with her in the Night. It is true, her Mother told me that this did not go far, and that she found out only some short period in this manner, but it did not hold out very long: Thus this young Woman without any pains taken on her, hath meerly by a natural sagacity found out a method of holding discourse, that doth in a great measure lessen the misery of her deafness. I examined this matter critical'y, but only the Sister was not present, so that I could not see how the conversation past between them in the dark.

But before I give over writting concerning this place, I cannot hinder my self, from giving you an account of a conversation that I had with one of the most

most Celebrated persons that lives in it. I was talking concerning the credit that the Order of the *Jesuites* had every where; It was said that all the World mistrusted them, and yet by a strange sort of contradiction all the World trusted them, and tho it was well known that every *Jesuite* was truer to the Interests of his Order, than he could be to the Interests of any Prince whatsoever, yet those Princes that would be very careful not to suffer spies to come into their Courts or into their Councils suffered those spies to come into their breasts and Consciences: and tho Princes were not generally very tender in those parts, yet as they had oft as much guilt, so they had sometimes as much fear as other People, which a Dextrous spy knew well how to mannage: Upon which that person that pretended to be a zealous Catholick, added, that for their part they considered only the Character that the Church gave to a Priest; and if the Church qualified him to do the functions of a Priest, they thought it very needless to inquire after other personal Qualities, which were but common things, whereas the other was all Divine. On the Contrary, they thought it was so much the better to have to do with a poor Ignorant Priest: for then they had to do only with the Church, and not with the man. Pursuant to this, that persons Confessor was the greatest and the most notorious block head that could be found, and when they were asked why they made use of so weak a Man, they answered, because they could not find a weaker: and when ever they found one better qualified that way, if it were a groom or a footman that got into Priest's Orders, they would certainly make use of him. For they would ask Council of a friend; but they knew no other use of a Confessor, but to Confess to him, and to receive Absolution from him: and in so doing, they pre-

pretended they acted as became a true Catholick, that considered only the power of the Church in the Priest, without regarding any thing else.

So far have I entertained you with the short ramble that I made, which was too short to deserve the name of Travelling, and therefore the enquiries or Observations that I could make, must be received with the abatement that ought to be made for so short a stay: and all will be of a piece, when the remarks are as slight, as the abode I made in the places through which I past was short. I have avoided the troubling you with things that are commonly known, so if I have not entertained you with a long recital of ordinary matters, yet I have told you nothing but what I saw and knew to be true, or that I had from such hands, that I have very good reason to believe it: and I fancy that the things which made the greatest impression on my self, will be acceptably received by you, to whom, as upon many accounts, I owe all the expressions of esteem and gratitude that I can ever pay; so I had a more particular reason that determined me to give you, so full an account of all I saw and observed: for as you were pleased at parting to do me the Honour to desire me to communicate to you such things as appeared most remarkable to me, so I found such a vast advantage in many places, but more particularly at *Venice*, *Rome* and *Naples*, by the happiness I have of being known to you, and of being so far considered by you, that I could give a Copious Account both of your person and Studies, to those in whom your curious discoveries had kindled that esteem for you, which all the World payeth both to you and to your immortal enquiries into nature, which are among the peculiar blessings of this Age: and that are read with no less care and pleasure in *Italy* then in *England*.

This

This was so well received, that I found the great advantage of this Honour I did my self, in assuming the glorious Title of one of your friends, and I owe a great part of that distinction which I met with, to this favourable character that I gave my self; so that if I made any progress in the enquiries, that so short a stay could enable one to make, I owe it in so a peculiar a manner to you, that this return that I make is but a very small part of that I owe you, and which I will be endeavouring to pay you to the last moment of my life.

THE

BOOK III.

THE FIFTH LETTER.

From Nimmegen, *the* 20. *of* May 1686.

SIR,

I Thought I had made so full a point at the conclusion of my last Letter, that I should not have given you the trouble of reading any more Letters of the Volume of the former: But new Scenes and new Matter offering themselves to me, I fancy you will be very gentle to me, if I Engage you again to two or three Hours reading. From *Civita Vecchia* I came to *Marseilles*, where if there were a Road as Safe as the Harbour is covered; and if the Harbour were as large as it is convenient, it were certainly one of the most important places in the World; all is so well defended, that it is with respect either to Storms or Enemies the securest Port that can be seen any where. The Freedoms of this place, though it is now at the mercy of the Cittadel,

tadel, are such, and its scituation draweth so much Trade to it, that there one seeth another appearance of wealth then I found in any Town of *France*, and there is a new street lately built there, that for the beauty of the buildings, and the largeness of the street, is the Noblest I ever saw. There is in that Port a perpetual heat, and the Sun was so strong in the *Christians* week, that I was often driven off the Key. I made a Tour from thence through *Provence*, *Languedoc*, and *Dauphine*. I will offer you no account of *Nismes*, nor of the *Amphitheatre* in it, or the *Pont du Gar* near it; which as they are stupendious things, so they are so copiously described by many, and are so generally known to the *English* Nation, that if you have never gone that way your self, yet you must needs have received so particular a relation of them from those that have seen them on their way to *Montpelier*, that I judge it needless to enlarge upon them: Nor will I say any thing of the Soil, the Towns, or any other remarkable things that I found there.

I have a much stronger inclination to say somewhat, concerning the persecution which I saw in its rage and utmost fury; and of which I could give you many instances that are so much beyond all the common measures of barbarity and cruelty, that I confess they ought not to be believed, unless I could give more positive proofs of them, than are fitting now to be brought forth: and the particulars that I could tell you are such, that if I should relate them with the necessary circumstances of time, place, and persons, these might be so fatal to many that are yet in the power of their Enemies, that my regard to them restrains me. In short I do not think that in any Age there ever was such a violation of all that is sacred, either with relation to God or Man: And what I saw and knew there

from

from the firſt hand, hath ſo confirmed all the Idea's that I had taken from Books of the cruelty of that Religion, that I hope the impreſſion that this hath made upon me ſhall never end but with my life: The applauſes that the whole Clergy give to this way of proceeding, the many Panegyricks that are already writ upon it, of which, beſides the more pompous ones that appear at *Paris*, there are numbers writ by ſmaller Authors in every Town of any note, there; and the Sermons that are all flights of flattery upon this ſubject, are ſuch evident demonſtrations of their ſenſe of this matter; that what is now on foot may be well termed the Act of the whole Clergy of that Kingdom, which yet hath been hitherto eſteemed the moſt moderate part of the *Roman* Communion. If any are more moderate than others; and have not ſo far laid off human nature as not to go in entirely into thoſe bloody practiſes, yet they dare not own it, but whiſper it in ſecret as if it were half Treaſon: but for the greater part, they do not only magnifie all that is done, but they animate even the *Dragoons* to higher degrees of rage: and there was ſuch a heat ſpread over all the Country, on this occaſion, that one could not go into any Ordinary, or mix in any promiſcuous converſation, without finding ſuch effects of it, that it was not eaſie for ſuch as were toucht with the leaſt degree of compaſſion for the miſeries that the poor *Proteſtants* ſuffered, to be a witneſs to the Inſultings that they muſt meet with in all places. Some perhaps imagine that this hath not been approved in *Italy*, and it is true there were not any publick rejoycings upon it at *Rome*; no Indulgences nor *Te Deums* were heard of: And the *Spaniſh* faction being ſo prevalent there, it is not ſtrange if a courſe of proceedings, that is without an example, was ſet forth, by all that were of that intereſt, in its proper colours; of which I met with some instances my self, and could not but smile to see some of the *Spanish* Faction so far to forget their Courts of Inquisition as to argue against the Conversions by the *Dragoons*, as a reproach to the *Catholick* Religion. Yet the Pope was of another mind, for the Duke *d'Estrées* gave him an account of the Kings proceedings in this matter very copiously, as he himself related it. Upon which the Pope approved all, and expressed a great satisfaction in every thing that the King had done in that matter; and the Pope added, that he found some Cardinals [as I remember the Duke *d'Estrées* said two] were not pleased with it, and had taken the liberty to censure it, but the Pope said, they were to blame: The Duke *d'Estrees* did not name the two Cardinals, though he said he believed he knew who they were: and it is very likely that Cardinal *Pio* was one, for I was told that he spoke freely enough of this matter. I must take the liberty to add one thing to you, that I do not see that Great Monarch is to be so much blamed in this matter as his Religion is, which, without question, obligeth him to extirpate Hereticks, and not to keep his faith to them: so that instead of censuring him, I must only lament his being bred up in a Religion that doth certainly oblige him to devest himself of humanity, and to violate his faith, whensoever the cause of his Church and Religion requireth it: Or if there is any thing in this conduct that cannot be entirely justified from the principles of that Religion, it is this, that he doth not put the Hereticks to death out of hand, but that he forceth them, by all the extremities possible, to sign an abjuration, that all the World must needs see is done against their Consciences: and this being the only end of their miseries, those that would think any sort of death a happy conclusion of their sufferings, seeing no prospect of such a glorious issue out of

their

their troubles, are prevailed on by the many lingring deaths of which they see no end, to make Shipwrack of their faith: This appearance of mercy in not putting men to death, doth truly verifie the character that *Solomon* giveth of the tender mercies of the wicked, that they are cruel.

But I will stop here, though it is not easie to retire from so copious a subject, that as it affordeth so much matter, so upon many accounts raiseth a heat of thought that is not easily governed. I will now lead you to a Scene that giveth less passion.

I past the Winter at *Geneva*, with more satisfaction that I had thought it was possible for me to have found any where out of *England*: though that received great allaies from the most lamentable Stories that we had every day from *France*: but there is a sorrow by which the heart is made better. I ought to make the most publick acknowledgments possible for the Extraordinary Civilities that I met with in any one particular: but that is too low a Subject to entertain you with it. That which pleased me most, was of a more publick nature, before I left *Geneva*, the numbers of the *English* there was such, that I found we could make a small Congregation. For we were Twelve or Fourteen, so I addressed my self to the Councel of Twenty five for liberty, to have our own worship in our own Language, according to the *English* Liturgy. This was immediately granted in so obliging a manner, that as there was not one person that made any exception to it, so they sent one of their body to me, to let me know that in case our number should grow to be so great, that it were fit for us to assemble in a Church, they would grant us one, which had been done in Queen *Maries* reign: but till then we might hold our assemblies as we thought fit. So after that {time} during the rest of my stay there, we had every Sunday our devotions according to the Common Prayer, Morning and Evening: and at the Evening Prayer, I preacht in a Room that was indeed too large for our small Company, but there being a considerable number in *Geneva* that Understand *English* and in particular some of the Professors and Ministers, we had a great many strangers that met with us: and the last Sunday I gave the Sacrament according to the way of the Church of *England*, and upon this occasion I found a general joy in the Town, for this that I had given them an opportunity of expressing the respect they had for our Church, and as in their publick Prayers they always prayed for the Churches of *Great Brittain*, as well as for the King, so in private discourse they shewed all possible esteem for our Constitutions, and they spoke of the unhappy divisions among us, and of the Separation that was made from us, upon the account of our Government and Ceremonies with great regret and dislike. I shall name to you only two of their Professours, that as they are Men of great distinction, so they were the Persons with whom I conversed the most. The one is Mr. *Turretin*, a Man of great Learning, that by his Indefatigable Study and Labour has much worn out and wasted his strength; amidst all the affluence of a great plenty of Fortune to which he was born, one discerns in him all the modesty of a humble and mortified temper, and of an active and fervent charity, proportioned to his abundance or rather beyond it; and there is in him such a melting zeal for Religion, as the present conjuncture calls for, with all the seriousness of piety and devotion, which shews it self both in private conversation and in his most edifying Sermons by which he enters deep into the consciences of his Hearers. The other is Mr. *Tronchin*, a Man of a strong head, and of a clear and

correct

correct Judgment; who has all his thoughts well digested; his conversation has an engaging charm in it that cannot be resisted. He is a Man of Extraordinary virtue and of a readiness to oblige and serve all Persons, that has scarce any measures. His Sermons have a sublimity in them that strikes the hearer as well as it edifies him. His thoughts are noble, and his Eloquence is Masculine and exact, and has all the Majesty of the Chair in it, tempered with all the softness of persuasion, so that he not only convinces his Hearers, but subdues them and triumphs over them. In such Company it was no wonder if time seemed to go off too fast, so that I left *Geneva* with a concern, that I should not have felt in leaving any place out of the Isle of *Brittain*.

From *Geneva*, I went a second time through *Switzerland* to *Basile*: At *Avanche* I saw the Noble fragments of a great *Roman* Work, which seems to have been the *Portico* to some Temple: the heads of the Pillars are about four foot square of the *Jonick* Order: The Temple hath been dedicated to *Neptune* or some Sea god; for on the fragments of the *Architrave*, which are very beautiful, there are *Dolphins* and *Seahorses* in *bas-reliefs*; and the neighbourhood of the place to the Lakes of *Iverdun* and *Morat* maketh this more evident: there is also a Pillar standing up in its full height, or rather the corner of a building, in which one seeth the rests of a regular Architecture in two ranks of Pillars: If the ground near this were carefully search'd, no doubt it would discover more rests of that Fabrick. Not far from this is *Morat*; and a little on this side of it is a Chappel, full of the bones of the *Burgundians* that were killed by the *Switzers*, when this place was besieged by the famous *Charles* Duke of *Burgundy*, who lost a great Army before it, that was entirely cut off by the besieged; the inscription is very extraordinary, especially for that Age;

Age: for the bones being so piled up that the Chappel is quite filled with them: the inscription bears, that *Charles* Duke of *Burgundy*'s Army having besieged *Morat*, *Hoc sui Monumentum reliquit*, had left that Monument behind it. It cannot but seem strange to one that views *Morat*, to imagine how it was possible for a Town so situated, and so slightly fortified, to hold out against so powerful a Prince and so great an Army that brought Cannon before it. I met with nothing remarkable between this and *Basile*, except that I staid sometime at *Bern*, and knew it better; and at this second time it was, that my Lord *Advoyer d'Erlach* gave order to shew me the Original Records of the famous Process of the four *Dominicans*; upon which I have retoucht the Letter that I writ to you last year, so that I now send it to you with the corrections and enlargements, that this second stay at *Bern* gave me occasion to make.

Basile is the Town of the greatest extent of all *Switzerland*, but it is not inhabited in proportion to its extent. The *Rhine* maketh a crook before it: and the Town is situated on a rising ground, which hath a noble effect on the eye, when one is on the Bridge, for it looketh like a Theater. Little *Basile* on the other side of the *Rhine*, is almost a fourth part of the whole: The Town is surrounded with a Wall and Ditch, but it is so exposed on so many sides, and hath now so dreadful a Neighbour within a quarter of a League of it, the Fort of *Huningh*, that it hath nothing to trust to, humanly speaking, but its Union with the other Cantons. The maxims of this Canton have hindred its being better peopled than it is, the advantages of the Burgership are such, that the Citizens will not share them with strangers; and by this means they do not admit them. For I was told, that during the last War, that *Alsatia* was so often the seat of both Armies, *Basile* having then a neutrality, it might have been well filled, if it had not been for
this

this maxim. And it were a great happiness to all the Cantons, if they could have different degrees of Burgership, so that the lower degrees might be given to strangers for their encouragement to come and live among them: and the higher degrees which qualifie men for the advantagious Employments of the State, might be reserved for the ancient Families of the Natives. *Basile* is divided into sixteen Companies, and every one of these hath four Members in the little Council, so that it consisteth of sixty four: But of those four, two are chosen by the Company it self, who are called the Masters, and the other two are chosen by the Councel out of the Company; and thus as there are two sorts of Councellers, chosen in those different manners, there are also two chief Magistrates. There are two Burghermasters that Reign by turns, and two *Zunft-Masters* that have also their turns, and all is for life: And the last are the heads of the Companies, like the *Roman Tribunes* of the people. The Fabrick of the Stadt-House is ancient; there is very good Painting *in fresco* upon the Walls; one Piece hath given much offence to the *Papists*, though they have no reason to blame the Reformation for it; since it was done several years before it, in the year 1510. It is a representation of the Day of Judgement, and after Sentence given, the Devil is represented driving many before him to Hell, and among these there is several Ecclesiasticks. But it is believed that the Councel which sate so long in this place, acting so vigorously against the Pope, ingaged the Town into such a hatred of the Papacy, that this might give the rise to this representation. The more learned in the Town ascribe the beginning of the Custom in *Basile* of the Clocks anticipating the time a full Hour, to the sitting of the Councel, and they say that in order to the advancing of business, and the shortning their Sessions, they ordered their Clocks to be set forward an Hour, which continueth to this

day

day. The Cathedral is a great old *Gothick* building; the Chamber where the Councel sate, is of no great reception, and is a very ordinary Room: *Erasmus*'s Tomb is only a plain Inscription upon a great brass plate: There are many of *Holbens*'s Pictures, who was a Native of *Basile*, and was recommended by *Erasmus* to King *Henry* the VIII. the two best are a *Corpo* or *Christ* dead. which is certainly one of the best in the World: There is another Piece of his in the Stadt-House, for this is in the publick Library, of about three or four foot square; in which, in six several Cantons, the several parts of our Saviours Passion are represented with a life and beauty that cannot be enough admired; it is valued at ten thousand Crowns; it is in Wood, but hath that freshness of Colour on it, that seems peculiar to *Holbens*'s Pencil. There is also a Dance that he painted on the Walls of an House where he used to drink, that is so worn out that very little is now to be seen, except shapes and postures: but these shew the exquisiteness of the hand. There is another longer Dance that runneth all along the side of the Convent of the *Augustinians*, which is now the *French* Church, which is Deaths Dance; there are above threescore figures in it at full length of Persons of all ranks, from Popes, Emperors and Kings, down to the meanest sorts of People, and of all Ages and Professions, to whom Death appeareth in an insolent and surprizing posture, and the several passions that they express are so well set out, that this was certainly a great design. But the *fresco* being exposed to the Air, this was so worn out some time ago, that they ordered the best Painter they had to lay new Colour on it, but this is so ill done that one had rather see the dead shadows of *Holbens*'s Pencil, than this course work. There is in *Basile* a Gun-Smith that maketh Wind-Guns, and he shewed me one that as it received at once Air for ten shot, so it had this particular to it, which he pretends is his own Invention, that he can discharge all the Air that can be parcelled out in ten shot at once, to give a home blow. I conf.ss those are terrible instruments, and it seems the interest of Mankind to forbid them quite, since they can be imployed to assassinate persons so dextrously, that neither noise nor fire will discover from what hand the shot cometh. The Library of *Basile* is, by much the best in all *Switzerland*, there is a fine collection of Medals in it, and a very handsome Library of Manuscripts; the Room is Noble, and disposed in a very good method. Their Manuscripts are chiefly the *Latine* Fathers, or *Latine* Translations of the *Greek* Fathers, some good Bibles, they have the Gospels in *Greek* Capitals, but they are vitiously writ in many places: There is an infinite number of the Writers of the darker Ages, and there are Legends and Sermons without number. All the Books that were in the seueral Monasteries at the time of the Reformation were carefully preserved; and they believe that the Bishops who sate here in the Council, brought with them a great many Manuscripts which they never carried away. Among their Manuscripts I saw four of *Huss*'s Letters that he writ to the *Bohemians* the day before his death, which are very devout, but excessively simple. The Manuscripts of this Library are far more numerous than those of *Bern*, which were gathered by *Bongarsius*, and left by him to the publick Library there: They are indeed very little considered there, and are the worst kept that ever I saw: But it is a Noble collection of all the ancient *Latine* Authors, they have some few of the best of the *Roman* times, writ in great Characters, and there are many that are seven or eight hundred years old.

There is in *Basile* one of the best collections of Medals that ever I saw in private hands; together with a Noble Library, in which there are Manuscripts of good antiquity that belong to the Family

of

of *Fefch*, and that goeth from one Learned Man of the Family to another: For this Inheritance can only pafs to a Man of Learning, and when the Family produceth none, then it is to go to the publick. In *Bafile* as the feveral Companies have been more or lefs ftrict in admitting fome to a Freedom in the Company, that have not been of the Trade, fo they retain their priviledges to this day. For in fuch Companies that have once received fuch a number that have not been of the Trade as grew to be the majority, the Trade hath never been able to recover their intereft. But fome Companies have been more cautious, and have never admitted any but thofe that were of the Trade, fo that they retain their intereft ftill in Government. Of thefe the Butchers were named for one, fo that there are always four Butchers in the Council: The great Council confifteth of Two-Hundred and Forty, but they have no power left them, and they are only affembled upon fome extraordinary occafions, when the little Council thinketh fit to communicate any important matter to them. There are but fix Baliages that belong to *Bazile*, which are not Employments of great advantage; for the beft of them doth afford to the Bailif only a Thoufand livres a year: They reckon that there are in *Bafile* Three Thoufand Men that can bear Arms, and that they could raife Four Thoufand more out of the Canton, fo that the Town is almoft the half of this State, and the whole maketh Thirty Parifhes. There are Eighteen Profeffors in this Univerfity; and there is a Spirit of a more free and generous Learning ftirring there, then I faw in all thofe parts. There is a great decency of habit in *Bazile* and the garb both of the Counfellers, Minifters, and Profeffors, their ftiff Ruffs, and their long Beards, have an Air that is Auguft: The appointments are but fmall, for Counfellers, Minifters and Profeffors have but a Hundred Crowns a piece: It is true many Ministers are Professors so this mendeth the matter a little: But perhaps it would go better with the State of Learning there, if they had but half the number of Professors, and if those were a little better incouraged. No, where is the rule of St. *Paul* [of Women having on their heads the badge of the authority under which they are brought, which by a phrase that is not extraordinary, he calleth power] better observed than at *Bazile*; for all the Married Women go to Church with a coif on their heads, that is so folded, that as it cometh down so far as to cover their eyes, so another folding covereth also their Mouth and Chin, so that nothing but the nose appears, and then all turns backward in a folding that hangeth down to their midleg. This is always white, so that there is there such a sight of white heads in their Churches as cannot be found any where else: The unmarried Women wear hats turned up in the brims before and behind; and the brims of the sides being about a foot broad, stand out far on both hands: This fashion is also at *Strasburg*, and is worn there also by the Married Women.

I mentioned formerly the constant danger to which this place is exposed from the neighbourhood of *Huninghen*; I was told that, at first, it was pretended that the *French* King intended to build only a small Fort there, and it was believed that one of the Burgo-masters of *Bazile*, who was thought not only the wisest man of that Canton, but of all *Switzerland*, was gained to lay all Men asleep, and to assure them that the suffering this Fort to be built so near them, was of no importance to them, but now they see too late their fatal error: For the place is great, and will hold a Garrison of Three or Four Thousand Men; it is a *Pentagone*, only the side to the *Rhine* is so large,

Bbb that

that if it went round on that fide, I believe it muft have been a *Hexagone*; the Baftions have all *Orillons*, and in the middle of them there is a void fpace, not filled up with earth, where there is a Magazine built fo thick in the Vault that it is proof againft Bombs; The Remparts are ftrongly faced, there is a large Ditch, and before the Cortine, in the middle of the Ditch, there runs all along a Horn-work which is but Ten or Twelve foot high; and from the bottom of the Rampart, there goeth a Vault to this Horn-work, that is for conveying of Men for its defence; before this Horn-work there is a half Moon, with this that is peculiar to thofe new Fortifications, that there is a Ditch that cuts the half Moon in an Angle, and maketh one half Moon within another: beyond that there is a Counter-Scarp about Twelve foot high above the Water, with a covered way, and a *glacy* defigned, though not executed. There is alfo a great Hornwork befides all this, which runs out a huge way with its out-works towards *Bazile*; there is alfo a Bridge laid over the *Rhine*, and there being an Ifland in the River, where the Bridge is laid, there is a Horn-work that filleth and fortifieth it. The Buildings in this Fort are beautiful, and the Square can hold above Four Thoufand Men; the Works are not yet quite finifhed, but when all is compleated, this will be one of the ftrongeft places in *Europe*: There is a Cavalier on one or two of the Baftions, and there are half Moons before the Baftions, fo that the *Switzers* fee their danger now, when it is not eafie to redrefs it. This place is fcituated in a great Plain, fo that it is commanded by no rifing ground on any fide of it. I made a little Tower into *Alface*, as far as *Mountbelliard*; the Soil is extream rich, but it hath been fo long a Frontier Country; and is, by confequence, fo ill peopled, that it is in many places over-grown with Woods:

In

In one respect it is fit to be the seat of War, for it is full of Iron-works, which bring a great deal of Money into the Country. I saw nothing peculiar in the Iron-works there (except that the sides of the great Bellows were not of Leather but of Wood, which saves much Money) so I will not stand to describe them. The River of the *Rhine*, all from *Bazile* to *Spire*, is so low, and is on both sides so covered with woods, that one that cometh down in a Boat hath no sight of the Country: The River runneth sometimes with such a force, that nothing but such Woods could preserve its Banks, and even these are not able to save them quite, for the Trees are often washed away by the very Roots, so that in many places those Trees lye along in the Channel of the River: It hath been also thought a sort of a Fortification to both sides of the River, to have it thus faced with Woods, which maketh the passing of Men dangerous, when they must march for sometime after their passage through a *defilé*. The first night from *Bazile* we came to *Brisac*, which is a poor and miserable Town, but it is a noble Fortification, and hath on the *West-side* of the River, over which a Bridge is laid, a regular Fort of Four or Five Bastions. The Town of *Brisac* riseth all on a Hill which is a considerable heigth; there were near it two Hills, the one is taken within the Fortification, and the other is so well levelled with the ground, that one cannot so much as find out where it was; All the ground about for many miles is plain, so that from the Hill, as from a Cavalier, one can see exactly well, especially with the help of a Prospect, all the motions of an Enemy in case of a Siege: The Fortification is of a huge compass, above a *French* league, indeed almost a *German* league; the Bastions are quite filled with Earth, they are faced with brick, and have a huge broad Ditch full of Water around them,

them, the Counterscarp, the covered way, which hath a palisade within the *Parapet*, and the *Glacy*, are all well executed; there is a half Moon before every Cortine: the Bastions have no *Orillons* except one or two, and the Cortines are so disposed that a good part of them defendeth the Bastion. The Garrison of this place in time of War must needs be Eight or Ten Thousand Men; there hath not been much done of late to this place only the Ditch is so adjusted that it is all defended by the flanks of the Bastions. But the noblest place on the *Rhine* is *Strasburg*: It is a Town of a huge extent, and hath a double Wall and Ditch all round it; the inner Wall is old and of no strength, nor is the outward Wall very good, it hath a *Fauſſebraye*, and is faced with Brick Twelve or Fifteen Foot above the Ditch: the Counterscarp is in an ill condition, so that the Town was not in case to make any long resistance; but it is now strongly fortified. There is a Cittadel built on that side that goeth towards the *Rhine*, that is much such a Fort as that of *Huningh*, and on the side of the Cittadel towards the Bridge, there is a great Horn-work that runs out a great way with out-works belonging to it; there are also small Forts at the two chief Gates that lead to *Alsace*; by which the City is so bridled that these can cut off all its communication with the Country about, in case of a revolt; the Bridge is also well Fortified; there are also Forts in some Islands in the *Rhine*, and some Redoubts: so that all round this place, there is one of the greatest Fortifications that is in *Europe*.

Hitherto the Capitulation with relation to Religion hath been well kept, and there is so small a number of new Converts, and these are for the greatest part so inconsiderable, they not being in all above Two Hundred as I was told: The *Lutherans* for the greatest part retain their animosities almost

to

to an equal degree both against *Papists* and *Calvinists*. I was in their Church, where if the Musick of their Psalms pleased me much, the irreverence in singing, it being free to keep on or put off the Hat, did appear very strange to me: The Churches are full of Pictures, in which the chief passages of our Saviours life are represented; but there is no sort of religious respect payed them, they bow when they name the Holy Ghost, as well as at the name of *Jesus*; but they have not the Ceremonies that the *Lutherans* of *Saxony* use, which Mr. *Bebel*, their Professor of Divinity, said was a great happiness, for a similitude in outward rites might dispose the ignorant People to change too easily. I found several good People both of the *Lutheran* Ministers and others, acknowledge that there was such a corruption of morals spread over the whole City, that as they had justly drawn down on their heads the plague of the loss of their liberty, so this having toucht them so little they had reason to look for severer strokes: One seeth, in the ruine of this City, what a mischievous thing the popular pride of a free City is: they fancied they were able to defend themselves, and so they refused to let an *Imperial* Garrison come within their Town; for if they had received only Five Hundred Men, as that small number would not have been able to have opprest their Liberties, so it would have so secured the Town that the *French* could not have besieged it, without making War on the Empire: but the Town thought this was a diminution of their Freedom, and so chose rather to pay a Garrison of Three Thousand Souldiers, which as it exhausted their Revenue, and brought them under great Taxes, so it proved too weak for their defence when the *French* Army came before them. The Town begins to sink in its Trade, notwithstanding the great circulation of Money that the expence of the Fortifications

fications hath brought to it; but when that is at an end, it will sink more sensibly, for it is impossible for a place of trade, that is to have always Eight or Ten Thousand Souldiers in it, to continue long in a Flourishing State. There was a great animosity between two of the chief Families of the Town, *Dittrick* and *Obrecht*, the former was the Burgomaster, and was once almost run down by a Faction that the other had raised against him; but he turned the tide, and got such an advantage against *Obrecht*, who had writ somewhat against the conduct of their affairs, that he was condemned and Beheaded for writing Libels against the Government. His Son is a Learned Man, and was Professor of the Civil Law; and he to have his turn of revenge against *Dittrick*, went to *Paris* last Summer, and that he might make his Court the better, changed his Religion. *Dittrick* had been always looked on as one of the chief of the *French* Faction, though he had been at first an *Imperialist*, so it was thought that he should have been well rewarded; yet it was expected that to make himself capable of that, he should have changed his Religion, but he was an antient Man, and would not purchase his Court at that rate: so without any reason given, and against the express words of the Capitulation, he was confined to one of the midland Provinces of *France*, as I remember it was *Limosin*; and thus he that hath been thought the chief cause of this Towns falling under the power of the *French*, is the first Man that hath felt the effects of it. The Library here is considerable, the Case is a great Room very well contrived, for it is divided into Closets all over the body of the Room, which runs about these as a Gallery, and in these Closets all round there are the Books of the several Professions lodged apart; there is one for Manuscripts in which there are some of considerable Antiquity. I need say nothing to you of the vast heighth, and the *Gothick* Architecture of the Steeple and of the great Church, nor of the curious Clock where there is so vast a variety of motions, for these are well known. The *bas reliefs* upon the tops of the great Pillars of the Church are not so visible, but they are surprizing; for this being a Fabrick of Three or Four Hundred Years old, it is very strange to see such representations as are there. There is a Procession represented, in which a Hog carrieth the Pot with the Holy Water, and Asses and Hogs in Priestly Vestments follow to make up the Procession; there is also an Ass standing before an Altar, as if he were going to Consecrate, and one carrieth a Case with Reliques, within which one seeth a Fox, and the trains of all that go in this Procession, are carried up by Monkies. This seems to have been made in hatred of the Monks whom the Secular Clergy abhorred at that time, because they had drawn the Wealth, and the following of the World after them, and they had exposed the Secular Clergy so much for their ignorance, that it is probable after some Ages, the Monks falling under the same contempt, the Secular Clergy took their turn in exposing them in so lasting a representation to the scorn of the World. There is also in the Pulpit a Nun cut in Wood, lying along, and a Frier lying near her with his Breviary open before him, and his hand under the Nuns habit, and the Nuns feet are shod with Iron Shoes. I confess I did not look for these things, for I had not heard of them; but my Noble Friend Mr. *Ablancourt* viewed them with great exactness, while he was the *French* Kings Resident at *Strasburg*, in the company of one of the Magistrates that waited on him; and it is upon his credit, to which all that know his eminent sincerity, know how much is due, that I give you this particular.

From *Strasburg* we went down the *Rhine* to *Philipsburg*,

lipsburg, which lieth at a quarter of a miles distance from the River, it is but a small place, the Bastions are but little; there is a Ravelline before almost all the Cortines, and there lye such Marishes all round it, that in these lieth the chief strength of the place. The *French* had begun a great Crown-work on the side that lieth to the *Rhine*, and had cast out a Horn-work beyond that; but by all that appears it seems they intended to continue that Crown work quite round the Town, and to make a second Wall and Ditch all round it; which would have Enlarged the place vastly, and made a compass capable enough to lodge above Ten Thousand Men; and this would have been so terrible a Neighbour to the *Palatinate* and all *Franconia* that it was a Master-piece in *Charles Lewis*, the late Elector *Palatine*, to Engage the Empire into this Siege. He saw well how much it concerned him to have it out of the hands of the *French*, so that he took great care to have the Duke of *Lorrain*'s Camp so well supplied with all things necessary during the Siege, that the Army lay not under the least uneasiness all the while. From thence in three Hours time we came to *Spire*, which is so naked a Town that if it were attacked, it could not make the least resistance. The Town is neither great nor rich, and subsisteth chiefly by the *Imperial* Chamber that sitteth here, though there is a constant dispute between the Town and the Chamber concerning Priviledges; for the Government of the Town, pretends that the Judges of the Chamber, as they are private Men, and out of the Court of Judicature, are subject to them; and so about a year ago they put one of the Judges in Prison; on the other hand the Judges pretend that their Persons are sacred. It was the consideration of the Chamber that procured to the Town the neutrality that they injoyed all the last War. I thought to have seen the forms of this Court, and the way of

laying

laying up, and preserving their Records, but the Court was not then sitting. The Building, the Halls and Chambers of this Famous Court are mean beyond imagination, and look liker the Halls of some small Company, then of so great a body; and I could not see the places where they lay up their Archives: The Government of the City is all *Lutheran*, but not only the Cathedral is in the hands of the Bishop and Chapter, but there are likewise several Convents of both Sexes, and the *Jesuites* have also a Colledge there. There is little remarkable in the Cathedral, which is a huge building in the *Gothick* manner of the worst sort. The Tombs of many Emperours that lie buried there, are remarkable for their meanness; they being only great Flag-stones layed on some small Stone ballisters of a foot and a half high: There are also the marks of a ridiculous Fable concerning St. *Bernard*, which is too foolish to be related, yet since they have taken such pains to preserve the remembrance of it, I shall venture to write it. There are from the Gate all along the *Nef* of the Church up to the Steps that go up to the Quire, Four round Plates of Brass, above a foot Diameter, and at the distance of Thirty foot one from another; laid in the pavement, on the first of these is ingraven: *O Clemens*; on the second, *O Pia*; on the third, *O Felix*; and on the fourth, *Maria:* The last is about Thirty Foot distant from a Statue of the Virgins; so they say that St. *Bernard* came up the whole length of the Church at four steps, and that those four plates were laid where he stept: and that at every step he pronounced the word that is engraven on the Plate, and when he came to the last, the Image of the Virgin answered him. *Salve Bernarde:* upon which he answered, *let a Woman keep silence in the Church,* and that the *Virgins* Statue has kept silence ever since, this last part of the Story is certainly very credible.

He

He was a man of Learning that shewed me this; and he repeated it so gravely to me, that I saw he either believed it, or at least that he had a mind to make me believe it: and I asked him as gravely if that was firmly believed there, he told me that one had lately writ a Book to prove the truth of it, as I remember, it was a *Jesuit*: he acknowledged it was not an Article of Faith, so I was satisfied.

There is in the Cloister an old *Gothick* representation of our Saviours Agony in Stone, with a great many Figures of his Apostles, and the Company that came to seize him, that is not ill Sculpture, for the Age in which it was made, it being some Ages old. The *Calvinists* have a Church in this Town, but their numbers are not considerable: I was told there were some ancient Manuscripts in the Library, that belongeth to the Cathedral; but one of the Prebendaries to whom I addressed my self, being, according to the *German* custom, a man of greater quality than learning, told me he heard they had some ancient Manuscripts, but he knew nothing of it, and the Dean was absent, so I could not see them, for he kept one of the keys. The lower Palatinate is certainly one of the sweetest Countries of all *Germany:* It is a great Plain till one cometh to the Hills of *Heidelberg*: the Town is ill scituated, just in a bottom between two ranges of Hills, yet the Air is much commended: I need say nothing of the Castle, nor the prodigious Wine Cellar, in which, though there is but one celebrated Tun that is seventeen foot high, and twenty six foot long, and is built with a strength liker that of the ribs of a ship, than the Staves of a Tun; yet there are many other Tuns of such a prodigious bigness, that they would seem very extraordinary if this vast one did not Eclipse them. The late Prince *Charles Lewis* shewed his capacity in the peopling and and settling this State, that had been so entirely ruined, being for many years the Seat of War, for in four years

years time he brought it to a Flourishing condition: He raised the Taxes as high as was possible without dispeopling his Country, and all mens Estates were valued, and they were taxed at five *per cent* of the value of their Estates; but their Estates were not valued to the rigour, but with such abatements as have been ordinary in *England* in the times of Subsidies; so that when the Son offered to bring the Taxes down to two *per cent* of the real value; the Subjects all desired him rather to continue them as they were. There is no Prince in *Germany* that is more absolute than the *Elector Palatine*, for he layeth on his Subjects what Taxes he pleaseth, without being limited to any forms of Government. And here I saw that which I had always believed to be true, that the Subjects of *Germany* are only bound to their particular Prince, for they swear Allegiance simply to the Elector, without any reserve for the Emperor, and in their Prayers for him they name him their Soveraign. It is true the Prince is under some ties to the Emperor, but the Subjects are under none. And by this *D. Fabritius*, a learned and judicious Professor there, explained those words of *Pareus*'s Commentary on the *Romans*, which had respect only to the Princes of the Empire: and were quite misunderstood by those who fancied that they favoured Rebellion; for there is no place in *Europe* where all rebellious Doctrine is more born down than there. I found a great spirit of moderation with relation to those small controversies that have occasioned such heat in the *Protestant* Churches reigning in the University there, which is in a great measure owing to the prudence, learning, and the happy temper of mind of *D. Fabritius*, and *D. Miek*; who as they were long in *England*, so they have that generous largeness of Soul, which is the Noble Ornament of many of the *English* Divines. Prince *Charles Lewis* saw that *Manheim* was marked out by Nature to be the most important place of all his Territory, it being

ing scituated in the point where the *Neckar* falleth into the *Rhine:* So that those two Rivers defending it on two sides, it was capable of a good Fortification: It is true the Air is not thought wholsome; and the Water is not good, yet he made a fine Town there, and a Noble Cittadel with a regular Fortification about it, and he designed a great Palace there, but he did not live to build it. He saw of what advantage Liberty of Conscience was to the peopling of his Country, so as he suffered the *Jews* to come and settle there, he resolved also not only to suffer the three Religions tolerated by the Laws of the Empire to be professed there, but he built a Church for them all three, which he called the Church of the Concord, in which both *Calvinists,* *Lutherans* and *Papists* had, in the order in which I have set down, the exercise of their Religion, and he maintained the peace of his Principality so entirely, that there was not the least disorder occasioned by this tolleration: This, indeed, made him to be lookt on as a Prince that did not much consider Religion himself: He had a wonderful application to all affairs, and was not only his own chief Minister, but he alone did the work of many.

But I were Injust, if I should not say somewhat to you of the Princely vertues and the Celebrated probity of the present Prince Elector upon whom that Dignity is devolved by the extinction of so many Princes that in this Age composed the most numerous Family of any of that rank in *Europe*. This Prince as he is in many respects an honour to the Religion that he professes, so is in nothing more to be commended by those who differ from him, than for his exact adhering to the promises he made his Subjects with relation to their Religion, in which he has not even in the smallest matters, broke in upon their establisht Laws, and though an Order of Men, that have turned the World upside down, have great Credit

with

with him, yet it is hitherto visible that they cannot carry it so far, as to make him do any thing contrary to the established Religion; and to those sacred promises that he made his Subjects. For he makes it appear to all the World that he does not consider those as so many words spoken at first to lay his people asleep, which he may now explain and observe as he thinks fit; but as so many ties upon his Conscience and Honour, which he will Religiously observe. And as in the other parts of his life he has set a Noble Pattern to all the Princes of *Europe*, so his exactness to his promises, is that which cannot be too much commended: of which this extraordinary Instance has been communicated to me since I am come into this Countrey. The Elector had a Procession in his Court last *Corpus Christi* day, upon which one of the Ministers of *Heidelberg* preacht a very severe Sermon against Popery, and in particular, taxed that Procession, perhaps, with greater plainness than discretion: This being brought to the Elector's ears, he sent presently an Order to the Ecclesiastical Senate to suspend him. That Court is composed of some Secular Men, and some Churchmen, and as the Princes authority is delegated to them, so they have a sort of an Episcopal jurisdiction over all the Clergy. This Order was a surprise to them as being a direct breach upon their Laws and the Liberty of their Religion? so they sent a Deputation to Court, to let the Elector know the reasons that hindred them from obeying his Orders, which were heard with so much Justice and Gentleness, that their Prince instead of expressing any displeasure against them, recalled the Order that he had sent them. The way from *Heidelberg* to *Frankfort*, is, for the first twelve or fifteen miles, the beautifullest piece of ground that can be imagined; for we went under a ridge of little Hills that are all covered with Vines, and from them, as far as the eye can go, there is a beautiful Plain of Corn-fields and Meadows, all sweetly divided and inclosed with rows of Trees, so that I fancied I was in *Lombardy* again, but with this advantage, that here all was not of a piece, as it is in *Lombardy*: but the Hills as they made a pleasant inequality in the prospect, so they made the Air purer, and produced a pleasant Wine: The way near *Darmstat*, and all forwards to *Frankfort*, becometh more wild and more sandy: There is a good Suburb on the *South-side* of the *Main* over against *Frankfort*, which hath a very considerable Fortification; there is a double Wall, and a double Ditch that goeth round it, and the outward Wall, as it is regularly fortified, so it is faced with Brick to a considerable heighth. The Town of *Frankfort* is of a great extent, and seemed to be but about a third part less then *Strasburg*: The three Religions are also tolerated there; and though the number of the *Papists* is very inconsiderable, yet they have the great Church, which is a huge rude building; they have also several other Churches, and some Convents there. There are several open squares for Market places, and the Houses about them look very well without. Among their Archives they preserve the Original of the *Bulla Aurea*, which is only a great Parchment writ in *High Dutch*, without any beauty answering to its Title: and since I could not have understood it, I was not at the pains of desiring to see it, for that is not obtained without difficulty. The *Lutherans* have here built a new Church, called *St. Catherin's*, in which there is as much painting as ever I saw in any *Popish* Church, and over the high Altar there is an huge carved Crucifix, as there are painted ones in other places of their Church. The Pulpit is extream fine of Marble of different colours very

well

well polished and joyned. I was here at a Sermon where I understood nothing, but I liked one thing that I saw both at *Strasburg* and here, that at the end of Prayers, there was a considerable interval of silence left, before the conclusion, for all peoples private devotions. In the House of their publick Discipline, they retain still the old *Roman Pistrina* or Hand-mill, at which lewd Women are condemned to grind, that is, to drive about the Wheel that maketh the Millstones go. There is a great number of *Jews* there, though their two Synagogues are very little, and by consequence the numbers being great, they are very nasty. I was told they were in all above twelve hundred. The Women had the most of a tawdry Imbroidery of Gold and Silver about them that ever I saw, for they had all Mantles of Crape, and both about the top and the bottom, there was a border above a hand breadth of imbroidery. The Fortification of *Frankfort* is considerable, their Ditch is very broad, and very full of Water; all the Bastions have a Counter-mine that runneth along by the brim of the Ditch; but the Counterscarp is not faced with Brick as the Walls are, and so in many places it is in an ill condition; the covered Way and *glacy* are also in an ill case: The Town is rich, and driveth a great Trade, and is very pleasantly scituated. Not far from hence is *Hockam* that yieldeth the best Wine of those parts. Since I took *Frankfort* in my way from *Heidelberg* to *Mentz*, I could not pass by *Worms*, for which I was sorry. I had a great mind to see that place where *Luther* made his first appearance before the Emperor, and the Diet, and in that solemn audience expressed an undaunted zeal for that Glorious Cause in which God made him such a blessed Instrument. I had another piece of Curiosity on me which will, perhaps, appear to you somewhat ridiculous. I had a mind to see a Picture

Picture that, as I was told, is over one of the *Popish* Altars there, which one would think was Invented by the Enemies of Transubstantiation to make it appear ridiculous. There is a Windmill, and the Virgin throws *Christ* into the Hopper, and he comes out at the eye of the Milne all in Waters, which some Priests take up to give the People. This is so course an Embleme, that one would think it too gross even for *Laplanders*; but a Man that can swallow Transubstantiation it self, will digest this likewise. *Mentz* is very nobly scituated, on a rising ground a little below the conjunction of the two Rivers, the *Rhine*, and the *Main* ; it is of too great a compass, and too ill Peopled to be capable of a great defence: There is a Cittadel upon the highest part of the Hill that commandeth the Town ; it is compassed about with a dry Ditch that is considerably deep. The Walls of the Town are faced with Brick and regularly fortified, but the Counterscarp is not faced with Brick, so all is in a sad condition ; and the Fortification is weakest on that side where the Elector's Palace is. There is one side of a new Palace very nobly built in a regular Architecture , only the *Germans* do still retain somewhat of the *Gothick* manner. It is of a great length , and the design is to build quite round the Court, and then it will be a very magnificent Palace, only the Stone is red; for all the Quarries that are upon the *Rhine*, from *Bazile* down to *Coblentz*, are of red Stone, which doth not look beautiful. The Elector of *Mentz* is an absolute Prince ; his Subjects present Lists of their Magistrates to him , but he is not tied to them , and may name whom he will: The Ancient Demeasne of the Electorate is about Forty thousand Crowns : But the Taxes rise to about Three hundred thousand Crowns ; so that the Subjects here are as heavily taxed as in the *Palatinate:* There is

Twelve

Twelve thousand Crowns a year given the Elector for his privy Purse, and the State bears the rest of his whole expence: It can Arm Ten thousand Men, and there is a Garison of Two thousand Men in *Mentz*: This Elector hath three Councels, one as he is Chancellour of the Empire, consisting of three Persons; the other two are for the Policy and Justice of his Principality. He and his Chapter have Months by turns for the Nomination of the Prebends. In the Month of *January* he names, if any dies, and they chuse in the Room of such as die in *February*, and so all the Year round. The Prebendaries or *Domeheer's* have about Three thousand Crowns a year a piece. When the Elector dieth, the Emperor sendeth one to see the Election made, and he recommendeth one, but the Canons may chuse whom they please; and the present Elector was not of the Emperors recommendation. Besides the Palace at *Mentz*, the Elector hath another near *Frankfort*, which is thought the best that is in those parts of *Germany*: The Cathedral is a huge *Gothick* Building; there is a great *Cupulo* in the *West-end*, and there the Quire singeth Mass: I could not learn whether this was done only because the place here was of greater reception than at the *East-end*, or if any burying place and endowment obliged them to the *West-end*. Near the Cathedral there is a huge Chapel of great Antiquity, and on the *North* Door there are two great Brass Gates with a long Inscription, which I had not time to write out, but I found it was in the Emperor *Lotharius's* time. There are a vast number of Churches in this Town, but it is poor and ill inhabited. The *Rhine* here is almost half an *English* mile broad, and there is a Bridge of Boats laid over it. From *Mentz* all along to *Baccharach* (which seems to carry its name (*Bacchi*

Ccc 3 *Ara*)

Ara) from some famous Altar that the *Romans* probably erected by reason of the good Wine that grows in the neighbourhood.) There is a great number of very considerable Villages on both sides of the River: Here the Rats Tower is shewed, and the People of the Country do all firmly believe the story of the Rats eating up an Elector, and that though he Fled to this Island where he built a small high Tower, they pursued him still, and swimmed after him, and eat him up: And they told us that there were some of his Bones to be seen still in the Tower. This extraordinary Death makes me call to mind a peculiar and unlooked for sort of Death, that carried off a poor Labourer off the ground a few days before I left *Geneva*. The foot of one of his Cattel, as he was ploughing, went into a nest of Wasps, upon which the whole swarm came out, and set upon him that held the Plough, and killed him in a very little time; and his body was prodigiously swelled with the poyson of so many Stings.

But to return to the *Rhine*, all the way from *Baccharach* down to *Coblents*, there is on both sides of the River hanging grounds, or little Hills, so laid as if many of them had been laid by Art, which produce the rich *Rhenish* Wine: They are indeed as well exposed to the Sun, and covered from Storms, as can be imagined; and the ground on those Hills, which are in some places of a considerable heighth, is so cultivated that there is not an inch lost that is capable of improvement, and this bringeth so much wealth into the Country, that all along there is a great number of considerable Villages. *Coblentz* is the strongest place that I saw of all that belong to the Empire; the scituation is Noble, the *Rhine* running before it, and the *Moselle* passing along the side of the Town; it is well fortified, the Ditch is large, the Counterscarp is high, and the
covered

covered way is in a good condition; both Walls and Counterscarp are faced with Brick, and there are Ravelines before the Cortines; but on the side of the *Moselle* it is very slightly fortified, and there is no Fort at the end of the stone Bridge that is laid over the *Moselle*, so that it lieth quite open on that side, which seemeth a strange defect in a place of that consequence: But though the Fortifications of this place are very considerable, yet its chief defence lieth in the Fort of *Hermanstan*, which is built on the top of a very high Hill, that lieth on the other-side of the *Rhine*; and which commandeth this place so absolutely, that he who is Master of *Hermanstan*, is always Master of *Coblentz*. This belongeth to the Elector of *Triers*, whose Palace lieth on the *East*-side of the *Rhine*, just at the foot of the Hill of *Hermanstan*, and over against the point where the *Moselle* falleth into the *Rhine*, so that nothing can be more pleasantly scituated; only the ground begins to rise just at the back of the House with so much steepness that there is not Room for Gardens or Walks. The House maketh a great shew upon the River, but we were told that the Apartments within were not answerable to the outside. I say we were told for the *German* Princes keep such forms, that, without a great deal of ado, one cannot come within their Courts, unless it be when they are abroad themselves; so that we neither got within the Palace at *Mentz*, nor this of *Hermanstan*. It is but a few Hours from this to *Bonne*, where the Elector of *Collen* keepeth his Court; the place hath a regular Fortification, the Walls are faced with Brick; but though the Ditch, which is dry, is pretty broad, the Counterscarp is in so ill a condition, that it is not able to make a great defence. This Elector is the Noblest born, and the best provided of all the *German* Clergy, for he is Brother to the great *Maximilian* Duke of *Bavaria*; and besides *Collen*, he hath
                                                                        Liege,

Liege, *Munster*, and *Hidelsheim*, which are all great Bishopricks: He hath been also Six and Thirty years in the *Electorate*: His Palace is very mean, consisting but of one Court, the half of which is cast into a little Garden, and the Wood-yard is in the very Court; the lower part of the Court was a stable; but he hath made an apartment here that is all furnished with Pictures: where, as there are some of the hands of the greatest Masters, so there are a great many foils to set these off, that are scarce good enough for Signposts.

The Elector has a great many gold meddals, which will give me occasion to tell you one of the Extravagantest pieces of forgery that perhaps ever was; which happened to be found out at the last siege of *Bonne*: for while they were clearing the ground for planting a battery, they discovered a Vault in which there was an Iron Chest that was full of meddals of gold to the value of 100000 Crowns; and of which I was told the Elector bought to the value of 30000 Crowns. They are huge big, one weighed 800. Ducats, and the gold was of the fineness of Ducat gold; but though they bore the Impressions of *Roman* Meddals, or rather Medaillons they were all Counterfeit; and the imitation was so coursely done that one must be extream Ignorant in Meddals to be deceived by them. Some few that seemed true were of the late *Greek* Emperours. Now it is very unaccountable what could induce a Man to make a forgery upon such mettle, and in so vast a quantity, and then to bury all this under ground, especially in an Age in which so much gold was ten times the value of what is at present for it is judged to have been done about Four or Five Hundred Years ago.

The Prince went out a hunting while we were there, with a very handsome Guard of about Fourscore Horse, well mounted; so we saw the Palace, but where not suffered to see the Apartment where
he

he lodged: There is a great Silver Cafolette gilt, all set with Emeralds and Rubies, that though they made a fine appearance, yet were a Compofition of the Princes own making: His Officers alfo fhewed us a Bafon and Ewer, which they faid were of Mercury fixed by the Prince himfelf; but they added that now for many Years he wrought no more in his Labouratory. I did not eafily believe this, and as the weight of the Plate did not approach to that of Quick-Silver, fo the Medicinal Virtues of fixed Mercury, if there is any fuch thing, are fo extraordinary, that it feemed very ftrange to fee Twenty or Thirty Pound of it made up in two pieces of Plate. A quarter of a mile without the Town, the beft Garden of thofe parts of *Germany* is to be feen, in which there is a great variety of Water-works, and very many Noble Allies in the *French* manner, and the whole is of a very confiderable extent; but as it hath no Statues of any value to adorn it, fo the Houfe about which it lieth in, is in ruines: and it is ftrange to fee that fo rich and fo great a Prince, during fo long a Regence, hath done fo little to Enlarge or beautifie his Buildings. *Bonne* and *Coblentz* are both poor and fmall Towns. *Collen* is three Hours diftant from *Bonne*, it is of a prodigious extent, but ill built and worfe Peopled in the remote parts of it; and as the Walls are all in an ill cafe, fo it is not poffible to fortifie fo vaft a compafs as this Town maketh, as it ought to be, without a charge that would eat out the whole Wealth of this little State. The *Jews* live in a little Suburb on the other fide of the River, and may not come over without leave obtained, for which they pay confiderably. There is no exercife of the *Proteftant* Religion fuffered within the Town, but thofe of the Religion are fuffered to live there, and they have a Church at two miles diftance. The Arfenal here, is fuitable to the Fortifications, very mean, and ill furnifhed. The Quire of the great Church is as

high

high in the roof, as any Church I ever saw; but it seemeth the Wealth of this place could not finish the whole Fabrick, so as to answer the heighth of the Quire, for the Body of the Church is very low: Those that are disposed to believe Legends, have enough here to overset even a good degree of credulity, both in the story of the three Kings, whose Chappel is visited with great devotion, and standeth at the East end of the great Quire; and in that more copious Fable of the Eleven Thousand *Ursulins*, whose Church is all over full of rough Tombs, and of a vast number of Bones that are piled up in rows about the Walls of the Church: These Fables are so firmly believed by the *Papists* there, that the least sign which one giveth of doubting of their truth, passeth for an infallible mark of an Heretick. The *Jesuites* have a great and noble Colledge and Church here. And for *Thauler's* sake I went to the *Dominicans* House and Church; which is also very great. One grows extreamly weary of walking over this great Town, and doth not find enough of entertainment in it: The present subject of their discourse is also very melancholy: The late Rebellion that was there, is so generally known, that I need not say much concerning it. A report was set about the Town, by some Incendiaries, that the Magistrates did eat up the publick Revenue, and were like to ruine the City; I could not learn what ground there was for these reports, for it is not ordinary to see reports of that kind fly, through a body of Men, without some foundation: It is certain this came to be so generally believed, that there was a horrible disorder occasioned by it: The Magistrates were glad to save themselves from the storm, and abandoned the Town to the popular fury, some of them having been made sacrifices to it; and this rage held long: But within this last year, after near two years disorder, those that were sent by the Emperor and Diet to Judge the matter,

having

having threatned to put the Town under the *Imperial Bann*, if it had stood longer out, were received; and have put the Magistrates again in the possession of their Authority, and all the chief Incendiaries were clapt in Prison: many have already suffered, and a great many more are still in Prison; they told us that some executions were to be made within a week when we were there. *Dusseldorp* is the first considerable Town below *Collen*, it is the Seat of the Duke of *Juliers*, who is Duke of *Newburgh*, eldest Son to the present *Elector Palatine*. The Palace is old and *Gothick* enough; but the *Jesuits* have their a fine Colledge, and a noble Chappel, though there are manifest faults in the Architecture; the *Protestant* Religion is tolerated and they have a Church lately built here within these few years, that was procured by the intercession of the Elector of *Brandenburgh*, who observing exactly the liberty of Religion that was agreed to in *Cleve*, had reason to see the same as duly observed in his Neighborhood, in favour of his own Religion. The Fortification here is very ordinary, the Ramparts being faced but a few foot high with Brick. But *Keiserswert*, some hours lower on the same side, which belongeth to the Elector of *Collen*, though it is a much worse Town then *Dusseldorp*, yet is much better fortified; it hath a very broad Ditch, and a very regular Fortification; the Walls are considerably high, faced with Brick, and so is the Counterscarp, which is also in a very good condition. The Fortification of *Orsoy* is now quite demolished. *Rhineberg* continueth as it was, but the Fortification is very mean, only of Earth, so that it is not capable of making a great resistance. And *Wesel*, though it is a very fine Town, yet is a very poor Fortification, nor can it ever be made good, except at a vast expence; for the ground all about it being sandy, nothing can be made there that will be durable, unless the foundation go very deep, or that

it

it be laid upon Pilory. In all thefe Towns one fees another air of Wealth and Abundance than in much richer Countries that are exhaufted with taxes. *Rees* and *Emmerick* are good Towns, but the Fortifications are quite ruined. So that here is a rich and populous Country, that hath at prefent very little defence, except what it hath from its fcituation. *Cleve* is a delicious place, the fcituation and profpect are charming, and the Air is very pure, and from thence we came hither in three hours.

I will not fay one word of the Country into which I am now come, for as I know that is needlefs to you on many accounts, fo a Picture that I fee here in the Stadthoufe, puts me in mind of the perfectest Book of its kind that is perhaps in being, For Sir *William Temple*, whofe Picture hangeth here at the upper end of the Plenipotentiaries that negotiated the Famous Treaty of *Nimmegen*, hath indeed fet a pattern to the World, which is done with fuch life, that it may juftly make others blufh to copy after it, fince it muft be acknowledged, that if we had as perfect an account of the other places, as he hath given us of one of the leaft, but yet one of the Nobleft parcels of the Univerfe, Travelling would become a needlefs thing, unlefs it were for diverfion; fince one findeth no further occafion for his curiofity in this Country, then what is fully fatisfied by his rare performance. Yet I cannot give overwriting, without reflecting on the refiftance that this place made, when fo many other places were fo bafely delivered up, though one doth not fee in the ruines of the Fortification here, how it could make fo long a refiftance: yet it was that that ftem'd the tide of a progrefs that made all the World ftand amazed; and it gave a little time to the Dutch to recover themfelves out of the confternation, into which fo many blows, that came fo thick one after another, had ftruck them.

But then the World faw a change, that though it hath

hath not had so much Incense given to it, as the happy conjuncture of another Prince hath drawn after it, with so much excess, that all the topicks of flattery seem exhausted by it, yet will appear to posterity one of the most surprizing Scenes in History, and that which may be well matched with the recovery of the *Roman* State after the Battel of *Canne*. When a young Prince, that had never before born Arms, or so much as seen a Campagne, who had little or no Council about him but that which was suggested from his own thoughts, and that had no extraordinary advantage, by his Education either for literature or affairs, was of a sudden set at the head of a State and Army, that was sunk with so many losses; and that saw the best half of its Soil torn from it; and the powerfullest Enemy in the World, surrounded with a Victorious Army that was commanded by the best Generals that the Age hath produced, come within sight, and settle his Court in one of the best Towns, and had at the same time the greatest force both by Sea and Land, that hath been known, united together for its destruction. When the Inhabitants were forced, that they might save themselves from so formidable an Enemy, to let loose that which on all other occasions, is the most dreadful to them; and to drown so great a part of their Soil for the preservation of the rest; and to complicate together all the miseries that a Nation can dread, when to the general consternation with which so dismal a Scene possessed them, a distraction within doors seemed to threaten them with the last strokes; and while their Army was so ill disciplined, that they durst scarce promise themselves any thing from such feeble Troops, after a Peace at Land of almost Thirty Years continuance; and while their chief Ally, that was the most concerned in their preservation, was, like a great paralitick body, liker to fall on those that it pretended to support, and to crush them, then to give them

Ddd any

any confiderable affiftance: When I fay a young Prince came at the head of all this, the very prolpect of which would have quite dampt an ordinary courage, he very quickly changed the Scene, he animated the Publick Councils with a generous vigour; he found them finking into a feeblenefs of hearkning to Propofitions for a peace, that were as little fafe as they were honorable, but he difpofed them to refolve on hazarding all, rather than to fubmit to fuch Infamous terms. His credit alfo among the populace feemed to Infpire them with a new life; they eafily perfuaded themfelves that as one WILLIAM Prince of ORANGE had formed their State, fo here another of the fame name feemed marked out to recover and preferve it. It was this Spirit of Courage which he derived from his own breaft, and infufed into the whole People, as well as into the Magiftracy that preferved this Country. Some thing there was in all this that was Divine. The Publick Councils were again fetled, and the People were at quiet when they faw him vefted with a full authority for that time with Relation to peace and war, and concluded they were fafe, becaufe they were in his hands. It foon appeared how faithfully he purfued the Intereft of his Country, and how little he regarded his own. He rejected all Propofitions of Peace that were hurtfull to his Country, without fo much as confidering the advantages that were offered to himfelf, (in which you know that I write upon fure grounds.) He refufed the offer of the Soveraignty of its Chief City, that was made to him by a folemn Deputation, being fatisfied with that Authority which had been fo long maintained by his Anceftors with fo much glory, and being juftly fenfible, how much the breaking in upon eftablifhed laws and liberties, is fatal even to thofe that feem to get by it. He thus began his publick appearance on the ftage, with all the difadvantages that a Spirit afpiring to true Glory could wifh for; fince it was Vifible that

he

(39)

he had nothing to truſt to, but a good cauſe, a favorable Providence, and his own Integrity and Courage; nor was ſucceſs wanting to ſuch Noble beginnings; for he in a ſhort time, with a Conduct and Spirit beyond any thing that the World hath yet ſeen, recovered this State, out of ſo deſperate a diſtemper, took ſome places by main force, and obliged the Enemy to abandon all that they had acquired in ſo feeble a manner. And if a raw Army had not always ſucceſs againſt more numerous and better trained Troops, and if the want of Magazins and Stores in their Alliés Country, which was the chief Scene of the War, made that he could not Poſt his Army, and wait for favourable circumſtances, ſo that he was ſometimes forced to run to action, with a haſt that his neceſſities impoſed upon him; yet the forcing of the beginnings of a Victory out of the hands of the greateſt General of the Age, the facing a great Monarch with an Army much inferior to his, when the other was too cautious to hazard an ingagement, and in ſhort the forming the *Dutch* Army to ſuch a pitch that it became viſibly Superior to the *French*, that ſeemed to have been fed with Conqueſts; and the continuing the War, till the Prince that had ſacrificed the quiet of *Europe* to his GLORY, was glad to come and treat for a Peace in the Enemies Country, and in this very place, and to ſet all Engines on work to obtain that, by the mediation of ſome, and the jealouſies of other Princes; all theſe are ſuch performances that poſterity will be diſpoſed to rank them rather among the *Idea*'s of what an imaginary Hero could do, then with what could be really tranſacted in ſo ſhort a time, and in ſuch a manner. And in concluſion every place that belonged to theſe States, and to their Neighbours along the *Rhine*, together with a great many in *Flanders*, being reſtored; theſe Provinces do now ſee themſelves under his happy Conduct, re-eſtabliſhed in their former peace and ſecurity. And though ſome ſcars of ſuch

deep

deep wounds do still remain, yet they find themselves considered on all hands, as the Bulwark of *Christendom*, against the fears of a new Monarchy, and as the preservers of the peace and liberty of *Europe*.

Here is a Harvest, not for forced Rhetorick, or false Eloquence, but for a severe and sincere Historian, capable of affording a work that will far exceed all those luscious Panegyricks of mercenary pens; but a small or a Counterfeit Jewel must be set with all possible advantages, when a true one of great value needs only to be shewed. I cannot end with a greater subject, and I must acknowledge my self to be so inflamed with this hint, that as I cannot after this bring my pen down to lower matters, so I dare not trust my self too long, to the heat that so Noble an Object inspires, therefore I break off abruptly.

YOURS.

AD-

ADDENDA.

Ad Page 210. *l.* 22.

The same learned Person has since my first conversation with him upon this subject, suggested to me two passages of *Festus Pompeius*, that seem to determine this whole matter; and that tell us by what names those *Catacombs* were known in the *Roman* time, where abouts they were, and what sort of Persons were laid in them, we have also the designation by which the bearers were commonly known, and the time when they carried out the dead bodies; and it appears particularly by them that in the repositories of which that author makes mention, there was no care taken to preserve the bodies that were laid in them from rotting. His words are. *Puticulos antiquissimum genus sepulturæ appellatos, quod ibi in puteis sepelirenter homines: qualis fuerit locus quo nunc cadavera projici solent, extra portam Esquilinam; quos quod ibi putescerent, inde prius appellatos existimat puticulos Ælius Gallus, qui ait antiqui moris fuisse, ut patres familias in locum publicum extra oppidum mancipia vilia projicerent, atque ita projecta, quod ibi ea putescerent, nomen esse factum puticuli.* The other passage runs thus. *Vespæ & Vespillones dicuntur, qui funerandis corporibus officium gerunt, non à minutis illis volucribus, sed quia vespertino tempore eos efferunt, qui funebri pompa duci propter inopiam nequeunt.* All this agrees so exactly to the thoughts that a general view of those repositories give a Man, that it will not be hard to persuade him that those burying places that are now graced with the pompous title of Catacombs, are no other then the *Puticoli* mentioned by *Festus Pompeius*, where the meanest sort of the *Roman* Slaves were laid, and
so

so without any further care about them were left to rot.

Ad page 278. *l.* 1.

I have since my being in *Naples* instructed one that was going thither in this particular, and have received this account from him; that he had taken care to plumm the water at the furthest pillar of *Caligula*'s bridge on the *Puzzolo* side; and found it was seven fathom and a half deep; but he adds that the Watermen assured him, that that on the other side before *Baia* the water was 26. fathom deep; but as he had not a plummet long enough to try that, so he believed a good deal ought to be abated; for the Watermen had assured him that the water was ten fathom deep on the *Puzzolo* side, though upon tryal he found it was only seven and a half; and by this measure one may suppose that the water is 20. fathom deep on the other side; so that it is one of the most astonishing things that one can think of that pillars of brick could have been built in such a depth of water.

F I N I S.